The West Bank and Gaza St

Written in a clear and easy-to-follow style, this revealing text examines the contemporary political geography of the West Bank and Gaza Strip. Descriptive in nature, it documents the changes and developments since 1967 as well as the recent disengagement from Gaza. The book is supplemented by numerous maps and covers issues including:

- demography
- Jewish settlements
- water and natural resources
- transport infrastructure
- planning
- partition plans for Jerusalem
- settlement policy
- the Separation Fence
- the Palestinian State.

One of the first books to tackle this contentious subject from a geographical rather than a political or historical perspective, this essential text will be of huge interest to both undergraduate and graduate students studying the Israel–Palestine conflict.

Elisha Efrat is Emeritus Professor of Geography at Tel Aviv University. He has held posts in Israel's Ministry of the Interior as Head of the Department of National and Regional Planning and has written more than 200 articles on Israeli issues. His previous publications include *Israel – a Contemporary Geography* (1996) and *Physical Planning Prospects in Israel during 50 Years of Statehood* (1998).

The West Bank and Gaza Strip

A geography of occupation and disengagement

Elisha Efrat

LONDON AND NEW YORK

First published 2006
by Routledge
2 Park Square, Milton Park, Abingdon, Oxon OX14 4RN

Simultaneously published in the USA and Canada
by Routledge
270 Madison Ave, New York, NY 100161

Routledge is an imprint of the Taylor & Francis Group

Typeset in Times New Roman by
Keystroke, Jacaranda Lodge, Wolverhampton
Printed and bound in Great Britain by
TJ International Ltd, Padstow, Cornwall

British Library Cataloguing in Publication Data
A catalogue record for this book is available from the British Library

Library of Congress Cataloging in Publication Data
The West Bank and Gaza Strip : a geography of occupation and disengagement / Elisha Efrat.
p. cm.
Includes bibliographical references and index.
ISBN 0–415–38544–X (hardback) – ISBN 0–415–38545–8 (pbk.)
1. Arab-Israeli conflict 1993–Occupied territories. 2. Israel–Government policy–West Bank. 3. Israel–Government policy–Gaza Strip. 4. Israel–Politics and government–1993– . 5. West Bank–Politics and government. 6. Gaza Strip–Politics and government. 7. Palestinian Arabs–Politics and government. 8. Military occupation–Social aspects–West Bank. 9. Military occupation–Social aspects–Gaza Strip. I. Title.
DS119.76E38 2005
956.95′3044–dc22
2005018144

ISBN10: 0–415–38544-X (hbk)
ISBN10: 0–415–38545–8 (pbk)

ISBN13: 9–78–0–415–38544–2 (hbk)
ISBN13: 9–78–0–415–38545–9 (pbk)

Contents

Plates

All photographs courtesy Israel Government Office.

Figures

Tables

Introduction

This book, dealing with contemporary geographical issues and politics of the West Bank and the Gaza Strip, is an attempt to describe current events against the background of the geographical space in which they took place, and is based on the follow-up, record, and study of the main events that have occurred between 1967 and the first years of the twenty-first century. The book explores methodically the policies, facts, and figures from the perspective of geography, and offers a clear presentation of data that everybody should be aware of. The point of departure in this book is professional and pragmatic, with a study of the land and how it is affected by human beings, and, in this case, how the activities of various Israeli authorities have affected the territories occupied in June 1967, in the West Bank and the Gaza Strip.

Since the Six Day War in 1967 the geography of Israel has changed radically, for example in borderlines, the new layouts of towns and villages, the distribution of population in the occupied areas, the mass immigration of Russian Jews, the increase in number of the Israeli Arab population, the growth of Jerusalem, the national and regional planning of the infrastructure, and – above all – the attempts at negotiation with the Palestinians under fire and terrorism, with the hope for a possible freedom in the region. The two last decades have been the most intensive and dynamic ones Israel has ever experienced, both in the number of events and in their rapid occurrence. Since the beginning of the 1990s most of the changes that have occurred have taken place beyond the official "Green Line" borders, including such issues as territory, settlement, rural and urban development land use, housing, etc. These issues have left their mark on the occupied territories of Judea, Samaria, and the Gaza Strip, and created spatial and demographic changes, but with a flimsy connection to the social and economic fabric that exists within Israel. It seems that despite the tremendous investments that the Israeli government has made in the territories, there is no great likelihood of continuing them in the future because of their demographic, social, and ethnic complexity.

The outcome of the terrorism and the activities of the right-wing government in the last decade has brought to the fore political and territorial matters that the State of Israel was compelled to address. The occupation of territory, the settlement of areas across the borders for the purpose of controlling them or turning them into a bargaining card in peace negotiations, the massive investments in the physical infrastructure of the occupied areas to the detriment of Israel's development within the "Green Line" that marked the boundary of Israel as determined by the Armistice Agreement of 1949, and such political and urban acts as the creation of "Greater Jerusalem" – all these exemplify how geography interacts in the current period. There is no period as fitted as the recent two decades for facilitating a proper investigation, description, and analysis of the geographical aspects of contemporary events in the background of the history of Israel's occupation.

The public in Israel and in the world does not seem to be sufficiently aware of the economic, social, demographic, and physical implications of the occupation. Over the decades, while the Israelis have engaged in ideological disputes for and against a Greater Israel, a civil occupation has been taking shape, under the auspices of the military administration, with the aim of turning the occupied territories into an inseparable part of the State of Israel. These activities have been going on, slowly but steadily, with the sanction of all Israeli governments, left and right, and with the co-operation of all authorities, military and civil.

Beginning in the 1970s, a systematic effort has been made to shape a new reality. First, hundreds of thousands of acres were expropriated by the army for military or public purposes, declaring the land abandoned property or State land. Most of it was slated for settlement. At the same time, countless military and civil regulations and laws were passed in order to skirt the obstacles clearly while preserving a façade of law and order. The land and the Israelis who settled on it were awarded a special civilian status in a territory officially under military control, along with *de facto* annexation of enclaves scattered throughout the West Bank. Israel has been using every trick to pursue its goals while pretending that everything is above board and legal. Tracts of land were amassed after being put to various tests, and taken over by the State, which built settlements on them and set aside huge land reserves, sometimes much larger than the core settlement, to enable them to expand. Vast expanses of unused land, criss-crossed by glistening asphalt roads, are parts of the master plan for small Israeli settlements. Most of the outposts have been built on this land, so that even those established without a permit have been approved by the military establishment after the fact, on orders of the political echelon.

According to various estimates, 50–60 per cent of Judea and Samaria are in the hands of Israel and the settlers. Apart from tracts that have been declared State land, large expanses have been expropriated for military use. Broad stretches of land are off-limits to Palestinians, building near major highways is prohibited, and Palestinians cannot live near settlements or military installations. Many areas have been declared nature reserves and cannot be used for agriculture or other purposes.

The facts on the ground are blithely ignored by most of the Israeli public, as if they were trivialities compared to the political-military controversy, which seemingly takes precedence over everything else. But settlers in the West Bank comprise only 12 per cent of the population. Population density and birth rates are there much higher among Palestinians than among Jews. Despite all the land expropriated by the Israeli government in this region, housing and development projects benefit only the settlers and not the local inhabitants, who are suffering from an acute shortage of land zoned for building. The Palestinians are on the verge of strangulation as their land reserves dwindle and building permits are denied.

Israel consumes 500 million cu. m of water from the mountain aquifer for every 100 million cu. m allocated to the Palestinian sector. An Israel settler in the territories gets three to five times as much water for home consumption as a Palestinian. The elaborate network of approach roads in the territories is topographically illegal, and a fortune has been spent to serve tiny clusters of settlers in different parts of the Gaza Strip.

There are in this region two hostile populations living one on the top of the other in enclaves. One gets everything, for ideological reasons and in direct contradiction to theories of logical planning, not to mention political, social, and human logic, while the other gets nothing, and its living space is steadily shrinking. The occupation in Judea, Samaria, and the Gaza Strip drives home the realization that the occupied territories are the source of and breeding ground for the appalling deterioration this country has experienced in every sphere of life since the end of 2000. The public is paying in money, in blood, in social stamina, and emotionally for the absurd reality. These are citizens who trust the policy-makers and their decisions, whose life has been disrupted and whose personal and national future is being put at such risk to such an extent that soon the damage may be irreversible.

The chapters in this book treat subjects of great interest and importance for life in Israel and in the occupied territories today, and are divided into three main parts: The West Bank, Jerusalem, and the Gaza Strip. They deal with such issues as Jewish and Arab settlements, water, land, roads, separation fences, demography, planning, disengagement, and peace. They analyze the future Palestinian State alongside the results of the occupation and its delusions, and many others from a geographical standpoint.

E. Efrat
Jerusalem, August 2005

1 The scope of geography and occupation

The attitude to occupation is mostly political, juristic, economic, demographic, or administrative, but rarely geographical, rarely taking into account the meaning of physical changes that take place in an occupied region and all their consequences regarding the population that has to live under conquest. The link between geography and occupation does not have deep roots in academic literature, and features of terrain, land use, population distribution, or ethnic diversity are aspects of geography that have not received particular attention in the theme of occupation. Empirical studies have been less than successful in establishing a clear link between the geographic distribution of physical and human facts and occupation. While occupation is engaged first and foremost with territory, it turns out to be an issue that has geographical significance, describes and analyzes the influence of people, army, and occupier on its environment, and the impact of the changes they make in the natural and physical landscape when they use a region for their own occupational purposes.

Occupation, in traditional law, refers generally to the acquisition of territory by the victorious State in a war at the expense of the defeated State. Some authorities identify occupation with the provisional conquest of territory resulting from successful military operation, and describe the legal process of transferring title as subjugation, if the defeated State is totally annexed by the occupier, or as cession, if the defeated State retains its identity and agrees by treaty to the alteration of the territorial status quo in favor of the victor. According to another view, the term "occupation" is dissociated from the physical appropriation of territory during hostilities and used as a synonym for subjugation. In either case, occupation is associated with the principle of traditional international law that sovereign States may resort to in war at their discretion and, by military victory, achieve territorial and other gains that will be recognized as having legal validity. The State acquiring territory by occupation is regarded as the successor, with certain qualifications, to the rights and duties previously appertaining in the territory. Private rights, interests, and property in the territory are not affected by the change of sovereignty, and legal rules applicable to such matters remain in effect until altered by the legislative authority of the new sovereign.

While occupation is generally followed by annexation of territory, it was understood by international law in the nineteenth century that sovereign States were free to make war for reasons of State and consequently had the right to annex occupied territory. Title could not, however, be claimed until occupation was complete, that is, until the defeated State surrendered or lost all capability to resist further. Some international lawyers held that, after occupation was complete, title did not pass to the victor until the defeated State had ceded it by treaty or other States had generally recognized the change.

Annexation is a formal act whereby a State proclaims its sovereignty over territory hitherto outside its domain. Unlike cession, where territory is given or sold by means of a treaty, annexation is a unilateral act made effective by actual possession and legitimized by general recognition. Annexation is frequently preceded by occupation, a process by which a State ousts the existing government within a territory and places in authority its own military forces, thus setting up conditions of military occupation. Occupation and annexation may be limited to only a portion of territory of a State but such acquisition is usually effected by cession and by means of a treaty. An official announcement of an annexation, before occupation has been completed, has long been deemed irregular and, according to the widely accepted Stimson doctrine of 1932, annexation following completed occupation should not be recognized if the occupier has violated an antiwar obligation. The formalities of annexation are not defined by international law; whether it is done by one authority or another within a State is a matter of constitutional law. In international law annexation is the formal act by which a State declares its title to a territory. It differs from acquisition in that a State may acquire territory without formal annexation, by means of prescription, or uncontested occupation of territory of another State over a long period of time, by accretion, or adding to its territory on a river or maritime frontier through the operation of natural forces, or by discovery and occupation of unclaimed territory.

From a geographical point of view, occupation is usually executed by a massive penetration of military forces into a territory, by dominating roads and junctions, strategic points, important regional and environmental sites, and also towns and villages in which most of the population is concentrated. The occupation of a region can be executed in different ways, but in most cases it does not match with its internal structure and form. Occupation is executed more rapidly and is generally carried out violently and against the nature of the environment and against the whole fabric of its settlements and artificial networks. Occupation is not a constructive action but a move of destruction and exploitation of the existing infrastructure of a region by the occupying country for its specific aims. On the one hand it uses the geographical elements of the territory for purposes of dominance, and on the other hand it misuses them in their natural layout, and creates a military fabric of its own, which may be separated from or be in contrast with the traditional surroundings. As the military fabric imposes itself on the existing physical elements of a region, it not only destroys it but also leaves behind it remnants, after the occupation comes to an end, that are harmful to the natural environment.

Communications arteries such as roads, railway lines and all kinds of transportation means are the most important elements in an action of engagement. A communications artery is a geographical linear element that allows the occupier rapid penetration into a region in a relatively short time and in a most effective way. The capturing of a communications axis provides dominance over the inter-relationships and economic connections between cities and villages and control over population movements in the area. A regional road system connects population, dwellings, economic and social relationships and is, therefore, the main target in any invasion. The axis dominance is also used for conveying combat matériel, goods and army troops: it is a channel that can be opened or closed intermittently according to the occupier's decisions and benefits, and enables the occupier to direct the daily life of the population under occupation. While a communications system is usually constructed in a branched form, its dominance enables the occupier to control large areas with minimal military forces. Instead of distributing troops to all parts of a region, it is sufficient to dominate the main arteries and road junctions. The reason why dominance on communications axes makes occupation easier is that roads are usually aligned according to topography and such physical elements as soil composition, slope gradients, mountain passages, water resources, climatic conditions, land uses, settlements, etc. If no reasonable road system exists in an area efficient enough for the occupier's needs, the latter may construct a new communications system of its own with arteries and by-passing roads, parallel with or even in contrast to the existing one, on condition that its access to all parts of the occupied region will be safe and efficient.

Territorial occupation is also connected with seizure of land. Occupation needs land for its own uses, such as military camps, engineering installations, places for arms and ammunition storage, training fields, and administration buildings that cannot be combined with civilian land uses in towns, villages, or even in open space. The land uses of an occupier are typically exploitative and are aimed at providing urgent needs and services, to enforce dominance in the occupied territory, and are far from being oriented to civilian sustainable development. There is no doubt that occupation causes damage to agricultural land, especially when the army has, for instance, to clear an area to widen its field of view for safeguarding the surroundings against attacks. Military occupational land uses do not fit local outline schemes or civilian detailed building plans, because they are different in their style and construction, they have a monotonous appearance, and are usually anomalous in the nature and in the history of a region. An occupied region creates a new fabric of sites that have nothing in common with the geographical features of a natural region.

Territorial occupation is also engaged with the exploitation of water resources, especially in arid or semi-arid regions. The dependence on water resources gives the occupier the power of directing the life, economy, and agricultural production of a region, and to provide for its own needs in the ruling territory. Occupation of water resources is executed by seizing land under which the aquifers lie, where rain water is accumulated and where the upper installations, the wells, the drilling pumps, and the conveying water network are. This kind of occupation administers water supply, controls reservoirs, and even keeps water resources as an economic and strategic means for more efficient dominance of the population that is under occupation.

Territorial occupation is connected with the conquest of towns and villages. The geographical layout of settlements in a region demonstrates the interrelationships between people and the environment and the artificial fabric that people have created for their existence. Such interrelationships develop gradually over time by the adaptation of people to their surroundings, which shape over periods of time an optimal form of land use that suits the local population. Some settlements function as service centers for the region, and their rate of growth is determined by their regional position and their economic power which creates a hierarchy of settlements of different size. The occupation of towns and villages, or their encirclement by walls or ditches, as a means of disconnecting them from their surroundings, is an effective way for the occupier to gain control over the majority of a region's population through a few occupied cities and villages. The occupation of towns and villages holds and prevents local development, is not constructive, and in the best case succeeds in maintaining a restraining situation.

There is also a way of dominating an occupied region by an initiated penetration of rural and urban population into it and by establishing there a separate layout of settlements under military administration. In such a case the occupier may dominate a region by creating many *faits accomplis*. Such an imposed settlement layout is from the geographical point of view far from ideal, because the best parts of a region are usually taken by the local inhabitants, and what remains for the occupier are no more than marginal areas of low economic potential. Such an imposed settlement layout may entail serious geographical deficiencies regarding agricultural soil, water resources, and adjustment to main communications arteries. It is hard to imagine a deeper change in a region than a new imposed artificial layout of settlements with settlers who have not lived there before, who are outsiders in the region, who have had no relationship to it in the past, and who since the military occupation have decided to make their life there for political and economic reasons. If such a layout includes outposts and remote fringe settlements that have been established for political purposes, the result will be unreasonable and far from having any geographical logic.

Territorial occupation causes damage to the natural landscape. Occupation does not consider nature and landscape values and certainly not ecological sites with special fauna and flora as important elements that have to be protected. These are neglected by the occupier because its actions are typically drastic, exploitative, short-range, and based on aims that do not consider the efforts invested by the local inhabitants in the slow and gradual development of their region. Therefore, tree felling, soil erosion, land dissection, irrational land-use, waste of building remnants after evacuation – all these are signs of a military and occupied landscape, whether it is under occupation or abandoned later on. Terrible environmental damage is being inflicted on large areas in occupied regions in Israel. Millions of cubic metres of soil, with tens of thousands of trees, thousands of acres of orchards and groves, tens of thousands of acres of natural growth, greenhouses, archaeological sites and wells, as well as the fabric of life of hundreds of people, are being crushed. A desperate thought comes to mind: before the fate of a disputed land is resolved, there will be nothing left to fight about, and then a great cry will be heard over the ruins.

When the Jewish settlers arrived in Judea and Samaria following the Six Day War, they found a strip of land that still preserved an amazing likeness to the landscape of Second Temple days, as far as this can be imagined, and even a likeness to the landscape of biblical times. Today one must search for the scenery, because it hides in the shadow of the controlling presence of the outposts, settlements, and by-pass roads. Love of land is the last thing one thinks of when encountering the sight of the region today. It is not the aesthetics of the settlements themselves but their impact and their associated infrastructure on their near and distant surroundings, especially the landscape that has been used for agriculture and grazing for thousands of years. Settlements were spread over large territories and their houses were scattered in every direction, slicing up the typical landscape and damaging cliffs and hills. The landscape is broken from every direction with heavy equipment, the hills lose their soil and vegetation, and the slopes become naked waste ground. Israel decided in April 2005 to transfer garbage beyond the "Green Line" and dump it in the West Bank for the first time since 1967. The project was launched despite international treaties prohibiting an occupying State from making use of occupied territory unless it benefits the local population. The dump operators planned to deposit some ten thousand tons of garbage from the Sharon region every month in what was known as the largest quarry in the West Bank. The initiative started out as a plan to rehabilitate a 4-acre plot in a quarry by filling it with building waste, junk, and shredded tyres. It evolved into a huge project spread over dozens of acres for household garbage. Israel's construction and operation of the dump appeared to be in violation of international law, as it involves transferring garbage to territory defined as occupied. Experts warned that the dump would jeopardize the mountain aquifer, one of the largest freshwater sources in Israel and the West Bank.

It seems that the occupation of the West Bank and the Gaza Strip – until the end of 2005 still the only regions in the world under occupation by a neighboring country – realizes the scope of geography of occupation. In these two regions, which were once to be a Palestinian State, we find all the typical elements of occupation mentioned above – capturing of a territory, disregarding land ownership, dominating water resources, ruling over rural and urban local population, establishing new types of settlements with settlers who come from outside, erecting outposts in remote and peripheral areas in order to seize more land, by-passing local communications arteries and constructing separate road networks, creating *faits accomplis* to establish arbitrary borderlines and all these in conflict and clashes with the strong national emotions of the Palestinian people under occupation, and have been the cause of two Intifadas and terrorism.

2 The West Bank: a Jewish–Arab struggle for sovereignty

Background

The West Bank, or Judea and Samaria as it is called in Israel, is a part of western Palestine which during the period 1948–67 was under Jordanian rule, when it was referred to as the West Bank, as distinct from the East Bank of the Jordan which formed the core of the Hashemite Kingdom of Jordan. To the north of it are the Gilbo'a hills and the Valley of Yesreel, in the west it borders on the Plain of Sharon, the Jerusalem Corridor and the Judean Lowlands, and in the south is the Arad region. Between Israel's War of Independence of 1948 and the Six Day War of 1967, the region of Judea and Samaria was bounded by an armistice line between Israel and Jordan, but no physical links connected it with the State of Israel. After 1948 the region no longer had access to the Mediterranean Sea or to the Coastal Plain and the Gaza Strip; its only link was with the Kingdom of Jordan to the east. The armistice line caused changes in the pattern of towns and villages that were reflected in their number, population, interrelationship and eastward orientation. Geographical changes in the settlement pattern were the result of the unnatural political conditions, which affected the physical, economic and social factors of this area. For 19 years, from Israel's War of Independence in 1948 until the Six Day War in 1967, the area was virtually isolated from its natural surroundings, being cut off from the more densely populated and highly developed parts of Israel by an armistice line.

Judea constitutes the southern part of the area. The western slopes of the Judean Mountains have been included in the State of Israel since 1948, as have their southern slopes which form part of the Arad region. Mount Hebron forms a wide crest with a syncline on each side, the lowland in the west and the desert in the east. Rising to an altitude of 3,000 ft (1,000 m) it runs in a northeast to southwest direction. To the west a tectonic fold line provides a gradual 900–1,500 ft (300–500 m) ascent. In the east another fold forms the transition from the crest to the Judean Desert. The Samarian Hills in the north, on the other hand, are entirely included in what was formerly known as the West Bank. The Hills of Samaria fall gradually from the south. They extend from the Mountains of Jerusalem up to the Yesreel Valley in the north, and border on the Jordan Valley in the east and the Coastal Plain in the west. In contrast to the Hebron Mountains, the Samarian Hills, whose average height is 1,650 ft (550 m), are dissected by rifts and valleys underlining the topographical differences between one section and another. Economically and politically Samaria was less isolated and maintained close ties with the East Bank. Although Samaria and Judea each have distinct geographic, demographic, and economic characteristics, they should nevertheless be regarded as a single entity. The region has an area of 2,296 sq. miles (5,878 sq. km), constituting 21 per cent of western Palestine, and extends along 75 miles (120 km) from north to south with an average east to west width of 25 miles (40 km). The armistice line of 1948 was fixed according to the disposition of Jewish and Arab forces at the end of the 1948 war and determined the administrative and political boundaries of the region. In the east the earlier international border runs along the course of the Jordan River down to the Dead Sea (Fig. 2.1).

In the Hebron Mountains the dispersion of the villages is linear and concentrated, owing to the geographical features of the area. To the east the influence of the desert is very noticeable; the annual precipitation is between 4 and 12 in. (100 and 300 mm), the vegetation is scanty, there are few springs and little soil. All these factors severely limit the extension of human settlement beyond a line of 3.1 miles (5 km) east of the mountain crest. To the south, the influence of the Negev Desert penetrates some distance into the Hebron Mountains, and as result the number of villages falls off as one nears the border of the desert.

The villages in the Hebron Mountains are dispersed along a line parallel to the watershed, but at some distance from it, near deposits of good soft building stone. The villages also refrained from settling on fertile land on the plateau. To the west, a number of villages are located along a tectonic axis parallel to the general orientation of the mountain. Their position on the edge of the mountainous backbone ensures geographical advantages and adequate supplies of spring water. The larger villages, of three to five thousand inhabitants, are found mainly in the southwest, while in the central part of the region the average village has only five hundred to a thousand inhabitants. The larger population of the border villages may be explained by the need for protecting the settled farmers against the predations of desert nomads and by the gradual intermingling, over the years, of farmers and nomads in settlements that enjoy favorable soil and water conditions. The settlement pattern in the Hebron Mountains has, therefore, crystallized along well-defined axes, as a result of the geographical character of the hill country and its agricultural possibilities.

The pattern of settlement in Samaria is more scattered and covers almost the entire area. The broken mountainous topography has resulted in a network of villages located on hilltops and mountain spurs, where they dominate the surrounding country. The valleys are as a rule not settled, since they contain fertile sedimentary soil suitable for intensive cultivation. The wide dispersion of villages in the Samaria Hills is made possible by the presence of a large number of springs, as a result of many fault lines that are characteristic of these mountains. The villages are generally small and only a few have as many as three to five thousand inhabitants.

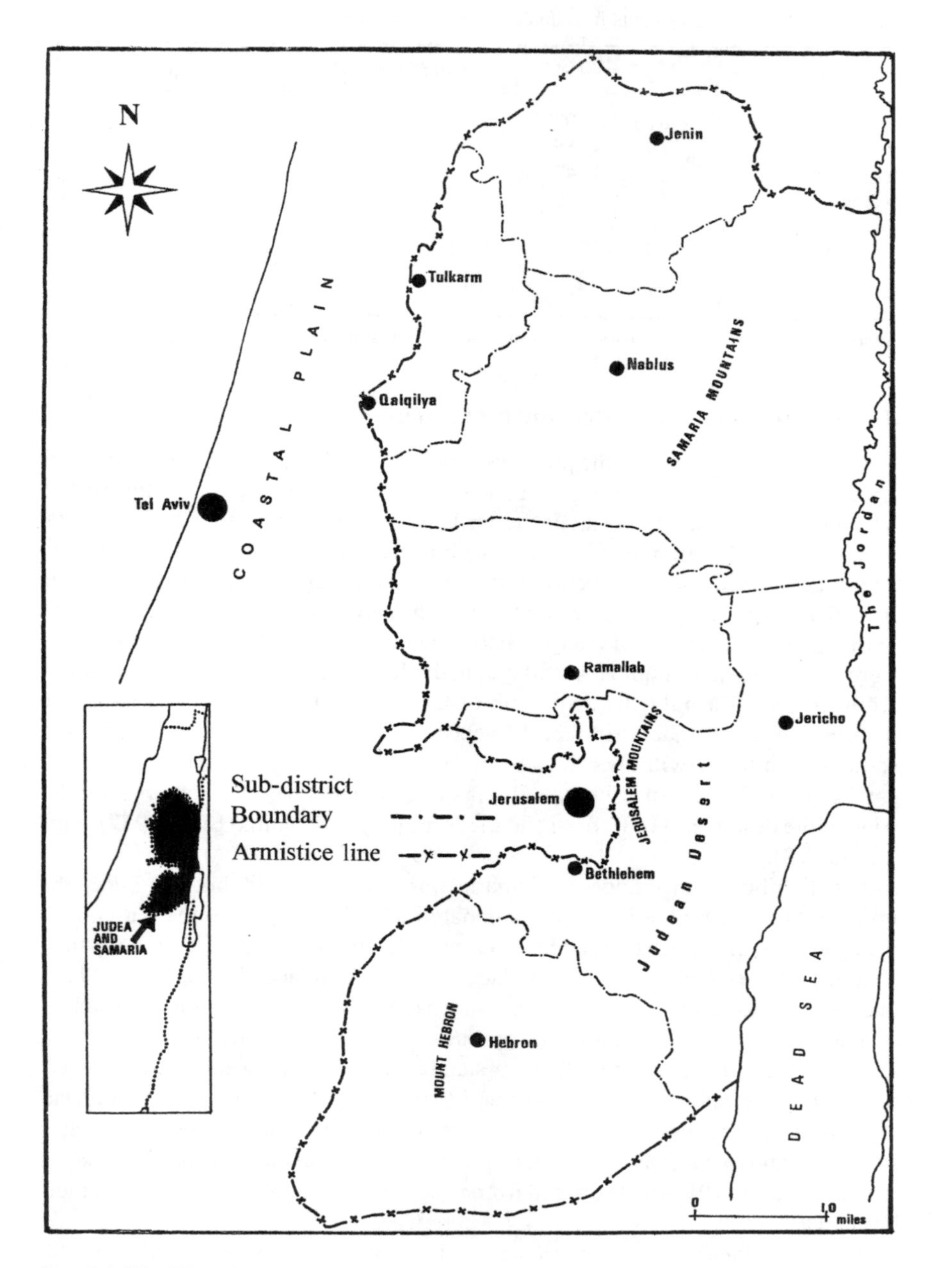

Fig. 2.1 The West Bank

Table 2.1 Village settlements in Judea and Samaria by sub-district

Sub-district	*1947*	*1967*	*Total increase*	*Percentage increase*
Nablus	91	97	6	6.5
Jenin	29	55	28	89.0
Tulkarm	34	42	8	23.5
Ramallah	56	70	14	25.0
Jerusalem	34	66	32	94.0
Hebron	20	66	46	230.0
Total	264	396	132	50.0

Source: Mandatory Village Statistics, 1945 and Statistical Abstract of Israel 1970, No. 21.

Judea and Samaria under Jordanian rule

Against the background of the physical conditions in the region, it is interesting to compare the number of villages in Judea and Samaria at the end of the British Mandate (1947) and at the end of the Jordanian rule (1967) (Table 2.1). The total increase was 132 villages (50 per cent) but the increase for Samaria was only 25 per cent, while the corresponding figure for Judea reached 144 per cent. While most of the new villages in Judea were small, they are nevertheless a striking feature in the spatial distribution of villages in this region. It can also be seen that there was a great increase in the number of villages in the Jerusalem and Hebron sub-districts, while in Samaria only the Jenin sub-district showed a striking increase. The distribution shows that during the 19 year period there was a tendency to further settlement in Judea, with special stress laid on settling the frontier with Israel in the south and southwest. An effort was also made to strengthen border settlement at the edge of the desert, east of Hebron and the Jerusalem Mountains (Efrat, 1977) (Figs 2.2 and 2.3).

The distribution of villages in Samaria was more balanced, but there, too, the north and the west were favored as compared with the east. As to the settlements near the armistice line, they underwent considerable demographic and physical changes. The armistice line cut the villages off from their lands in the Coastal Plain, and the villages began therefore to cultivate patches of land in the hills. The lack of markets in the west and the absence of roads to the east brought about a decline in agriculture and the lowering of living standards. Some villages turned eastward toward the interior of the region. The emigration of young villagers to the Persian Gulf countries raised the living standards of the inhabitants, leading to grater prosperity and to the construction of new buildings, so that the same border villages which in the late 1940s had suffered from isolation later revived and increased their built area.

In spite of these artificial settlement activities, there was little change in the geographic distribution of the villages. Only a few new settlements succeeded in gaining a foothold on the threshold of the desert or on the shore of the Dead Sea. Nor were many new settlements established in the Jordan Valley, owing to unfavorable soil conditions and lack of water resources.

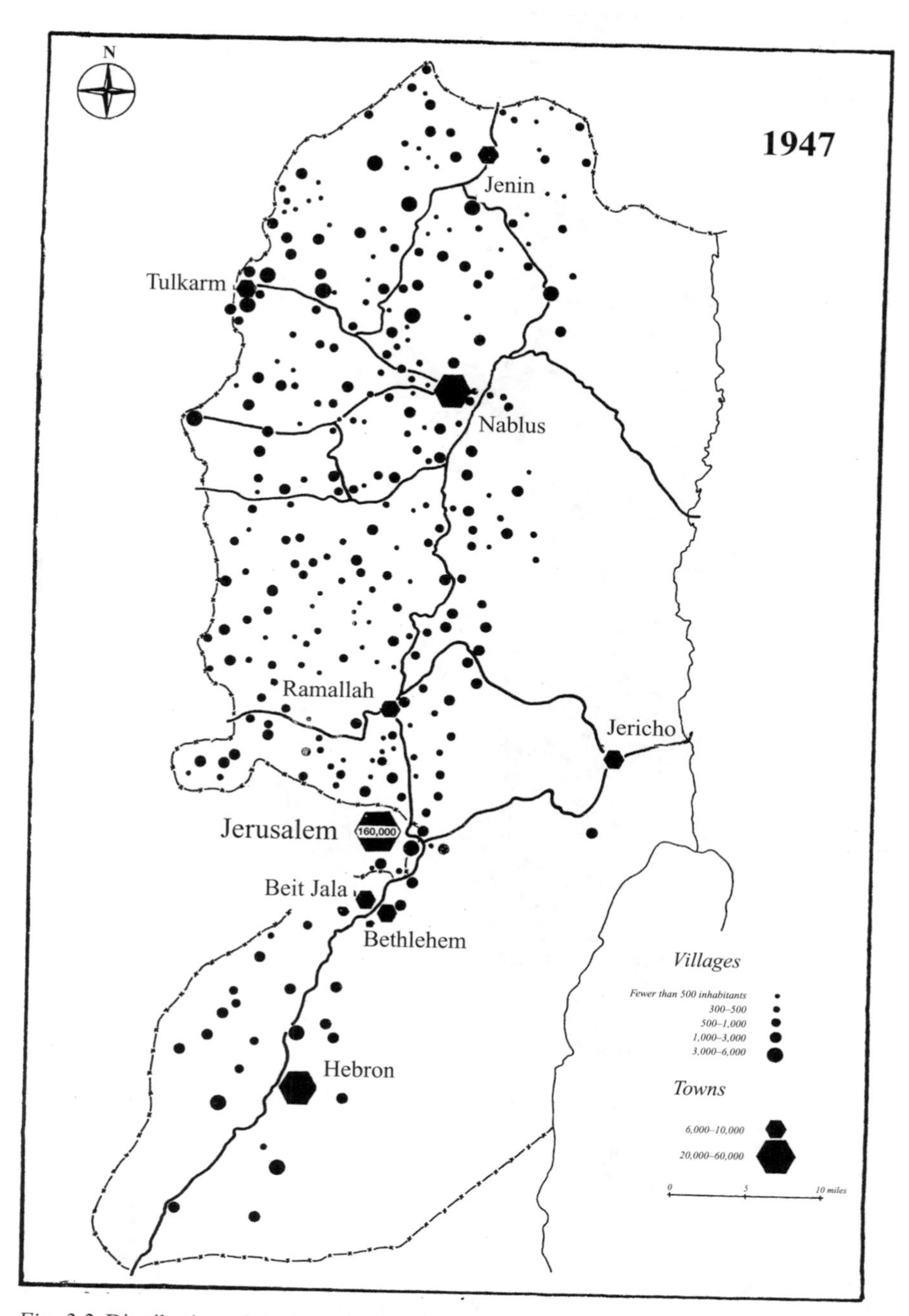

Fig. 2.2 Distribution of Arab settlements in the West Bank 1947

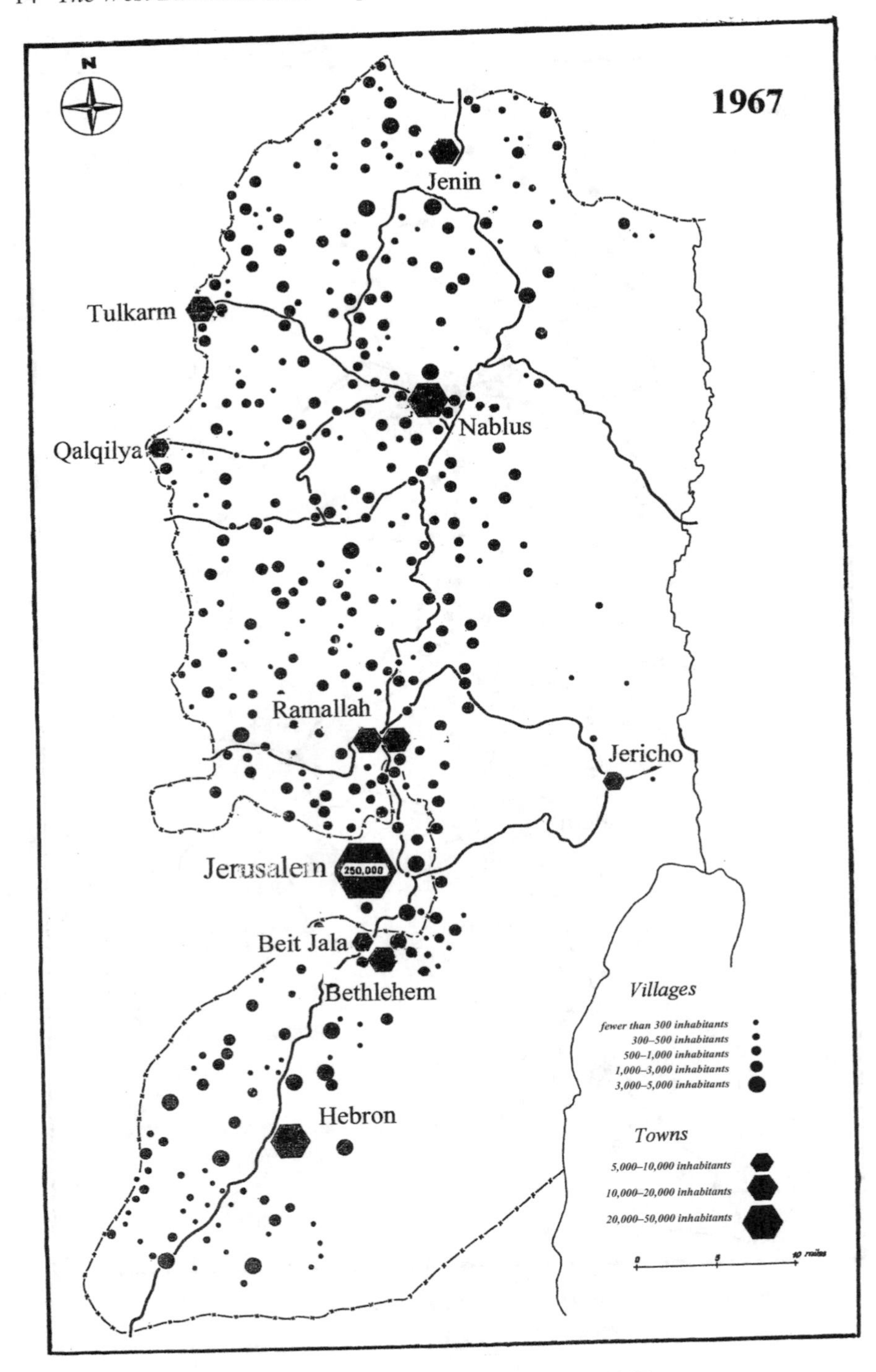

Fig. 2.3 Distribution of Arab settlements in the West Bank 1967

Table 2.2 The population of Judea and Samaria by sub-district

Sub-district	*1947*	*1967*	*Percentage increase*
Nablus	62,500	152,400	144
Jenin	49,000	78,000	60
Tulkarm	35,000	72,300	106
Ramallah	50,700	88,800	75
Jerusalem	39,400	88,400	124
Hebron	47,000	118,300	151
Total	283,600	598,500	111
Judea	86,400	206,700	139
Samaria	197,200	391,800	99

Source: Estimate based on Mandatory Village Statistics, 1945, rounded off to the nearest hundred. Figures of Population Census, 1967, Statistical Abstract of Israel, 1970, No. 21.

A comparison of the village population between the years 1947 and 1967 reveals some striking features. In 1947 the rural population numbered 283,600, and in 1967, after the increase of 111 per cent in 19 years, it had risen to 598,500 (Table 2.2). There is a striking difference between the rate of increase in Judea (139 per cent) and in Samaria (99 per cent), which is probably due to the internal migration of refugees and to the settlement of nomads. While in 1947 the population was more or less uniformly distributed among the several sub-districts, the figures for 1967 show a marked change in Nablus and Hebron sub-districts. The population of the Hebron sub-district rose by 151 per cent and that of Nablus by 144 per cent – that is, the highest population growth took place in the two principal centers of the region, one in the south and the other in the north, and especially along the armistice line. It should also be noted that during the British Mandate regime there was a normal distribution of the population among the villages, only a few of which numbered fewer than 500 or more than 3,000 inhabitants, the majority lying in the 500 to 1,000 range. Today this distribution has been distorted by the marked increased of small villages.

The geographical patterns of Arab settlements and towns

There are various approaches to the question of settlement in Judea and Samaria, some traditional and obsolete, others more modern and ambitious. The Arab agricultural settlement in Judea and Samaria is a primary geographical phenomenon resulting from the physical nature of the region and its technological under-development. However, the location of these settlements, their dispersion pattern and the manner in which their physical conditions have been exploited to enable the inhabitants to support themselves and to keep to their way of life may be used as a starting point for all other settlers in the region, even if they come equipped with the most modern knowhow and technology.

The dispersion of the villages in the Hebron Mountains is not freely ramified like that of the plains or in the valleys, but is linear, clustered, and concentrated, owing to the limitations imposed by nature and by the mountainous topography. These limit the eastward expansion of settlement beyond a line passing through a few large villages located close to the Judean Desert. In the south, the desert influence of the Negev is very noticeable. It penetrates the southern ridges of the Hebron Mountains and makes itself felt by the decrease in rainfall and population density. As one approaches the threshold of the desert toward the west, the concentration of settlements is limited by morphological and geographical forces. A number of villages are strung out along the backbone of the Hebron Mountains in a northeast direction, parallel to the crest of the mountains.

The villages on the mountain crest take advantage of the local topography, avoid the main highway as much as possible, and do not encroach on agricultural land. As the conditions on the plateau are relatively favorable for agriculture, the villages are located at the edge of the plateau, at a convenient distance from the fields, and preferably in areas, between the mountain crest and the slopes, where soft building stone is available and cultivation terraces can easily be built. In the north, the village network is bounded by the descent of the Hebron Mountains towards the Jerusalem Mountains. The village pattern of the Hebron Mountains can be seen as tending to crystallize and cluster along well-defined axes, owing to the character of the mountain and the location of areas suitable for cultivation.

The dispersion of settlements in Samaria is different from that in Judea. While Judea is sparsely populated, with most of the villages located on two or three longitudinal axes, in Samaria the settlements are more widely dispersed. Here, too, the settlement pattern is influenced by climate, topography, soil, water, and roads. There is a sharp division between the rainy Mediterranean climate in the west and the semi-arid desert climate in the east. The dividing line fits more or less with the 12 in. (300 mm) rain line, and there are almost no Arab settlements east of this line. Owing to the topography of the Samarian Hills, which are open to the west, the Mediterranean climate and consequently the boundaries of the agricultural area penetrate farther east than in Judea. There are no Arab settlements in the semi-arid Jordan Valley except in the south Jericho, which was in the past founded on an oasis.

The nature of the terrain in Samaria determines the location of the settlements, which are situated mainly on the hilltops, on the spurs or on the anticlines, which afford them relative security. There are also villages in valleys or on their fringes. Villages in the hilly terrain are found mainly in the western part of the Samarian Hills, following the mountain spurs which descend in the direction of the Coastal Plain, and also in the eastern part, near the threshold of the desert. In central Samaria, on the other hand, near the longitudinal valleys, the villages are located in the middle or at the foot of the slope. The same holds good for the area south of Nablus and the whole region between Nablus and Jenin, where better security and greater ease of cultivation enabled the villages to choose a lower location. The lower the topography, the more scattered are the villages. The dispersion is fairly even between Ramallah and Nablus, and less so between Nablus and Jenin.

In contrast to the Hebron and the Jerusalem Mountains, only one-third of the villages in Samaria are located on hilltops, while over 20 per cent are at the foot of

Plate 2.1 A typical Arab village in Samaria

or at the edge of a valley. The soil found in the valleys is an important factor for the villages in the Samarian Hills. The valleys themselves are not settled, since they contain fertile sedimentary soil suitable for intensive cultivation. The wide dispersion of villages in the Samaria Hills was also made possible by the abundance of springs, which are the result of many fault lines characteristic of this region.

The traditional Arab settlement in Judea and Samaria demonstrates that the climate frontier of the desert constitutes a barrier to the extension of the settlements and causes the concentration and sedentary population at the edge of the desert, which is evidenced by both the size of the villages and the extension of their landholding. The dispersion of the settlements, particularly in Judea, is governed almost entirely by the geographical factors, and no evidence can be found of artificial or Arab-planned development activity, such as that in the new Jewish settlement areas. Here, where human endeavor is more important than the natural conditions, there has been almost no development. The villages in this area and their interrelationship show no signs of any special co-ordination, but signs rather of isolation and dependence on the immediate local resources of soil, water, and means of communication.

In Judea the geographical dispersion of towns coincides generally with the watershed and follows the line Hebron, Bethlehem, Jerusalem, Ramallah, and Al-Bira. These towns are the administrative, commercial, marketing, and service centers for the surrounding villages. Jerusalem has the additional function of being the capital of both Judea and Samaria, while Hebron is the main center for the southern hills. Bethlehem and Beit Jala to the south, and Ramallah and Al-Bira to the north, serve as secondary centers which depend on the capital, particularly as regards their economy. The town distribution pattern in Judea is linear and is characterized by the division of functions between the various towns (Fig. 2.4).

In Samaria, on the other hand, the towns developed either on the hills facing the Valley of Yesreel and the Sharon Plain or at focal points and crossroads of intra- and interregional traffic arteries. The dispersion pattern of the towns emphasizes the central position of Nablus, the capital of Samaria, with Jenin to the north, Tulkarm to the west, and Qalqilya to the southwest. The towns of Samaria are not particularly large, but they are not a very important factor in the population of the region.

The urban population increased at a rate of only 42.6 per cent, as compared with the rise of 111 per cent in the rural population (Table 2.3). Thus, the urbanization index, which indicates the proportion of urban inhabitants in towns of a region as against the rural, is very low, and the rural population increase is still predominant. All the towns were small in the past. The main centers, such as Hebron and Nablus, did not exceed 42,000 inhabitants. During this period, two villages, Qalqilya and Al-Bira, were raised to the status of towns, but their population did not reach the 10,000 mark. The rate of growth of towns was lower in Judea and Samaria, while in the villages the position was reversed. The reason may have been that the towns in Judea had less commercial and social connection with Transjordan than did their counterparts in Samaria. The greater part of the urban population increase was accounted for by the migration of refugees or by the movement from village to town, and to a smaller degree by the internal growth of the town itself. East Jerusalem did not grow, and there was a continuous trickle of population to the neighboring towns and villages, such as Ramallah and Al-Bira. Jericho was an exception, owing to its location on the main route between Transjordan and Jerusalem and to its being a winter resort.

Table 2.3 The urban population of Judea and Samaria

Town	*1947*	*1967*	*Percentage increase*
Jenin	4,000	8,346	109.0
Nablus	23,250	41,537	78.0
Tulkarm	8,000	10,157	27.0
Qalqilya	(5,850)	8,922	52.0
Ramallah	5,000	12,030	141.0
Al-Bira	(2,920)	9,568	228.0
East Jerusalem	65,000	65,857	–
Bethlehem	9,000	14,439	60.0
Beit Jala	3,700	6,041	63.0
Hebron	24,600	38,091	55.0
Jericho	3,000	5,200	73.0
Total	154,320	230,188	42.6

Source: Estimate based on Mandatory Village Statistics, 1945, rounded off to the nearest hundred. Population Census, 1967, Statistical Abstract of Israel, 1970, No. 21. Qalqilya and Al-Bira were villages in 1947. East Jerusalem comprises those parts of Jerusalem annexed in 1967 to “Greater Jerusalem”.

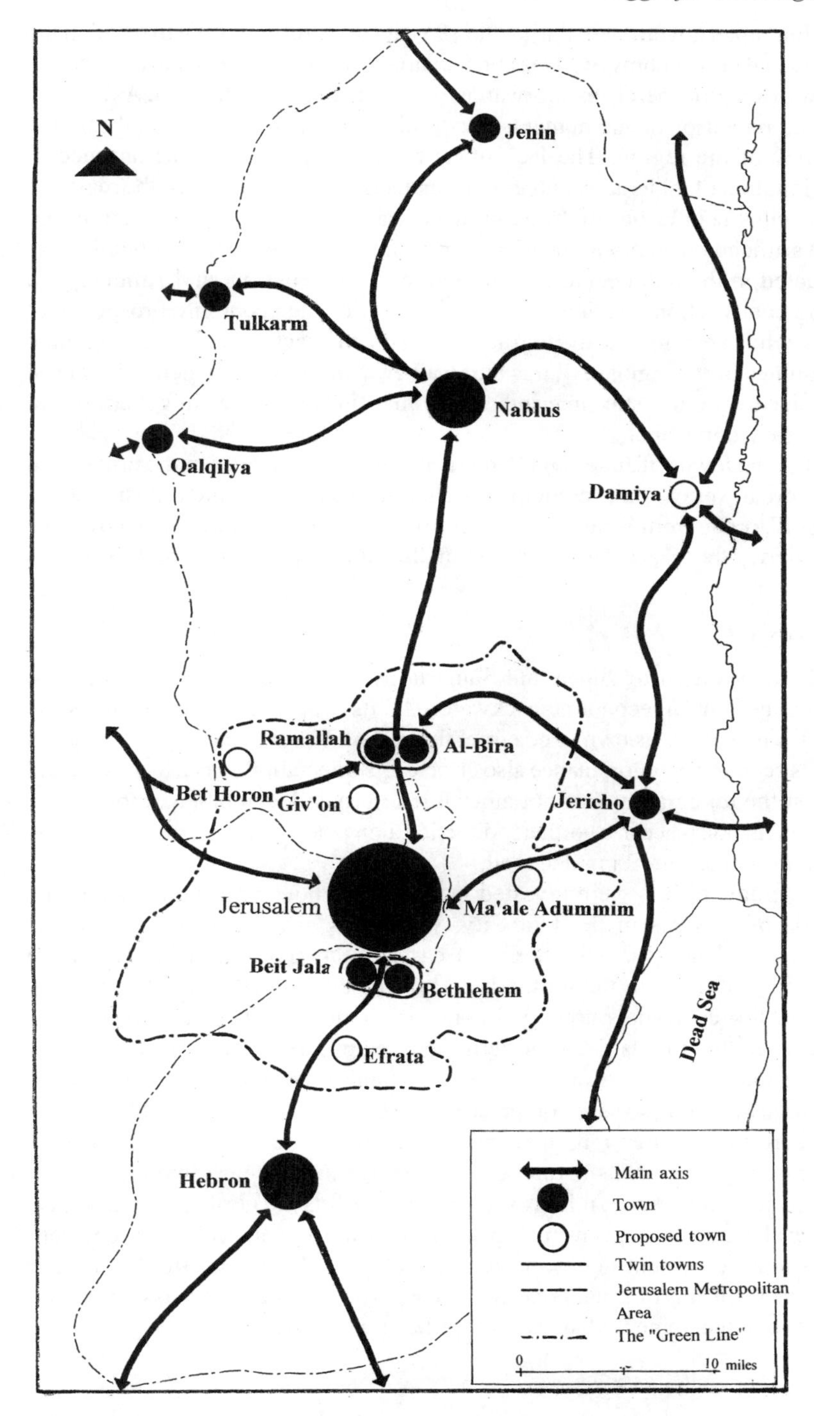

Fig. 2.4 Zones of influence and interrelationship axes in the West Bank according to the first master plan (1970)

The Jordanian government during the 19 years of its rule did little to develop the resources and the economy of Judea and Samaria, or to encourage physical planning, as it saw this region merely as a forward area on the frontier with Israel. As a result, the development of the settlements was limited and determined mainly by the geography of the region. The lack of new water supplies and the absence of the exploitation of mineral resources or of industrial development left the region to contend with the influence of the desert in the east, with a mountainous terrain and with an artificial boundary in the west, north, and south. New neighborhoods were constructed in the main centers of attraction, East Jerusalem and Amman, and building construction was intensified as a result of the economic prosperity of persons who were forced to migrate owing to the lack of suitable economic opportunities in the region. All this led to a new pattern of settlement, influenced on one side by the armistice line and on the other side by the lack of governmental economic encouragement

Most of the towns of Judea and Samaria experienced changes in the orientation of their urban sprawl and municipal boundaries as result of the armistice lines sealing off Jordan from Israel. An analysis of the building trends revealed by some of them during the 19 years may serve as an illustration of the general development.

East Jerusalem

With the annexation of Judea and Samaria by the Hashemite Kingdom, East Jerusalem became an economic backwater. All its supply lines were centered on Amman, which drew its own goods from the port of Aqaba and Beirut. The loss of the city's economic predominance also affected its orientation. Since to the east and southeast the topography was not amenable to urban development, most of the development took place in a northerly direction along the mountain crest and on both sides of the Jerusalem–Ramallah road.

Considerable efforts were invested in improving housing conditions and the standards of services in the Old City, which has always been the adequate commercial and industrial facilities in the eastern section of Jerusalem. This led to the rezoning of areas in the northern part of the city which had formerly been designated for residential purposes. In view of altered conditions the government of Jordan set about replanning the Jerusalem region, fixing its boundaries along a circular line stretching from Qalandiya airfield in the north to the village of Sur Bahir in the south, so as to comprise an area of 32,500 acres (130,000 dunams).

East Jerusalem under Jordanian rule therefore had to adapt to the artificial boundaries hemming in its natural expansion. Turning its back upon its natural economic base in the west, it had to spread out towards the north, south, and east. The main planning concepts were dispersion along the mountain crest, the development of new settlement nodes on the flat flanks of the central ridge and their connection by means of a main road along the north–south axis by-passing the Old City and the development of an eastern traffic artery to Transjordan.

Hebron

At one time Hebron had consisted of the inner core of the Old City and some few buildings around it, all straddling the main highway. At the beginning of the twentieth century further developments were carried out to the northeast along the highway to Bethlehem and Jerusalem. The new more spacious and taller buildings also enhanced the town's economic activities. The main expansion, however, took place during the 19 years of Jordanian rule when the city received a population increment of about 13,500. Its standard of living rose, not least because of the influx of funds from emigrants returning from the oil principalities. About 1,800 new houses were built in this period, about five hundred of them in the surrounding agricultural area. Most of the development was still along the Jerusalem highway, over a stretch of three miles (about 5 km) and at a depth of 600 ft (about 200 m) either way. To the southeast, however, the city expanded by only about one mile (1.6 km), having been cut off from Be'ersheva, the marketing center of the Bedouins.

Nablus

The original core of Nablus, the largest city in Judea and Samaria after Jerusalem, is a compact, unplanned warren of buildings hemmed in between two mountains. The influx of refugees from the Coastal Plain provided a considerable impetus for expansion, while at the same time the city lost its western zone of influence. It therefore had to develop an eastward orientation and strengthen its economic and social ties with Amman. The regional road leading to the east was expanded and the town began to spread out in a new direction previously barred by the presence of an ancient tel, a power station, and a prison. Over six years, from 1961 to 1967, over a thousand homes were built, many of them with money earned in Kuwait. The building boom also spread to the refugee camps and the suburbs on the Nablus–Amman and Nablus–Jerusalem highways.

Ramallah

Until 1947 Ramallah was densely built up, along the road to Al-Bira and about half a mile (800 m) to the north and to the south of it. Again, with the growing wealth of the population earned in foreign fields, new and better-spaced buildings went up, and the satellite town of Al-Bira began to be developed. As buildings sprawled over onto formerly agricultural areas, these were retroactively annexed to form part of the municipal boundaries. Though the new developments are totally unplanned they show a certain orientation towards Jerusalem, especially its northern neighborhoods, which have begun to merge with Ramallah into a continuous built-up strip along the mountainous crest. As for urban settlement in this region, there have been signs of urbanization. The towns are relatively large and are located along the main traffic artery of the mountain. The towns of Judea and Samaria form a kind of mirror image north and south of Jerusalem. Bethlehem and Beit Jala are opposite to

Ramallah and Al-Bira, while Hebron, the Hebron Mountain capital, is the counterpart of Nablus, the northern capital. The remaining towns are located as bridge points pointing towards the neighboring regions: Jericho towards Transjordan, Jenin towards the Valley of Yesreel, and Tulkarm towards the Sharon Plain.

These few examples are enough to indicate that the towns of Judea and Samaria responded in different ways to the region's severance from its natural outlets and surroundings, each according to its specific regional functions and geographic conditions. It may, moreover, be noted that they were all affected by the exogenous economic factor of emigration to the Arab oil principalities, despite sporadic urban growth. No attempt was made to adopt a modern approach to land uses, zoning, and the construction of modern, functional neighborhoods. The towns developed without an appropriate industrial base or adequate public institutions. Many of the residents still have an agrarian background, being landlords and farmers. Physical expansion thus did not go hand in hand with the development of urban functions and occupations. Moreover, the city boundaries were mostly determined haphazardly through the incorporation of rural areas on which buildings happened to be put up, so that the towns tend to sprawl out at low density.

To sum up, between 1949 and 1967 the West Bank was bounded by the armistice line between Israel and Jordan with no physical or economic links connecting it with the State of Israel. In 1947, as mentioned above, there were 264 Arab villages in the West Bank, which had grown to 396 by the end of the Jordanian rule in 1967, a rise of 50 per cent. The increase in rural population during the same period was even more pronounced: from 283,600 to 598,500, or 111 per cent. This growth took place mainly in the Hebron and the Jerusalem districts, rather than in the northern parts of the region, probably as a result of the internal migration of refugees and the settlement of nomads.

Arab agriculture in the West Bank is a primary geographical phenomenon resulting from the physical nature of the region. The location of the villages, their distribution pattern, and the manner in which the physical conditions have been exploited to enable the inhabitants to sustain themselves and to preserve their way of life may be taken into consideration by all new settlers in this region, even if equipped with modern technologies. Most villages are located on the mountain crest, a plateau favorable for agriculture, and on soft terraces with relatively deep soil; they take advantage of the local topography, avoid main highways, and do not encroach on agricultural land. The traditional Arab village in the Judean and Samarian Hills demonstrates the role played by the climate frontier as a barrier to the extension of villages, and explains the concentration and sedentary population at the edge of the desert.

The distribution of towns fits generally with the watershed and follows the line of Hebron, Bethlehem, Ramallah, Nablus, and Jenin. These towns constitute administrative, commercial, marketing and service centers for the surrounding villages, with Jerusalem having the additional function of being the regional capital. All in all, traditional Palestinian settlement in the West Bank has been widespread and deep-rooted, and has occupied most of the cultivable land.

First steps in the physical planning of the West Bank

The sovereign territory of the State of Israel, as established by the 1949 armistice, amounted to 8,086 sq. miles (about 20,700 sq. km). The occupation of the West Bank brought an additional 2,296 sq. miles (5,878 sq. km) under Israel's control, nearly a third of the country's territory. Prior to 1967, Israel's population stood at 2,750,000; following the Six Day War some 600,000 West Bankers, amounting to 22 per cent of Israel's population, came under occupation. In the West Bank considerable demographic changes have taken place with substantial emigration abroad, on the one hand, and immigration from the similarly liberated Gaza Strip, on the other.

All these changes presented new problems in the field of settlement, agriculture, construction, communication, and in many other domains. The development of the new areas could not be left to chance, but had to proceed according to a predetermined plan, so that the resources invested could be used for the best possible effect. Side by side with the current handling of everyday problems, attention had to be paid to the reshaping of the entire region in line with its inherent development potential, so that within a few decades it might, especially on the physical plane, attain the standard that it deserved.

The planning guidelines set in the first plan prepared in 1970 were independent of the political aspect. As far as possible, an attempt has been made to co-ordinate and direct the projected development with physical, national, and regional considerations and forestall random, local decisions based on considerations of expediency. The physical master plan that was prepared designated the locations of existing and projected uses, indicating their functions in the overall structure (Fig. 2.4).

The underlying ideas of the proposed master plan were: development of agriculture for export; urban development of Jerusalem and its satellites with a proportional growth of the various other towns in the area and their adequate industrialization; settlement of the unpopulated Jordan Valley and the Dead Sea area and making it arable; expansion of agriculture wherever possible; utilization of the available groundwater resources; clearance of slums and refugee camps; the development of the economic rural functions of the bigger villages; improvement of inland and air communications; utilization of the tourist potential of the area for the benefit of the entire country; and development of the periphery of Samaria and Judea so that they might become integrated with the rest of the country.

The principal projects in the plan were urban development of the region, expansion of town planning and preventing of excessive straggling, detailed urban planning of the periphery of Jerusalem, strengthening the urban character of towns, the rehabilitation of refugee camps, suburban housing projects, and the proper location of central business districts. In view of the projected urban growth additional areas were required for town building, especially in those towns whose municipal boundaries seemed insufficient. Not only the former villages that had been converted into small towns – Qalqilya, Tulkarm – but also bigger distinctly urban settlements such as Jenin, Ramallah, and Bethlehem suffered a disadvantage.

The plan proposed to establish a new town west of Damiya bridge and near to the Jordan River, as an additional linkage between Transjordan and Nablus. The town had to be populated by refugees after the Palestinian Authority's decision to settle them there, as part of a political agreement with Israel. The plan also proposed to establish in Judea and Samaria regional councils, very similar to those in Israel, in order to administer groups of villages under one municipal authority that might put an end to the traditional rule of sheikhs and mukhtars. The plan proposed to minimize gradually the nomadic population in the Judean Desert and to establish there a few sites for the Bedouins which should in the future turn into permanent service centers as in the northern Negev.

It is hard to believe how different the reality in Judea and Samaria is today compared to what the planners envisaged after the Six Day War. It seems that for certain reasons the politicians hesitated to approve and to execute the planners' proposals, so as a result they left the region to other interested powers to penetrate into it under the guise of a new political and religious settlement movement, which in the frame of the military occupation regime created a situation quite opposite to the planners' guidelines.

The basic planning at the end of the 1960s did not take into account any need for Jewish settlement in Judea and Samaria, and certainly not any intensive building of houses for settlers, as happened later on. The planning approach at that time was to initiate development for the future in the whole region for the local inhabitants, together with a gradual economic growth which might create an interrelationship with Israel's economy in many aspects. When the Jewish settlement establishment desired to take over Judea and Samaria, it was confronted in 1967 with unequivocal facts: a local population of five to six hundred thousand which had settled in this region in the past in the most suitable sites, and which was not ready to abandon any piece of its own land willingly, even for financial compensation, and refusing to submit to the Israeli occupation activities. That is the basic ground of the conflict which exists nowadays between the Palestinians and the Israelis, and has done for more than 38 years.

In Greater Jerusalem the westward expansion to the Jerusalem Corridor, as well as the eastward growth of the city, had to be arrested, and building had to take place mainly in the center, the south, and the north. Some of these areas had then not yet assumed a distinctly urban character, particularly Beit Jala, Al-Bira, Qalqilya, and Tulkarm, which retained much of their rural aspect. The refugee camps inside and on the outskirts of the towns had turned into slums, so they had to be cleared, and inhabitants provided with suitable alternative accommodation. The expansion of suburban neighborhoods had to be anticipated, especially in the Jerusalem area where overcrowding, the rising standard of living, and the tendency to move to a more exclusive neighborhood seemed particularly important.

In the economic field, the plan was particularly concerned with the development of the Jordan Valley, the utilization of ground water, the development of export crops and industry and crafts in the rural area, the development of the Dead Sea shores, and of tourist and recreation areas, and the restoration of ancient sites. The Jordan Valley seemed fit for development because of both its sparse existing population and its rich alluvial soil. Craft and light industry had to be integrated in the rural areas to solve the projected unemployment of considerable portions of the agricultural labor force resulting from increasing mechanization. The Dead Sea is a rich source of minerals and has a considerable potential for the development of the tourist industry and health resorts. Tourist sites and natural amenities were proposed mainly in the mountainous parts near Jerusalem, Bethlehem, and Hebron.

In the field of communications the most important proposals were the national roads, the international airport at Atarot, and the domestic airfields. It also seemed necessary to remedy the physical defects due to 19 years of neglect and division along the "Green Line". Existing roads had to be linked up, and new roads built to connect Judea and Samaria. Extensive areas of land had to be reclaimed and the settlement in the periphery, including various villages and towns in Samaria, had to be developed with a new orientation on the Coastal Plain.

After the Six Day War in 1967, Jewish settlements were gradually established in Judea and Samaria. These were initially defense strongholds and military agricultural settlements. Later they achieved the status of permanent settlements. At the beginning the main concentration of settlements was in the Jordan Valley and the eastern slopes of the Samarian Hills, but later on more settlements were established in western Samaria.

The settlements planted in Judea and Samaria are political in nature, their main object being to obtain a hold on areas which may in the future face being cut off from the State of Israel. Most of the settlements are located today in the western and central parts of the region and at selected points in the hill country, where land was available and where there were fewer inhabitants, and where the existing population could be minimally affected.

The "Allon" plan

In 1967 the Minister of Labor, Yigal Allon, presented the cabinet with a plan for the country's future border, which proposed principles concerning peace arrangements with neighboring states. The plan stipulated a territorial compromise of the West Bank that would meet Israel's security requirements while taking into account the aspirations of the Arab population. It proposed to leave some 40 per cent of the area under Israel's sovereignty, with Israeli settlements along the Jordan Valley serving as a security belt. Though never accepted as an official doctrine, the plan exerted a considerable impact on Israel's settlement map as long as Labor remained in power.

Shortly after the war it became evident that Israel was looking towards border modifications on the Jordanian front. The significance of the "Allon" plan thus lay in its being the first comprehensive attempt to formulate a clear territorial status for Israel's most problematic border, that with Jordan. The boundaries of the plan, derived from topographic and demographic considerations, were set between two longitudinal axes, one along the Jordan River and the other along the eastern slopes of the Samarian Hills; between them lay an arable and a rather sparsely populated area; the 1967 census showed no more than 15,000 inhabitants, 5,000 of them in

Jericho. The envisaged width of the proposed settlement belt along the Jordan Valley ranged between 6 to 15 miles (9.6 to 24 km), and a security strip was to join Israel's sovereign territory through a broad stretch of several miles along the Jerusalem–Jericho axis (Fig. 2.5).

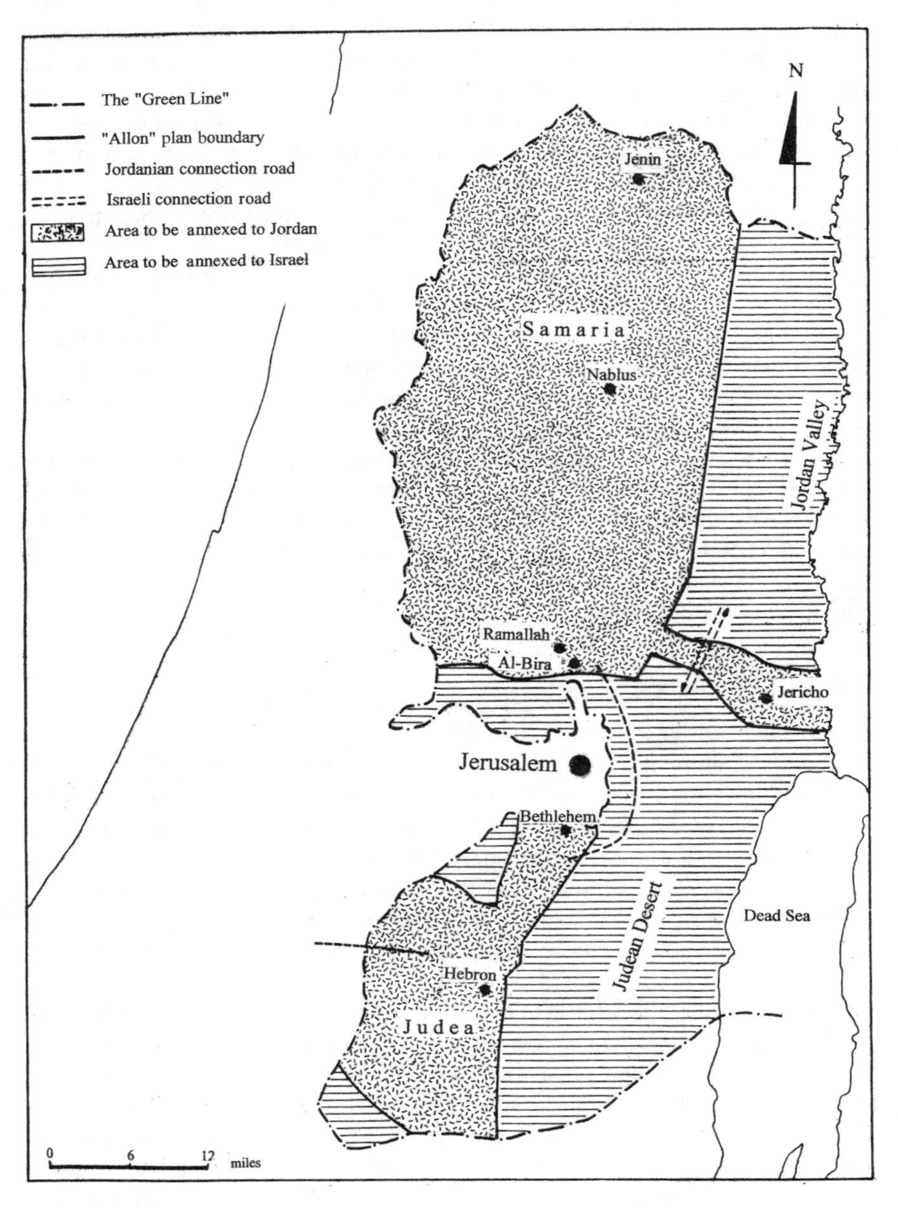

Fig. 2.5 The "Allon" plan

The plan posited a large Jewish population in many settlements along the Jordan and the slopes of the Samarian Hills, with agricultural settlements clustered around regional centers. The basis for this was the relative ecological advantage of the Jordan Valley for early ripe winter crops and tropical fruits. The settlement of the Jordan Valley was influenced by such factors as climate and the amount of water found locally, as well as the topography features of the land, as 37,500 acres (150,000 dunams) of land were found to be arable. Other key considerations were proximity to the Jordan River to secure the eastern border, as well as to the longitudinal roads; maximum population of uninhabited areas; and avoidance of occupation of land cultivated by Arabs. In the run-up to the 1973 elections the security rationale of the plan was underscored by Allon's fellow minister Yisrael Galilee, who drafted an ideological platform for the Labor Party, supporting the concentration of "security settlements" along the borders and rejecting Israel's return to the pre-1967 borders and the establishment of a Palestinian State in the West Bank.

When conceived, the "Allon" plan was a major innovation in Israeli strategic thinking. With the passage of time, however, it became outmoded. Rather than an asset, the concentration of settlements in a narrow strip of land came to be seen as a strategic liability that might restrict military training ability in the event of war; this skepticism regarding the utility of agricultural settlement as lines of defense in the occupied territories gained much ground after the October 1973 War, in which Israel was forced to evacuate its settlements on the Golan Heights hurriedly to prevent their seizure by the advancing Syrian army. Yet by 2004 Jewish presence along the Jordan Valley had expanded to some 6,000 settlers in 30 settlements.

Successive expansion plans

A second plan after the "Allon" plan was that of Defense Minister Moshe Dayan. Its aim was to reinforce Israeli control on the mountain crest with army camps, each stronghold to be connected with the area within the "Green Line" through a network of roads, water pipes, and electric cables. The idea behind the plan was implemented only in the Ezyon bloc, as difficulties in land acquisition emerged in other places. A third plan involved the reinforcement of the environs of Jerusalem, and was handled mainly by the ministerial committee on Jerusalem and the ministerial committee on settlement. Its aim was to broaden the Jerusalem Corridor northwards to the Bet Horon road and southwards to the Ezyon bloc. Another plan was connected with the erasure of the "Green Line". As the security border adopted by the government was along the Jordan River, it was decided to erase the previous border to the west of the Samarian Hills by means of almost contiguous Jewish settlement. Beginning in 1976, therefore, a few settlements were established beyond the "Green Line" as an extension of the settlement complex within Israel proper.

After the right-wing Likud Party came to power in 1977 the World Zionist Organization's Settlement Division prepared a comprehensive plan for the establishment of more settlements in the West Bank. This plan was a guiding document for the government policy regarding the settlements, and emphasized that the civilian presence of Jewish communities is vital for the security of the State, and there must be no doubt regarding the intention of Israel to hold the areas of Judea and Samaria forever; the way to do so should be a rapid settlement drive in these areas. This plan was completed in line with the Gush Emunim movement (see below) and the co-operation between the two bodies led to the establishment of many community settlements.

Another plan was prepared during the first Likud government at the end of the 1970s by Ariel Sharon as Minister of Agriculture. He prepared a plan that included a map delineating areas he believed to be vital for Israel's security, and should therefore be annexed. According to this plan only a small number of enclaves densely populated by Palestinians were not to come under Israel sovereignty. He recommended the establishment of settlements in these areas as a means of promoting annexation. Following this plan the government concentrated its effort on establishing settlements on the western slopes of Samaria and north of Jerusalem. These efforts reflected the belief that it might prevent the creation of a contiguous area populated by Arabs on either side of the "Green Line". While the settlements in the central mountain ridge were populated mainly by members and supporters of Gush Emunim, a great effort was made by the government to attract the general, non-ideological public to the settlements in western Samaria by guaranteeing them an approved standard of living there within a short distance of the Coastal Plain.

At the beginning of 1983 the Ministry of Agriculture and the World Zionist Organization published a master plan for settlements in the West Bank through the year 2010, which was also known as the Hundred Thousand Plan, owing to its aspiration to attract 80,000 new Israeli citizens by 1986, so that the Jewish population in the area, excluding East Jerusalem, would number 100,000. Twenty-three new communal and rural communities, as well as twenty "Nahal" army settlement sites, were planned for the additional population. In order to settle 100,000 Jews in Judea and Samaria, the government had to invest about US$ 3 billion. Presumably such an investment had to come at the expense of Galilee, Negev, and the development towns. As Israel's resources are in any case limited, any priority granted in one area would necessarily result in stagnation and regression in others. It should also be borne in mind that settling Jews in Judea and Samaria is contrary to the central Zionist goal, which is the establishment of a State in the Land of Israel that maintains a Jewish character and at the same time is democratic and just. The creation of a Jewish minority in Judea and Samaria is likely to produce another situation resembling that in the mountainous areas of Galilee. The plan was concerned primarily with reinforcing the existing settlement blocs and did not offer an orderly settlement mode. The pattern of the plan seemed to be a conglomeration of local solutions which did not coalesce into a rational regional alignment. During the period of the plan, the government achieved the objective in terms of the number of new settlements, but failed to meet the population forecast, since in 1986 the actual Jewish population was only 51,000.

Settlement activities continued at full pace under the newly elected Likud government in the years 1988–92. The population of the settlements increased during that time by 60 per cent. Ten new settlements were established and a tremendous wave of construction in the territories was carried out by this government, although it led to an open confrontation with the United States government, which decided to freeze guarantees it had promised to Israel as a part of the assistance to help absorb the wave of immigration of Russian Jews who came in the 1990s.

The Gush Emunim activities

Settlement activity in the West Bank has been carried out by Israel's two largest parties, Labor with its secular and socialist outlook, and Likud with its religious and nationalist stance. The former took a pragmatic approach to settlement, in line with Allon's concept of defensible borders, avoiding settlements in densely populated areas. Likud, conversely, was committed to the territorial ideology of "Greater Israel" and insisted on the right of Jews to settle everywhere in the territories, not least near major Arab population centers. A new kind of pioneer Zionism thus emerged, one that exhorted Israelis to exercise their rights in their historic homeland and used nationalist and religious justifications to this end. Those new settlers had to be highly motivated, since the regions in which they settled were densely populated by Palestinians, which made their endeavor a rather hazardous one.

The ultimate manifestation of the new settlers was provided by a new zealous movement established in 1974: Gush Emunim, meaning "Bloc of the Believers" or "Bloc of the Faithful". Emerging in a low point of Israel's national morale, shortly after the traumatic 1973 war, this radical extra-parliamentary movement inscribed on its ideological flag the acceleration of settlement activity in the "Greater Land of Israel", Judea and Samaria in particular. The Gush Emunim's approach to the occupied territories was religious, indeed messianic. It was not only convinced of Jewish ancestral rights over Jerusalem, Hebron, Nablus, Bethlehem, Shilo, and other places; it believed in the sanctity of the Land of Israel and maintained that, through settling in its historic homeland, the Jewish people, and not only Israel, was nearing its salvation.

The process of Jewish settlement in Judea and Samaria since 1967 has to be seen as a means of civil creeping occupation of a historic region which has been populated in the past hundred years by Arabs and Palestinians, and which after the Six Day War began to be resettled by Jews with the aim of changing it as an integral part of the "Greater Land of Israel". There were at that time many Israelis who were ready to execute this ideological, religious, and national aim, even for economic reasons, because it was then possible, among other things, to receive full subsidized housing on State land, almost without payment – and in a rural environment with a lot of open space nearby.

The military occupation of Judea, Samaria, and the Gaza Strip could be maintained under military rule only with the aid of a dependent gradual civilian settlement process. From past Zionist settlement experience it could be learned that the known land occupying system under the slogan "dunam after dunam" worked even without a general strategic scheme and even made it possible to execute spot settlement penetrations into relatively dense populated Arab regions and to dominate their territory. While the rural and urban Palestinian settlements on the mountain crest, on its slopes, and in the Gaza Strip's plain were historically sited on appropriate places from a geographical point of view, the Jewish settlements in these regions had to be content with relatively inferior sites on expropriated State land of unknown ownership.

Over the years the Jewish settlement in the territories created a dispersed layout of settlements which drove wedges between the Palestinian village blocs on the mountain crest and on their flanks and in the Gaza Strip, by basing at the same time its own settlements in the Ezyon, Ari'el, and Qatif blocs, and creating a chain of urban satellites around Jerusalem. It is hard to disregard the fact that the civilian-occupied sprawl in the region resulted by 2004 in the establishment of about 140 settlements in which more than 230,000 people reside.

In practical terms, Gush Emunim aspired to settle the mountain crest and the areas of dense Arab population. This meant the creation of territorial continuity between the West Bank and the State of Israel. The movement invoked the pioneering spirit that had animated the Jewish people in the past, and was evidently encouraged by the tradition that had developed in Israel whereby settlers have never abandoned their land of their free will. Their first actions were to revive the Ezyon bloc, occupied by the Jordanian Legion during the 1948–49 war, and to reinstate Jews in Hebron, where they had lived for centuries, through the establishment of the suburb of Qiryat Arba. The growing influence of this young guard, mainly within the religious community, but also among Likud supporters, led to the demand for the government to annex the occupied territories to the State of Israel.

The Gush Emunim embarked on its settlement policy with a vengeance. Already in 1974 it established the settlements of Ofra, Shilo, and Kefar Qedumim in the West Bank. As the Labor government was unable to agree on what measures should be taken against Gush Emunim, not least owing to the bitter personal rivalry between Prime Minister Yizhak Rabin and Defense Minister Shimon Peres, the movement could pursue its activities virtually undisturbed. In 1976 there were 220 Gush Emunim settlers in the territories, and it was clear that the government would not remove them. They even prepared an ambitious settlement plan aimed at settling a million Jews in a hundred locations in the course of one decade. The plan concentrated on places along the Jerusalem–Nablus axis and two or three lateral axes traversing the mountain region. Its underlying principles were maximum spread of settlements; transfer of resources from the Coastal Plain to the hills; the establishment of a company to invest in industrial enterprise; rapid development of profitable projects; and State seizure of land whose ownership was unclear.

By 1977 Gush Emunim had already set up 12 settlements in the hills, comprising together some 500 acres (2,000 dunams) of land. Each settlement consisted of a few inhabitants, employed outside the area and commuting to Jerusalem or the Coastal Plain; many settlers held on to their former dwellings as well. Likud's accession to power in 1977 changed this modest beginning and gave the Gush Emunim a tremendous boost. The late Prime Minister Menachem Begin had never hidden his deep sympathy for this messianic extra-parliamentary group. He viewed Gush Emunim as a selfless pioneering movement and, as head of the largest opposition party in the mid-1970s, supported their settlement activities. Now, with Likud in power, Gush Emunim was rapidly transformed from a small disruptive force on the sidelines of the Israeli political map into a mainstream movement (Fig. 2.6).

Encouraged by its new prowess, in 1978 the Gush prepared a second master plan for the settlement of 750,000 Israelis in the West Bank, the first 100,000 by 1981. The plan envisaged two central towns, Qiryat Arba and Ari'el, each with a population of 60,000, and four smaller towns of about 20,000 each, this in addition to 20 10,000-strong urban centers and 25 concentrations of community settlements. Through this extensive network of settlements the Gush Emunim hoped to create an irreversible reality in the territories, though it was obvious that such vast settlement activity would come at the expense of development in the Negev and Galilee, and even on the Golan Heights. The Gush Emunim's great plan effectively became the official policy of the World Zionist Organization and Israel's Ministry of Agriculture.

During Likud's first two years Gush Emunim succeeded in creating many settlements, though the percentage of Jews in the total West Bank population remained very low. Government policy sought to break up the territorial continuity of the Palestinian population by means of the Jerusalem-area settlements in the center, those of the Jordan Valley in the east, and of Gush Emunim in the heart of Samaria, in order to ensure that no autonomous entity above the level of local council would develop.

As noted earlier, an ambitious plan for the settlement of the West Bank, largely modeled on Gush Emunim's vision, was adopted in 1978 by the settlement Department of the World Zionist Organization and Israel's Ministry of Agriculture.

Plate 2.2 The Jewish settlement Talmon in Samaria

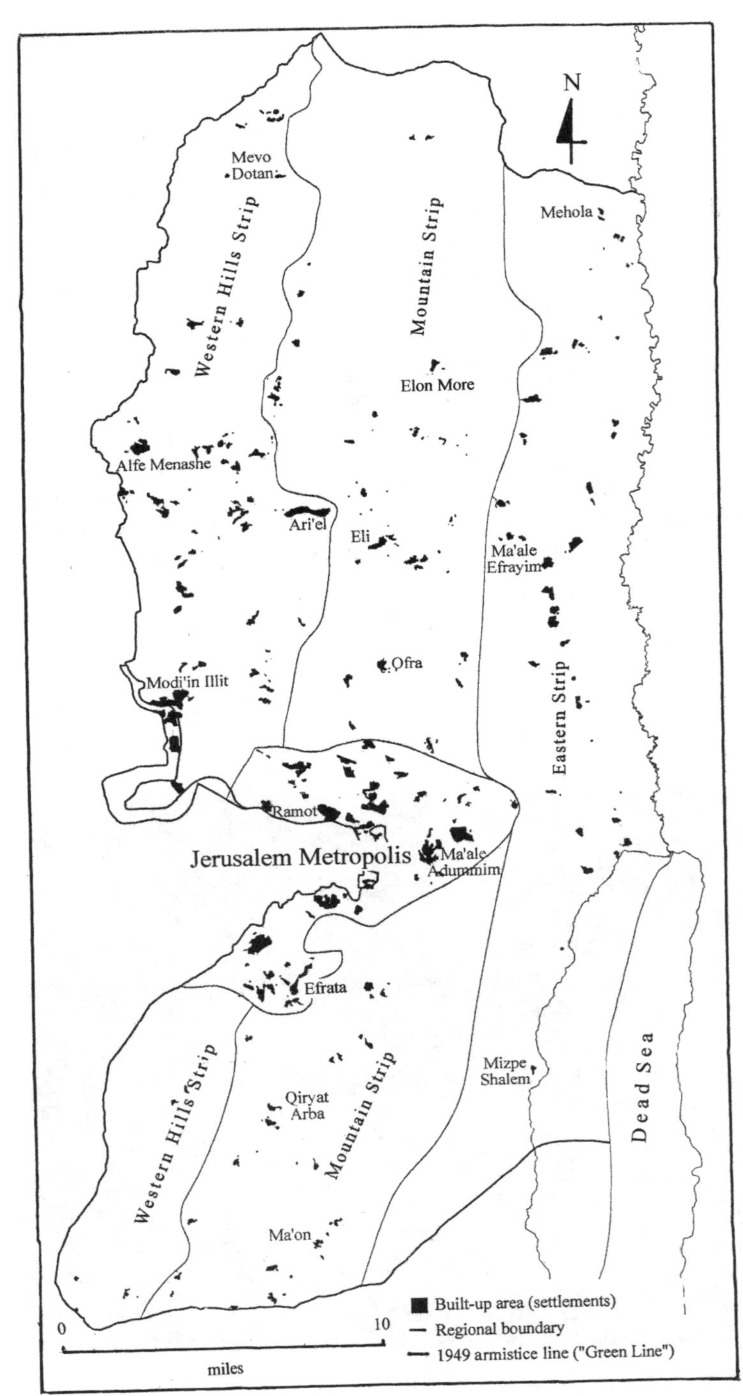

Fig. 2.6 Jewish built-up areas in the West Bank
Source: B'tselem, The Israeli Center for Human Rights in the Occupied Territories, 2002

Its aims were twofold: to settle 100,000 Jews in the territories between 1982 and 1987, and to increase their numbers to half a million by the year 2010. The plan provided for the creation in the main of urban settlements in the vicinity of the "Green Line"; these would not be based on a hard core of ideological settlers, as had been the case in the past, rather they would actually serve as residential suburbs of the Tel Aviv agglomeration and Jerusalem, offering their Israeli residents a high standard of housing at a relatively low cost.

An extended version of the plan proposed the preparation of land for 165 settlements over a 30-year period, so as to accommodate up to a million Jews in the territories. Five towns of ten to thirty thousand families each were to be established, as were 36 suburbs, each with 3,000 families, 65 communities of 400 families each, and another 60 collective and small holder settlements. The plan envisaged the construction of five to six thousand dwelling units per annum; the laying of 250 miles (400 km) of roads; the expansion of existing rural and urban settlements; the development of industrial zones at the rate of 10–125 acres (40–500 dunams) per annum, and continued acquisition of land. The areas identified for immediate implementation were Greater Jerusalem, the eastern slopes of the hills near Tulkarm, and south of Mount Hebron. The extended settlement plan did not concern itself with the empty areas east of the water divide, but aimed mainly at gaps between Palestinian villages. The model proposed was one settlement line to the east, loosely strung from north to south, and blocs of settlements to the west. The link between the blocs, and between the Jewish settlements in the territories and pre-1967 Israel, would be maintained by a new infrastructure of local and national roads that would not be integrated into existing Arab roads and would allow for settlement segregation.

In spite of the facts discussed above, it is hard to say that after a civilian creeping occupation there exists a full Jewish dominance in the territories. Actually, the situation is far from it, both in the size of the Jewish population residing in Judea and Samaria, compared to the three million Palestinians there, and also in the amount of land which has been seized by the settlers. Much more significant are the territorial issues that these settlements aroused regarding the future borderlines of the Palestinian State. After all, they succeeded in fragmenting the rural Palestinian village blocs into dozens of parts which will be very difficult to crystallize into a successive Palestinian territory. However, the continuing placement of most of the Jewish settlements in the region, their expansion and permanent growth, together with the outposts that were erected on top of hills in remote places as pioneer points, ensure that, unfortunately, more settlements may be added to this region in the future.

Types of Jewish settlements in the West Bank

The Israeli solution for the settlement of an entire region was to build a wide network of settlements, even if it ran contrary to the natural balance of population over a wider area, or if it involved establishing new settlements in previously uninhabited areas that might be less suitable for development than other places not settled by

Arabs. The only condition necessary for such settlement is a large investment of capital resources in order to bring about such changes in the natural environment as are needed to adapt it for settlement. This approach was first applied to a section of the Jordan Valley.

The Jordan Valley was one of the areas in the West Bank which had remained sparsely populated though it was potentially suitable for settlement. After the Six Day War the Israel settlement authorities immediately started to draw up plans with a view to settling Jews in the area. The plans were based on the establishment of a number of agricultural village settlements with the climatic advantage of the Jordan Valley: a mild winter and the possibility of growing tropical vegetables and fruits.

Thus an exceptional opportunity presented itself to develop an area by means of a comprehensive regional approach and to establish a group of settlements based on the physical characteristics of the Valley. It was also necessary to plan the infrastructure required for a continuous chain of settlements extending over the whole length of the Valley that would constitute a defense barrier parallel to the Jordan River and opposite Jordanian territory.

The Jordan Valley was estimated to contain 16,500 acres (66,000 dunams) of cultivable land, unevenly distributed along the length of the Valley. The northern part is more suitable for intensive cultivation than the southern part, near the Dead Sea shore, and therefore more settlements were established in the north than in the south. The settlement pattern was also influenced by the structure of the Valley. Settlements could be located either in the main Valley itself or in the lateral valleys which descend from the Judean Mountains and also contain soil suitable for cultivation. The availability of local water resources was less decisive, since it was possible to supply water by artificial means. The amount of land and water available determined the number of agricultural units and settlements that could be planned for the Valley. On the basis of the potential amount of land and water the number of agricultural settlements approached 30 (Fig. 2.7).

The settlements were necessarily located next to the cultivable areas. Most of them were at the beginning Nahal (Fighting Pioneer Youth) outposts, mostly changed into permanent settlements. The type of settlement was determined in each case by local conditions, such as soil and water, and by the type of pioneering organization providing the settlers. Owing to the comprehensive approach to the planning of the whole region, it was possible to bring in settlers from all sectors of the population, with varied backgrounds of agricultural knowledge and experience.

Agriculture, in its various branches, provided most of the employment in the region. Industries and crafts were established in co-operative settlements in order to supplement income and to provide alternative employment during slack seasons. Owing to the paucity of agricultural resources in the southern part of the Valley, the settlements there were based mainly on tourism. The settlement pattern in the Jordan Valley was more or less similar to that found in other parts of the country: a combination of farming and industry wherever this has been found to be necessary.

The regional settlement of the Jordan Valley was based, as already noted, on the political concept of a continuous chain of settlements parallel to the Jordan River

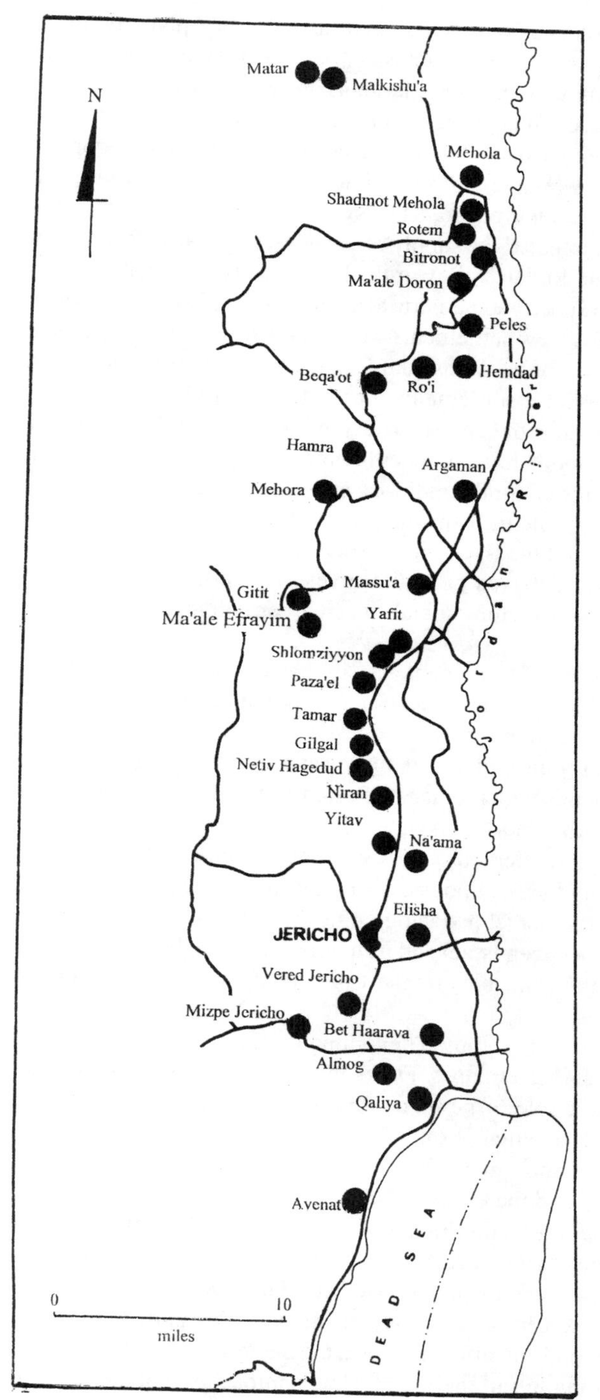

Fig. 2.7 Jewish settlements in the Jordan Valley

constituting a defense boundary in accordance with the "Allon" plan, avoiding Jewish settlement in those parts of Judea and Samaria which have a dense Arab population. The idea was that, with the aid of large-scale capital investment in the development of water resources and the use of agro-technical know-how that have not been available to the Arab farmers, it would be possible to raise large crops of winter vegetables and fruits which could be sold at high prices in the European markets. The settlement plan also ensured the geographical continuity of the settlements, which greatly facilitated the supply of services, as does the fact that all of them are close to either the Jordan Valley or the East Samaria highway.

Agricultural settlement in Judea and Samaria after the Six Day War has not been confined to the Jordan Valley. New settlements were established at many points in eastern Samaria and northwest of the Jerusalem Corridor, as well as in the Ezyon bloc, which was resettled. These settlements were of necessity established on unoccupied State land, and, since the greater part of the suitable land was already being cultivated in one way or other, the new settlements were in most cases set up in places with unfavorable agricultural conditions and often distant from existing roads. This raised difficult problems, especially regarding education and health services, electricity supply, and the like, which were not only a heavy burden on the national budget but also deterred potential investors – not to speak of the difficulty in maintaining a satisfactory social life in a community that does not exceed a few dozen souls.

No clear pattern of this type of settlement activity has emerged, and it did not form part of any regional plan, with the exception of a group of settlements in the Ezyon bloc, which were intended to form one cohesive unit. The settlements were established without a predetermined plan as to timing and location, the main object being political: to occupy lands which otherwise might some day be in danger of being cut off from the State of Israel.

The future of this type of settlement activity is not difficult to foretell. The settlements stand the test of changing political circumstances. Just as in the past, agricultural settlements within Israel had geographical significance when it came to determining the borders between Israel and its neighbors. It can be assumed that in the future as well the settlements beyond the 1949 "Green Line" will influence political territorial decisions.

The above outline indicates the common denominator of the various settlement bodies with regard to the Jerusalem area. Development should be based on the existing road network, the circle of new quarters within the municipal area of Jerusalem should be completed, villages should be built on the heights overlooking the city and in places which dominate the main traffic arteries connecting the mountains with the lowland and the Coastal Plain.

It may be concluded that the main difficulty encountered when planning the settlement of Judea and Samaria was that it was not empty but inhabited at that time by about 600,000 Arabs who were not prepared to leave any place of their own free will. In the contrast to past experience when Jews settled in other parts of the Land of Israel, the Arabs of Judea and Samaria were not at the mercy of absentee "effendi" landowners who were willing to sell their land. New approaches had therefore to be found to make settlement possible in this region, and the planners had to contend with innumerable constraints.

Traditional Arab settlement in the region was the most widespread and deep-rooted, and it occupied most of the cultivable land. It could not, however, serve as a model for modern Jewish settlement. The system of regional settlement has a history of success within the pre-1967 lines, is an accepted technique in other countries, and has given rise to well-defined settlement models. It is efficient and very promising but cannot serve as a model for all of Judea and Samaria, only for the Jordan Valley. This was its main weakness from a political point of view. The system of "spot" settlement had a wider application, and was perhaps more significant politically, but its economic and social weaknesses were so considerable as to raise doubts regarding its viability and its ability to achieve a spatial hold on the region, in the wider sense of the term. Of all types of settlement, urban settlement is the most compact in terms of population, the most economical with regard to land utilization, and generally also the one having the most promising economic future. Its main weakness is the huge cost because enormous sums have to be invested in preparing an urban infrastructure. To this must be added the doubt whether the necessary hundreds of thousands of people can be found for the urban settlement of the area.

It is interesting to note that the different approaches to settlement that have been described reflect the application of the settlement processes utilized in the Land of Israel over the twentieth century. When Zionist settlement first started, at the end of the nineteenth century, the traditional approach was predominant, and this constituted a challenge to the early Jewish settlers. The "spot" approach is reminiscent of the "stockade and tower" pioneer settlement of the 1930s, both on frontiers and in the midst of the Arab population. The regional approach brings to mind the settlement undertakings in the Valley of Yesreel and the Bet She'an Valley, and, later, in the Lakhish region and the northern Negev. The urban approach, which was first applied to the building of the development towns, was being repeated in Judea and Samaria.

The settlement map of today's Israel is fundamentally different from that of the 1950s and 1960s; it has been altered by the development of many additional Jewish settlements in the West Bank, by the internal migration of population to them, and by new priorities of regional development. The 1970s and 1980s were crucial in this respect, for it was then that Israel's ties with the occupied territories were forged and a new map was effectively drawn, influenced by the new political reality created by the Six Day War. Unlike earlier decades, settlement during the 1970s and 1980s was largely predicated on political, rather than economic, considerations. Executed on a mass scale, rural and urban, public and private, in areas whose ultimate fate remained unknown, it involved penetration into a crowded Arab settlement fabric by a new type of settlement. This, in turn, has generated a regrettable diffusion of new settlements and has cast serious doubts on whether Israel's new frontiers will allow the maintenance of national sovereignty and a democratic society.

The settlements established in the West Bank vary in several aspects, one being their social structure, or type of settlement: regular urban and rural, community and co-operative. Co-operative settlements are subdivided into three clear models, kibbutz, moshav, and co-operative moshav – they vary in terms of the level of equality and extent of co-operation in ownership of property, in general, and of means of production, in particular. These forms of settlements are the classic models, and accordingly most of the kibbutzim and moshavim in the West Bank were founded during the 1970s under the Labor Party governments and situated in areas within the "Allon" plan. The common feature of all the types of settlement, at least during the early phases, is their agricultural character, although since the 1980s many of these settlements have branched out into industry and tourism, while some of their members have begun to work as salaried employees in the adjacent urban centers.

Gush Emunim created a new type of settlement, the community settlement, suited to the hills, with their scarcity of land and water; each such settlement comprised some dozens of families and was based on private initiative and partial co-operation, with no obligation to work in the settlement itself; this also suited many residents who had no agricultural background. Most of the members of the community settlements are middle-class settlers employed in white-collar positions in nearby cities within Israel. By 1980 there were 18 Gush Emunim settlements in the West Bank, and the decade witnessed an extensive settlement effort in the hill country. By the time Israelis went to the ballots in 1981, the 7,000-strong Jewish population in the occupied territories had trebled. A decade later it had exceeded the 100,000 mark.

The remaining settlements are regular urban or rural settlements managed by local committees or councils elected by the residents. These settlements do not use any special procedure for membership or any co-operative financial framework. However, the smaller the settlement, the greater the homogeneity among its members. Among the largest of these settlements in homogeneous and demographic terms are the ultra-orthodox settlements, such as Betar Illit.

One of the claims made by Israel to justify the settlements, although they are prohibited by the Fourth Geneva Convention, is that the State does not transfer its citizens to the occupied territories. Israel argues that each citizen decides privately, of his or her own free will, to move to the settlement. In reality, however, all Israeli governments have implemented a vigorous and systematic policy to encourage Israeli citizens to move from Israel to the West Bank. One of the main tools used to realize this policy is the provision of significant financial benefits and incentives. Two types of benefit and incentives are granted by the government: support granted directly to the citizens by defining settlements as "national priority" areas, and support granted to local settlements in the West Bank in a manner that favors them in comparison to settlements inside Israel.

One of the main tools used to channel resources to the residents of the settlements is also the definition of most of the settlements in the West Bank as "development areas" or as "national priority" areas. Such a definition is also applied to settlements in Galilee or in the Negev. The current map of national priority areas and the relevant incentives and benefits was established in 1998 and was approved by the government. The purpose of the map of national priority areas is to encourage the generation remaining in these areas, to encourage initial settling by new immigrants, and to encourage the migration of veterans to the priority areas. The map is based principally on geographical criteria assuming that the scope of opportunities of citizens residing in the peripheral areas is in many respects limited by comparison to that in the center. While the geographical consideration might explain the inclusion in the periphery map of the Negev and Galilee, it cannot explain the inclusion of most of the settlements in the West Bank, a substantial number of which are adjacent or relatively close to Jerusalem and the cities of Tel Aviv metropolitan area, where many of the residents of the settlements are employed.

The benefits and incentives provided for the priority areas are granted by six government ministries: Housing and Construction; National Infrastructure; Education; Trade and Industry; Labor and Social Affairs; and Finance. The level of incentive varies according to the classification of each settlement as a class A or B category. The Ministry of Construction and Housing provides generous assistance for those who purchase a new apartment or build their own home in national priority areas. The Ministry also contributes to the development costs by means of a grant covering up to 50 per cent of expenses, according to the classification of the community and type of expense. The National Infrastructure Ministry through Israel Land Administration provides very high discounts from the value of the land in the payment of lease fees for residential construction, and a great discount on leasehold fees for industrial and tourism purposes. The Ministry of Education provides a range of incentives for teachers who work in priority areas, including promotion, participation in rental costs and travel expenses, and reimbursement of 75 per cent of tuition fees paid by teachers at institutions of higher education. The Ministry of Industry and Trade provides approved enterprises, pursuant to the Capital Investments Encouragement Law, to those defined as entitled to government support, with high grants and income tax benefits, and covers a significant portion of costs for the establishment of new industrial zones and the maintenance of existing zones, including significant discounts in land prices. The Ministry of Labor and Social Affairs provides social workers it employs in priority areas with a package of benefits that is almost identical to that provided to teachers. The Ministry of Finance, through the Income Tax Commission, provides the residents of certain locales in Israel with reductions in the payment of income tax at rates varying from 5 to 20 per cent. This benefit is not tied to the map of national priority areas. The Ministry decides on the discounts independently, through ordinances it enacts naming the communities to receive benefits and the level of the reduction (B'tselem, 2002).

Another source of financing by the government is the transfer of money to the local authorities, by two methods. The first is participation in the direct financing of specific services. The second is the provision of general grants by the Ministry of the Interior for the routine operation of the local authority, and even *ad hoc* grants enabling them to meet special needs. One of the mechanisms used by the government to favor local authorities in the West Bank is the channeling of money through the Settlement Division of the World Zionist Organization, whose sole purpose is to establish settlements in the territories occupied in 1967 and to support the continued development of these settlements.

The outposts

Besides the Jewish settlements in Judea and Samaria, another particular type of settlement has been developed there during the years, namely the outpost. The outpost settlements were established with financial assistance from several governmental ministries and with the army establishment, which turned a blind eye to them. They were established in the surroundings of selected settlements by setting caravans on desolate hills, and by adding to them a few tents and temporary structures, as happened in Itamar, Elqana, Bat Ayin, Talmon, Ma'ale Mikhmash, and others. Not all the Prime Ministers of Israel were happy with that kind of settlement, because they have been used by extremist settlers as a means to create *faits accomplis* in many parts of the West Bank. The former Prime Minister Ehud Barak at one time ordered all the outposts in the West Bank to be evacuated because he regarded them as a contempt of and contradiction to the law. In cases where the infringement of the law was less serious, only orders of work cessation were applied to the outposts, which brought them to a temporary halt and prevented wider expansion. At the time of Prime Minister Barak's tenure there existed in the West Bank about 40 outposts in different degrees of law infringement. Many of these outposts were approved by the governments in the past, some of them with a certain degree of illegality, but all the rest had no formal procedure for their establishment. The settlers declared repeatedly that most of the outposts were established according to the law, and, if some were not, they were approved legally later on, but this is far from the truth, a fact which is known to the Israel security establishment.

Plate 2.3 An outpost near Ma'on in southern Judea

Almost all the governmental, political, military and civil service echelons have been involved in one way or another in the establishment of the outposts. Prime Minister Sharon was the man who encouraged the settlers to hurry and quickly occupy the hills in this region. Former Prime Minister Ehud Barak prepared the ground for many of the outposts under an accord struck with the settlers that became known as "the outposts agreement". In the field itself, the Settlement Division of the World Zionist Organization helped with various operations and activities at the outposts, ranging from laying water pipes to providing mobile homes. The local and regional authorities in the West Bank also played a role in supporting the outposts. The Housing, Defense, and now-defunct Religious Affairs Ministries also offered a helping hand to the outposts, including building structures that would serve as synagogues, ritual baths, and kindergartens.

The Israel Defense Forces are deeply invested in the settlement enterprise. Even before a single settler family is evacuated, the army must untie its Gordian knot which has bound the settlers for many years. The Israel Defense Forces have accompanied the settlement enterprise from the start, when the big lie about the security value of the settlements was still prevalent. Some of the first settlements sprang forth from within army bases, a distorted phenomenon in itself, and the boundary is sometimes blurred to this day. Parts of the map of checkpoints and by-pass roads, conditions of closure and encirclement, as well as sections of the separation fence's route, were dictated by the leaders of the settlers and designed only to meet their wishes. Hardly a day goes by without a meeting between senior army officers and the settlers. A growing number of army commands in the field are residents of the territories. A large part of the army's activities are co-ordinated with the most violent and unruly group in Israeli society. Undoing this knot will be difficult: from an organizational and budgetary perspective this is a deep connection, which has also become an ideological connection over the years. The Israel Defense Forces commanders have internalized the feeling that it is the army of the settlers before being the army of the people. But this phenomenon may be coming to an end. After all the years in which the army groveled before the settlers and yielded to their very whim, the settlers' rebuff of the army may be a good sign.

Most governmental ministries provided the illegal outposts with massive assistance that may be estimated in millions of shekels. The Ministry of Education set up kindergartens in them and paid for the kindergarten teachers, the Ministry of Energy ensured that the outposts were connected to the electricity grid, and the Ministry of Housing financed construction of access roads. The Ministry of Defense and the army were also involved in the establishment of the outposts. Even today, the army still guards them, arguing that its job is to protect all Israeli citizens wherever they live. Regional brigade commanders and even senior officers reached a quiet agreement or understanding with the settlers regarding the existence of the outposts. Later on, the Israeli Civil Administration helped to connect the outposts to the infrastructure systems in the West Bank.

It is hard to define what is legal or illegal in construction in the territories, because the whole situation there is vague and complex and the settlers have taken full advantage of it. Many illegal buildings have been constructed not only in the outposts but even in the other settlements. Enforcement of the building law in this region is very lax. The Civil Administration has a formal supervision authority only outside the jurisdictions of the Jewish local councils, while, within those jurisdictions, the local councils are responsible for supervision, but they are very often the ones that do the illegal building (Fig. 2.8).

The establishment in 1992 of a new government headed by Yitzhak Rabin seemed to offer a real change in Israel's policy. The signing of the Declaration of Principles between Israel and the Palestinian Liberation Organization (PLO) in 1993 also indicated the government's intention to change its policy, although the Declaration did not explicitly prohibit the establishment of new settlements. It was only in the Oslo Accords 2, which were signed two years later, that the two sides state that neither side shall initiate or take any step that will change the status of the West Bank and the Gaza Strip pending the outcome of the permanent status negotiations. However, within a short period of time, it became clear that the change in policy was insignificant and that the new government intended to continue the development of settlements. The government made a promise to the United States that it would not establish new settlements and would halt the expansion of the existing settlements, with the exception of construction to meet the natural growth of the local population.

The exceptions in the government's guidelines effectively became the main tool permitting the continued building of settlements and growth of the Israeli population in the settlements which included also Greater Jerusalem. Moreover, the term "natural growth" was never precisely defined, and the vague nature of the term has allowed Israel to continue to expand the settlements while avoiding direct confrontation with the United States Administration. Under the same terms Israel had established new settlements as new neighborhoods of existing settlements. New settlements have been included in the area of jurisdiction of the adjacent settlement, even in cases of no territorial contiguity between two settlements. Another method employed in order to expand the settlements was the seizure of a new location by a group of settlers who installed caravans on the site. While this method was the settlers' initiative, without approval from the relevant authorities, the government generally refrained from evicting the settlers and demolishing the buildings they erected without permits. Overall, contrary to the expectations raised by the Oslo Accords, the Israeli government has implemented a policy leading to the dramatic growth of the settlements. Between 1993 and 2001 the number of housing units in the settlements in the West Bank, excluding East Jerusalem and Gaza Strip, rose from 20,400 to 31,400, an increase of approximately 54 per cent in seven years.

The illegality of the outposts in Judea and Samaria originates from their hurried creation in different areas of the West Bank and their political aim to create new irreversible situations in the region, as a political far-reaching step, to ensure the remaining of larger areas under Israeli sovereignty in the future, when a possible permanent agreement with the Palestinians will be signed, and to prevent meanwhile the creation of a territorial continuity of the Palestinian settlement blocs in the region. The establishment in a relatively short time of many outposts, which number

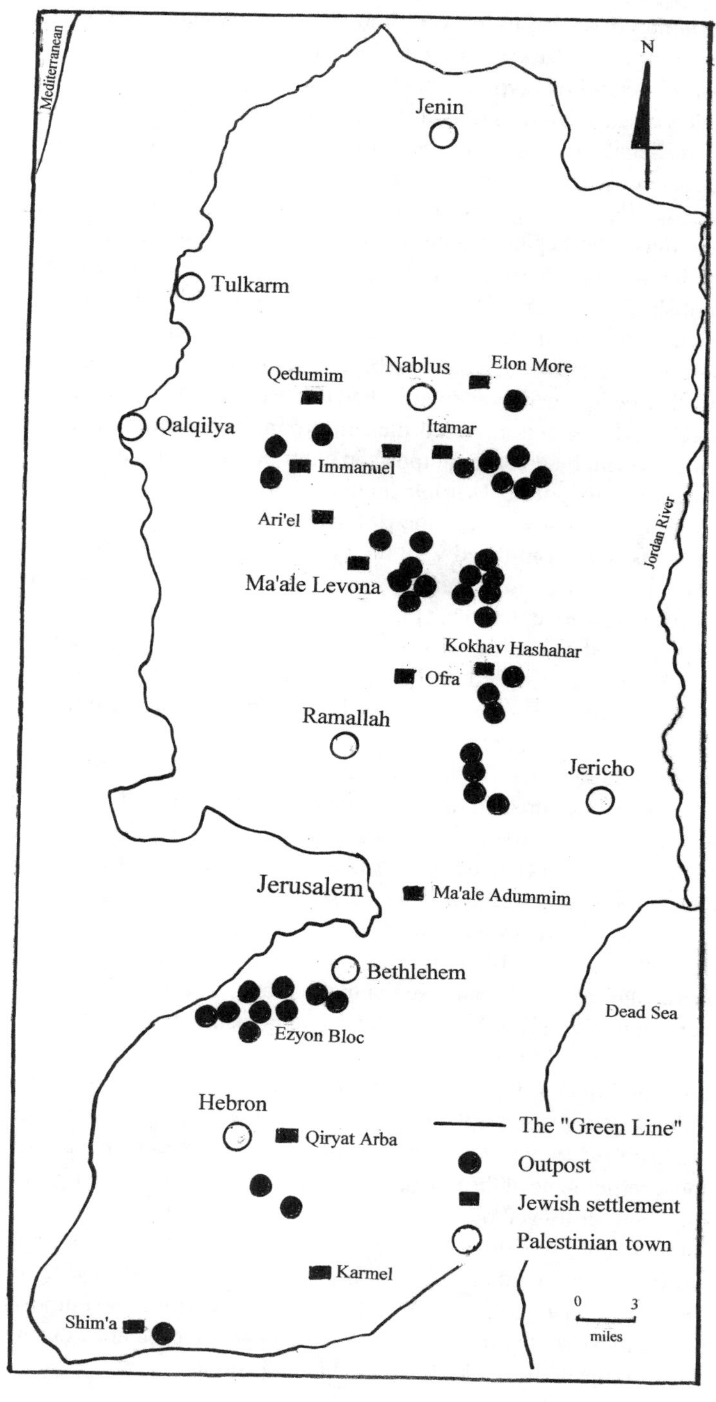

Fig. 2.8 Outposts in the West Bank

today more than a hundred, returns us to a well-known Zionist system of the 1930s, when many Jewish outposts were erected in the Land of Israel.

What is the history behind this type of settlement? At the end of the nineteenth century, the first Jewish immigration (Aliyah) to Palestine was considered by the Ottoman regime as illegal. According to the Ottoman law, every immigrant was allowed to stay in the country for a short time only, but in most cases a longer stay could be approved by paying a bribe. According to another Ottoman law, immigrants and settlers who began to build their house, but did not complete it, were punished by having it destroyed. According to this law, a house with a roof could not be demolished. Sometimes Turkish soldiers were ordered to demolish an illegal building which was in its first steps of construction, but then they were encircled by women who were set between the builders and the house because the soldiers were not allowed to touch women, they had to retreat, and then the settlers could finish the roof. Maybe this inspired the settlers in Judea and Samaria to implement the same system by erecting outposts in short periods of time.

Hurried construction, with political settlement that aims to seize as much land as possible in a region, is also known from the riot years of 1936–39. At that time many rapid settlements were completed with the vision of a future to redeem the Jewish Land of Israel. This system of land seizure by the erection of "tower and stockade" settlements was very common at that time. Those settlements were quite similar to the outposts of today, mainly in their first stage of establishment, intended to safeguard land purchased or seized by Jews, by enlarging existing settlement boundaries, and by ensuring that Arab attacks on the Jewish population would not hinder the entire Jewish settlement project.

In relatively desolate regions, such as the Bet She'an Valley and Upper and Lower Galilee, such settlements were erected rapidly, sometimes a settlement in one day. In order to establish a settlement in such circumstances, a tower and stockades made of wood were prepared in advance in one of the adjacent kibbutzim, and they were conveyed at night to the planned settlement site, surrounded by guarding posts, while inside the site a few barracks were built for the pioneering settlers. Most of the hurried settlements, such as kibbutz Hanita in northwestern Galilee, En Gedi near the Dead Sea in the east, or kibbutz Negba in the Negev, were established in desolate regions or along axes between existing Jewish settlements, or along strategic settlement lines that had to be fortified. About 50 such "stockade and tower" settlements were established during the 1930s. The encroachment of the three spot settlements Gevulot, Revivim, and Bet Eshel into the northern Negev, in order to study the area and to collect geographical information and facts, was a preparation for the 11 additional settlements of the northern Negev that were established in one night on 6 October 1946, followed by another seven settlements in 1947.

After the Six Day War in 1967, dozens of outposts were established in Judea and Samaria, as a means to seize land and hold it as long as the ownership was not decided. Unfortunately, the 1930s "stockade and tower" system of settling outposts in the West Bank has meanwhile proved its relative success and efficiency during recent years in the struggle between the Jews and the Palestinians.

The outposts established in Judea and Samaria are in daily public and political discussion in Israel. The left parties demand the evacuation of all the outposts in the region, while the settlers totally disagree, and even continue to build more constructions and lay roads. From inspections that were carried out by members of the "Peace Now" organization it has been revealed that in recent years dozens of outposts have been erected adjacent to many existing Jewish settlements in the region, about half of them at a distance of less than one mile (1.6 km) from the settlement outline border, and others 1.5 miles (2.5 km) from them or more. The outpost of Givot Olam, for instance, has been erected 2.5 miles (4 km) east of Itamar, and the outpost Har Kabir 3.5 miles (5.6 km) east of Allon More. Most of the outposts were erected far from their nearby settlement center, but so that they could claim the legitimacy of being related to a Jewish settlement, in practice to make it easier to connect them in a further stage to the settlement itself by building new constructions along an axis a few miles long.

If we assume that, in the frame of a permanent agreement between Israel and the Palestinians, all the outposts will remain on their sites and will be included in Israeli sovereign territory, it is doubtful if they will have any significance in the occupied territories, how much they will be able to enlarge the area which the Jews in the region are holding now, and how many Jewish people they will be able to absorb. A glance at the map of Judea and Samaria shows that most of the outposts have been erected in four main areas: on the western slopes of the Samarian and Bet El Hills; in the Ezyon bloc; and on the southern slopes of the Hebron Mountains adjacent to the "Green Line". Strenuous work has been done in western Samaria to erect as many of them as possible. Most of them were sited outside the adjacent official settlement boundaries in order to seize more territory, because it is one of the most important regions that Israel is interested in annexing in the future. In the Ari'el bloc, with the settlements that lie on the mountainous aquifer, Israel is anxious about losing parts of the areas in future negotiations, although they seem to be in a national consensus. The accumulated land which these outposts have seized stretches 5 miles (8 km) around them. The outposts that were erected around Nablus in eastern Samaria, a region in the periphery on the desert fringe, have added seized land to an accumulated length of 24 miles (38 km); in the Ezyon bloc 1.5 miles (2.5 km) and in the southern Hebron Mountains about 3.1 miles (5 km).

As said, the system of outpost erection in Judea and Samaria has in some senses succeeded. In many cases a single outpost led to the establishment of a permanent settlement on the site. There were only a very few cases in which an outpost has been evacuated and demolished by the governmental authorities and their settlers disengaged. The Israel governments face permanently the conflict between the main settlers' standpoint, as against the need to minimize their effect on the deepening occupation, without exposing the problem too much. This situation is repeated in every regime and causes the government to postpone its decisions regarding the outposts and to delay a solution to coming years when negotiations with the Palestinians will be in progress. But after all, it seems that the settlers' achievements in their outposts amounted to very little. They endangered their mission of settling in the "Greater Land of Israel" and damaged the general public atmosphere for a possible negotiation process with the Palestinians in the future.

In summer 2004 the Israel Defense Forces announced that, in accordance with the political decision, they had completed the evacuation of the illegal outposts. Apparently, after a lengthy period of quiet, regarding the evacuation of the illegal outposts, suddenly there were two developments. However, a quick check of the facts showed that outposts had been evacuated several times in the past. Further examination showed that outposts consisted of two or three empty mobile homes. Each outpost was inhabited by one family, but when the evacuation took place the families were not even there. There are also many "Potemkin outposts" meant to serve as bargaining cards, and also many genuine outposts. The estimate is that about 150 families are living in some twenty illegal outposts set up after 2001. Other methods of deception include the way the same outpost is given several names. Since they are illegal outposts, or unauthorized, they are not named by any committee. The deliberate obfuscation was discovered when aerial photos were thoroughly examined. The Ministry of Justice has lately prepared a report on the problem of illegal outposts on the West Bank that was presented to Prime Minister Ariel Sharon. One of the recommendations was to equate the laws regulating planning and construction on both sides of the "Green Line", in order to close the legal loop hole through which some of the outposts were set up. Another recommendation was that a tighter supervision of the funds used by local authorities in the settlements should start in order to prevent a diversion from the set budgets.

The year 2004 saw the evacuation of just two outposts in the territories, and three outposts were set up. There was also a significant expansion of another 12 existing outposts, with an additional 15 outposts said to house permanent residents. At the end of 2004 there were 99 outposts in the West Bank, and all of them grew to some extent. The built areas of these communities grew in 2004 by some 450 acres (1,800 dunams). There were at that time 3,500 housing units under construction throughout the West Bank. Tenders were published for the construction of 962 housing units, of which some two-thirds were in Betar Illit and Ari'el. Construction in 21 settlements was taking place outside the defined urban boundaries of the settlements. Large-scale construction was under way in more than 40 different settlements, with the biggest operation taking place in Ma'ale Adummim, Betar Illit, Alfe Menashe, Adam, and Har Gilo. Two new roads – Jerusalem to Noqedim and Nili to Ofarim – were being laid in the West Bank at that time, and another two – the trans-Samaria road and the Jerusalem to Jericho road – were being significantly expanded.

The unavoidable conclusion is that someone is trying to confuse the country's information system. The main reason is the negotiations the settlers plan to conduct about the outposts' future. Indeed, when settlers are pushed into the corner, they are usually ready to conduct negotiations with the intent of giving up something unimportant, but presented as significant for them, in exchange for rescuing something much more important.

The struggle between the government and the settlers is apparently heading for an explosion that will involve the Israel Defense Forces and other police forces. At present the settlers have the upper hand. The government talks a lot while the settlers act, on the basis of overall planning. They are better at maneuvering and establishing facts on the ground. The settlers opened a front which is aimed against the evacuation of the outposts which Prime Minister Sharon promised President Bush he would remove. Meanwhile, families have moved into one of the northwestern West Bank settlements that were earmarked for evacuation. According to one plan, the settlers will resettle a settlement while the authorities evacuate another one. In this way they intend to wear down the army.

As for the settlers' maneuverability methods, some settlers' leaders are saying they will be ready to talk about a compromise when it comes to the outposts. They will be willing to evacuate some outposts if others are recognized. The truth is that the government is afraid of the conflict involved in evacuating the outposts. The settlers are trying to prove that the same regime that wants to evacuate the outposts was part of their establishment and consolidation.

In February 2005 Israeli officials said that Israel will evacuate illegal outposts in the West Bank only after implementation of the disengagement from the Gaza Strip and the northern West Bank. Washington was not expected to pressure Israel on this issue prior to the disengagement. The Americans place higher priority on implementation of the disengagement which they describe as a dramatic opportunity and a historic decision. But the U.S. administration has warned Israel many times that its failure to keep the promise to remove all outposts established in the West Bank since March 2001 will harm relations between the countries and could have an impact on American aid to Israel.

A report submitted in March 2005 to Prime Minister Ariel Sharon essentially confirmed longstanding complaints by Palestinians and activists groups such as "Peace Now" that successive Israeli governments, including those after the Oslo Accords, have approved and financed for decades the establishment of outpost settlements on privately owned Palestinian land. This long awaited report into government support for illegal settlements in the West Bank described widespread State complicity, fraud and cynicism, illegal diversion of government funds, and illegal seizure of private Palestinian land. In many cases, said the report, the Defense Ministry, Attorney General, and the military forces' civil administration ignored settlers' incursions into property they did not own, backed by ministers and senior officials, to establish new settlements outside zoned areas in direct violation of government decisions and regulations and to exploit the sensitive security situation.

Many of the outposts built in the territories since March 2001 were established on lands that are not State-owned. Some are on private Palestinian land, and many others on lands of unknown ownership. The Israeli Housing Ministry was virtually indifferent to the question of who owned the land. Numerous governmental bodies were co-operating while committing blatant offenses to establish outposts, including bringing in mobile homes without proper permits, and connecting infrastructures to the outposts. A large share of the Housing Ministry's budget, allocated for the Rural Construction Administration, was directed to construction in the territories and for illegal outposts, but the budgets directed toward the outposts in recent years are unknown. The World Zionist Organization's Settlement Division established a large share of the illegal outposts and allocated lands against the Jordanian law that applies in the territories. This is how at last a hundred illegal outposts came into being, but this number does not reflect the actual number of outposts.

The report on the unauthorized settlement outposts in the territories exposed the occupation in all its ugliness. It revealed that settlers have been working underground for years in the branches of the government, that senior officials refused to divulge information, and that other officials acted contrary to the policies of their ministers. The U.S. administration suspected as much a long time ago, but was unsure whether the government was intentionally breaking the law and lying, or had lost control over what was going on and was required to make false statements about construction in the territories.

The report concluded that there is no need for a new law to enable the evacuation and dismantling of the outposts. It was recommended that severe punishments should be meted out to officials and others involved in violation of the law regarding construction on the territories, including jail sentences and steep fines. The government's failure to dismantle the outposts sent a message to settlers, soldiers, police, and the public in general that there was no real intention to evacuate illegal outposts, and that the political administration spoke in two voices. The report exposed an organized criminal conspiracy in which illegal outposts were established with taxpayers' money that was never earmarked for that construction, with ministers, Directors General, senior officials, and officers of the army involved. The systematic breaking of the law was known to successive attorneys general, and a number of complaints had been made in the past to the police about suspected criminal activity.

The report was supposed to help the law enforcement authorities to deal more effectively with the new outposts that go up. In effect, the State has already conducted legal proceedings against some of the outposts but the evacuation was postponed as soon as Sharon managed to persuade the Americans that fighting over them would take unnecessary energy before the disengagement from the Gaza Strip. In their struggle against the disengagement, the settlers have spoken about their great love for the people and the land. But when one looks at the outposts and settlements, and what their presence has done to the landscape and shape of the land, the conclusion is that what primarily drives them is not love for the land of Israel but mainly love for control over the Land of Israel.

The power that the settlers gained over the years could be seen very clearly in spring 2005 when the disengagement plan for the Gaza Strip and North Samaria had been approved by the government. The events in the Gaza Strip deteriorated into an overall violent conflict between two Jewish States with different goals. One is the State of Israel, and the other is the "State" of the settlers. Despite the profound ties between them, each of them feels threatened by the other. The State of Israel established the "State" of the settlers and, in the final analysis, the golem is rebelling against its creator. In the government and in the Knesset, the settlement movement has become the strongest political pressure group that Israel has ever known. The "State" of the settlers was provided with weapons, and now there is a fear that these weapons will be used against the Israel Defense Forces and the Israel police. On the ground, the settlers decided which State of Israel's laws should be observed in their "State", and which ones should be ignored. Thus, they fearlessly stole private lands belonging to their Palestinian neighbors, as well as lands defined "State lands". They cut down the Palestinians' olive trees and stole their fruit. None of these robbers has been indicted, and those who did get to the courts for acts of killing had their punishment mitigated. For a long time, the settlers have been behaving as though the State of Israel were a foreign government. They take what they can from the government, take over property and lands as far as possible, and ignore what is inconvenient for them. The "State" of the settlers is also taking safety measures to protect itself from the activities of the State of Israel. Settlers with knowledge in these fields are guiding their people as how to avoid the security services and how to behave in an investigation if they are arrested. These extremists, who are encouraged by the rabbis, are threatening the integrity of the military forces by calling on young religious men to refuse orders and even desert. The "State" of the settlers has only one goal, perpetuation of the occupation and domination of the Palestinian people.

The future of the "Green Line"

The "Green Line" as a border between Israel and Jordan was established after Israel's War of Independence in 1949, and separated Judea and Samaria and the Gaza Strip from the rest of Israel's territory. The line was thickened in the past by the establishment of the so-called Nahal settlements along it, populated by army units who combined security and military training with agricultural work. Only a few hundred miles of the line have been supported by new development regions that were established along it, such as Lakhish, Besor, and Ta'anach, mainly for the purpose of reinforcing border strips of land. The "Green Line" was very dominant as a border line between the two countries during the years 1948–67, till the outbreak of the Six Day War in 1967, which changed the region politically and territorially. Israel then unilaterally recognized the Jordan River as its eastern border, unilaterally converted the armistice line in the Golan Heights into a security border, and created a *de facto* border between Israel and Lebanon in the form of a narrow security zone, north of the 1923 international borderline.

In recent years, as the terrorist attacks initiated by the extreme Arab political groups Hamas and Islamic Jihad became more frequent, the "Green Line" which after 1967 had to be abandoned according to the Israeli "Greater Land of Israel" policy that insisted that no inner borders should exist within the whole territory – they led to the renewal of its security function as a zone line to safeguard Israel's population. It was realized that the "Green Line" was actually a broken border with many geographical and demographic shortcomings, which stem from its history in the years 1948–49, when it was first delineated, and from the geographical changes which have occurred along it since the Six Day War in 1967. Its weakness as a defense line for Israel may be demonstrated in four main domains: its great length; its twisted delineation in a difficult mountainous topography; the large Arab population which resides on both sides of it, with the Palestinians on its east side and the Israeli Arabs on the west; and the relatively sparse Jewish population which has settled adjacent to it through the years.

The "Green Line" which was finally delineated in 1949 as an armistice line between Israel, Egypt, Jordan, Syria, and Lebanon was actually a cease fire line agreed upon in Rhodes, and approved by military representatives of all the partners who participated in the 1948 war, with the mediation of U.N. observers. It expressed, more or less, the military situation of the positions that existed at a certain moment of cease fire, but it had not many security elements in it which could promise full defense to Israel from Arab infiltrations and terrorist attacks. It was delineated at that time with insufficient data on the geographical characteristics of the region through which it had to run. Furthermore, the "Green Line" encircled in Judea and Samaria an area of 2,296 sq. miles (5,878 sq. km), which demonstrated its great length relative to the territory which it comprised. In addition to that, the "Green Line" was dissected by many wadis of different width which were used by Palestinians as relatively easy infiltration axes.

Regarding the Arab population that resides along both sides of the "Green Line" it should be indicated, that at the time when the line was marked, there lived along it in Judea and Samaria about 60,000 people, while today the Arab population which lives within 1.25–2 miles (2–3 km) east of the line numbers about 200,000. Within the same distance of the west side of the line, but in Israel's territory, there live about 230,000 Arabs who have direct interrelationships with the Arab people in Judea and Samaria, and by that actually blur its character.

The Jewish population which resides adjacent to the "Green Line" in Israel's territory opposite to Judea and Samaria, within the same distance of 1.25–2 miles (2–3 km) west of it, numbers about 130,000 people, while that on the other side of the line in Judea and Samaria numbers about 100,000 settlers. It seems that the Jewish population along both sides of the "Green Line" made a big gap among the Arabs. The basic deficiencies of the "Green Line", intended to safeguard Israel from terrorism in its sovereign territory, were thereby demonstrated. As mentioned, the line was not properly delineated, it remained physically broken because of twisted topography, it was impossible to close it hermetically, it has a large Arab population on both sides of it, and it lacks a substantial Jewish population which might block the access of infiltrators or terrorists to Israel.

After the Six Day War there was a trend in Israel to disregard the existence of the "Green Line" by the development of new settlements along it in order to erase its existence in the area, but nowadays the "Green Line" has come to life again because of the new political circumstances and the need of Israel to defend itself against terrorism and the large number of Palestinian suicide bombers who pass through the "Green Line" quite easily, causing harm and casualties to the Israeli population. It seems that the "Green Line", in its geographical and demographic conditions, is unable to promise security, unless it is fortified as a sophisticated and perfect security zone, at least as the line between Israel and Jordan, or as the borderline between Israel and Syria. Such a step by the Israeli government might be very expensive, and perhaps even politically and economically not realistic, but for crucial security reasons the government came to this conclusion and decided in the year 2000 to build a strong fence, more or less parallel to the "Green Line", to defend itself from the current attacks, terror and sabotage.

The late Prime Minister Yitzhak Rabin declared in 1995 the need to separate the Arab population in Judea and Samaria from the Jewish one in Israel, and appointed a committee of experts to prepare a plan for a separation line east of the former "Green Line", but parallel to it, with all the necessary installations to provide Israel's security. With this act Israel joined the countries which have planned and constructed artificial separation borderlines to protect their territorial and economic security. It may be assumed that the separation line which Israel is building now in Judea and Samaria will not be able to close the border hermetically, because of the mountainous terrain and the strong interrelationship which exists between the West Bank and Israel regarding Israel's need for a workforce and the employment which the Arab population needs.

An effective partition line cannot be achieved by a hurried delineation, as in the recent case of Israel, but only after a long period of economic and demographic development on both sides. It is doubtful whether separation lines and artificial borders are able to prevent totally immigration of population from neighboring areas which are economically unequal. The immigration of foreigners who escape from hunger and poverty cannot be stopped even with the best means. Foreigners' desire for immigration will not change even if better separation lines are erected.

In the background of the Israel–Palestinian dispute is the old argument over the 1967 lines as a basis for the future border between the sides. Prime Minister Sharon correctly reckoned that the "Green Line" would return to the political picture, despite the enormous efforts to erase it. To prevent that, he equipped himself with two constraints: one was the letter from President Bush promising no return to the armistice line and considerations for the Israeli population centers in determining the border, and the other was the government decision about disengagement and that in any future agreement Israel would annex the main blocs of Jewish settlement, civilian settlements, security areas, and places where the State has additional interests.

The Palestinians' approach to setting the border is based on the legitimacy of United Nations decisions and the precedents of agreements reached between Israel and its neighbors which were based on full withdrawal, as in the case of Egypt, and the territorial exchanges, as in the case of Jordan. It is difficult to imagine a Palestinian leadership accepting a permanent agreement with a divided State in part of the West Bank. It is also difficult to imagine an Israeli leadership accepting full withdrawal, or nearly full withdrawal, from the territories, despite the readiness to leave the Gaza Strip. The conclusion therefore is that progress will at most be toward another interim agreement, and the dreams of a permanent agreement and declarations of an end to the conflict will apparently have to wait. Boundaries that are recognized by the world are the heart of any agreement. The world does not accept unilateral change of boundaries by any country, and not even dominance by occupation. The settlers are not aware of the danger and threat to the existence of the State of Israel as a country without recognized agreed and safe boundaries.

From the above some conclusions may be drawn concerning Judea and Samaria. Only a fundamental and economic solution in the territories, which will create more places of employment for the local population on the basis of positive interrelationships between the two people, will ensure the effectiveness of the separation line between Israel and the Palestinians, and no barriers, closure periods, watch posts, patrols, guard dogs, and electronic fences will solve the existing political problem. The new separation line which is now under construction as the alternative to the "Green Line" should not be closed hermetically, like that between Israel and Syria. It should be a temporary line to allow options for a final peace agreement on the revision for a borderline for the future Palestinian State, with the hope that "good fences make good neighbors".

The "Axis of the Hills" plan

In response to Israel's policy to defend its eastern borderline with the Palestinian region, a plan initiated by the Ministry of Housing in the 1990s was presented as a measure to ease the absorption of the 1990 wave of Jewish immigration to Israel. In reality its aim was to create an irreversible border on the map representing new demographic, economic, and political realities along the "Green Line". The government has been trying also to settle people more densely along the "Green Line" and "Judaize" the area. Both objectives were included in an original plan named "Axis of the Hills" settlement plan.

The plan focused on a narrow strip of land, 50 miles (80 km) long, at the edge of the "Green Line". It was wedged between the West Bank and the eastern Coastal Plain. The area, including the Arab town of Um Al-Fahm and surrounding villages, is inhabited by 150,000 Arabs and 40,000 Jews, and a decision was made by the Israeli government to settle 350,000 Jews in this area by the year 2005. The basic premise of the "Axis of the Hills" plan was to create a string of settlements parallel to the heavily populated coastal axis, in order to ease population pressure on the coastal center, especially between the city of Ashdod in the south and Hadera in the north. The plan also called for creating an economic infrastructure alongside these settlements because the designated area lacks industrial and economic support systems. In addition, it has been decided to build a national road known as the Crossing Highway which will cross the country from Galilee in the north to the Negev in the south. Without doubt this plan had a political basis, and, regardless of the type of peace agreement Israel may reach with the Palestinians in the future, these settlements, side-by-side with the Jewish settlements on the West Bank, will become interdependent and strengthen the border.

According to the plan the "Judaization" of the area had to occur in three stages, with the final stage reached in another few years, when it will have reversed the demographic composition from the present 82 per cent Arabs and 18 per cent Jews to 36 per cent Arabs and 64 per cent Jews; it will strive to settle the Jewish population between Kafar Qasem in the south to Um Al-Fahm in the north. The backbone of this plan is the Crossing Highway which will supply a necessary link between the settlements. The planners acknowledged that the decision to work on the highway was motivated by a desire to implement the plan. Without some east–west arteries to link the settlements to one another, it would be impossible to implement the plan which includes the building of new cities and thousands of square feet of industrial structures.

The plan also envisaged the building of four large centers which will offer the settlers commercial and industrial job opportunities, health services, cultural services, and a system of communications with the rural settlements to be built around them. The four centers in which the bulk of the work will occur are Modi'in, Rosh Ha'ayin, Kochav Ya'ir settlement cluster and Qazir-Harish in the Iron Valley. The settlement of Modi'in, expected to have a population of 160,000 by the year 2005, but numbering in 2004 not more than 55,000 inhabitants, will be a new city along the Jerusalem–Ben-Gurion airport highway. The population of Rosh Ha'ayin was expected to increase to fifty thousand by the year 2005. With a current population of 6,000, the Kochav Ya'ir settlement cluster is projected to have a population of 20,000 by the completion of the plan. For the fourth center, the plan called for the establishment of a new city, Qazir-Harish, with a projected population of 35,000.

Rural settlements built around each of the four urban centers will have between 1,000 and 4,000 residential units and will be connected by a new network of roads. The planned network of roads will cut through land and the administrative jurisdiction of Arab villages. The plan also called for constructing fourteen industrial complexes spread over an area of 1,340 hectares (13,400 dunams). The four urban centers were also expected to provide 25,000 new jobs for the settlers (Fig. 2.9).

The plan, aimed at settling 350,000 Jews in the strip on the border of the West Bank, is being implemented. Three steps were being undertaken by the Ministry of Housing. First, the most recent and apparently the final, routing of the north–south highway has been determined and building is in progress. The second was the founding of the town Qazir-Harish. The last was the decision to re-establish a regional council consisting of seven Arab villages which lack any municipal representation such as a local council. The planned council was unanimously opposed by the residents of the seven Arab villages, who believed that it might restrict their independence.

Requiem for the Jewish settlements

Since the Oslo Accords, which were signed between Israel and the Palestinians in 1994, the first symptoms of crumbling of the Jewish settlement layout in Judea and Samaria were felt at the end of the 1990s, expressed by the organization of groups of settlers toward a possible evacuation of Judea and Samaria in exchange for financial compensation or for alternative housing within Israel's "Green Line" territory. Self-organization of that kind was felt and reported from some of the settlements adjacent to the "Green Line", and from settlements in the Jordan Valley adjacent to the autonomous territory of Jericho. It may be estimated that tensions are appearing among other settlers, although not openly declared, but may increase as negotiations between Israel and the Palestinians accelerate.

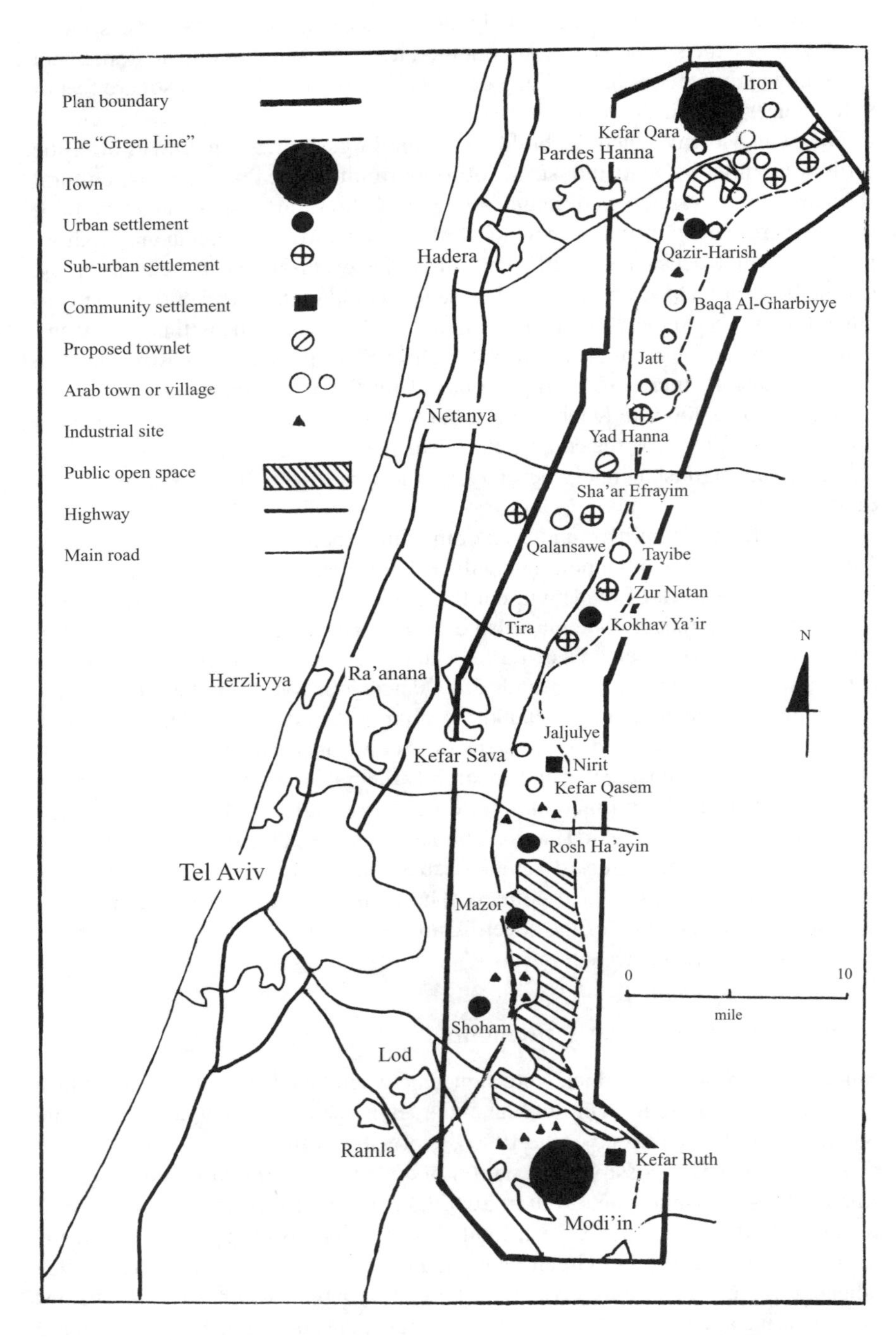

Fig. 2.9 The "Axis of the Hills" plan

A possible crumbling of the Jewish settlement layout in Judea and Samaria could have been expected a long time ago, and what was needed was a definite political situation to accelerate the process. The overwhelming refusal of extreme groups of Jewish settlers, and the resistance to the peace process of Palestinian extreme groups, such as Hamas and Islamic Jihad, create a situation from which a dynamic process of threat and danger in the occupied territory of Judea and Samaria has started.

Settlement in a geographical area for political interests by capturing a territory may succeed in certain conditions: when the number of settlers in the area is large enough to create a balance weighted against the local inhabitants; when the settlers are able to form a considerable dense population which can maintain connections among its parts; when the settlements in the area are established in a hierarchy according to size and function; when the settlement layout is executed by taking root on land, and most of the settlers are engaged in agriculture and local industry; and when the distribution of the settlements relies on main communications arteries which ensure free traffic between them. But, although many years have passed since the first establishment of settlements in Judea and Samaria, none of these basic conditions existed to justify Jewish settlement in this area.

The unofficial number of settlers in Judea and Samaria is about 230,000, equivalent to not more than 12 per cent of the Arab population: this does not create a meaningful counter-balance to the more than a million Arabs who live there. The Jewish birth rate in Judea and Samaria is high at 29 per thousand per annum, but against 40 per thousand per annum in the Arab population there is no chance of dominating the region demographically. Even the density of the Jewish population in Judea and Samaria is not very impressive: while the Arab density in this area is about 78 inhabitants per sq. mile (200 inhabitants per sq. km), that of the Jewish settlers is 16 per sq. mile (40 per sq. km) only. The dispersion of the Jewish settlements in Judea and Samaria is unequal too. Although 140 Jewish settlements have been erected, a relatively large number compared to the time when settlement in Judea and Samaria began in 1969, their distribution in the area remains very selective, except in the Jordan Valley and in the Ezyon bloc, where they demonstrate a complete dominance of their territory. In all other parts of the region this has not happened. In northern Samaria the number of Jewish settlers is quite low, and also in the western Judean Mountains and along the eastern flanks of Judea and Samaria. They are more conspicuous between Qalqilya and Nablus, and on the Bethel Hills north of Jerusalem. Even if no congested Arab urban or rural settlement existed in the region, it is doubtful whether such a pattern of Jewish settlements could maintain reasonable economic and social relationships. Also the hierarchy of Jewish settlements in Judea and Samaria has not been developed systematically, and especially not in a right proportion between urban and rural villages. While a territorial distribution of settlements needs a hierarchical layout of towns and villages of different size, the reality is that in Judea and Samaria about 65 per cent of the settlers reside in urban settlements which are almost equal in size, while the minority reside in small settlements of no more than a few hundred inhabitants. No primary town has been developed in the whole region as a capital. There are settlers who suppose that the town of Ari'el in Samaria, with its 20,000 inhabitants, is actually the capital of Jewish Samaria, but it is surrounded by several Jewish towns, such as Elqana with 3,500 inhabitants, Immanu'el with 4,800 inhabitants, and Qarne Shomron with 7,000 inhabitants, which compete to gain status as regional service centers in the region. Other towns in Judea such as Qiryat Arba, Efrata, and Ma'ale Adummim, do not have direct relationships with the Samarian towns, or between themselves (Fig. 2.10).

Even the putting down of roots on the land in most of the settlements seems to be very superficial. In most of the Jewish settlements along the western flanks of Judea and Samaria, and on the mountain crest, no agriculture has been developed, while industrial plants which were built in selected sites are not dominant as marketing centers for the region. Even in the Jordan Valley, which has good geographical conditions in climate, soil, and water for early fruit growing, production is not very high, much lower than in the southeastern Negev, a region in Israel's sovereign territory which lies in more difficult geographical conditions and is remote from the central parts of the country. Even exclusive Jewish dominance on the main roads in Judea and Samaria has not been fully achieved during these years. Despite the laying of new separate roads in the region, both peoples are using them for their own traffic, which creates a situation sometimes very unsafe for both sides. In general, the sparse dispersal of Jewish settlement in Judea and Samaria prevents linear and long-distance dominance by the existing road network, and the more this network has helped the settlers the more it has added to the commuting ability and the increase of motoring among the Palestinians.

The Jews who settled in Judea and Samaria for political reasons, and those who settled there for convenience, and the chance of getting housing and land at a low price, besides better utility and quality of life, are quite seperate groups. A study of their distribution in the region according to groups of settlers reveals that the militant and fanatic element among them, which organizes demonstrations and makes noise and trouble for the military and political bodies, is a very small proportion.

The division of settlers according to group and place of settlement could be elaborated according to geographical criteria, such as distance of residence from Arab nationalist centers and cities, and size of population in the different settlements. It was found that the most fanatic extreme and nationalistic element of Jewish settlers lives inside some Arab cities or adjacent to their municipal boundaries. Such an element is, for instance, to be found inside Hebron, in the adjacent town of Qiryat Arba with its 6,500 inhabitants. Another core, no less fanatic, whose origin is in the Gush Emunim movement of the mid-1970s, is to be found in two separate concentrations. One is near the city of Nablus, in a rectangle whose corners are Elon More in the northeast, Qarne Shomron in the northwest, Shilo in the southeast and Elqana in the southwest. In this area, including the townlets of Ari'el and Immanu'el, there exist 20 settlements with about 35,000 settlers. The second concentration of extremist settlers is to be found in the Bethel Hills, near the Arab cities of Ramallah and Al-Bira, in a rectangle whose corners are Ofra in the northeast, Halamish in the northwest, Almon in the southeast, and Bet Horon in the southwest. In this area there exist 15 settlements with a total Jewish population of about 13,000.

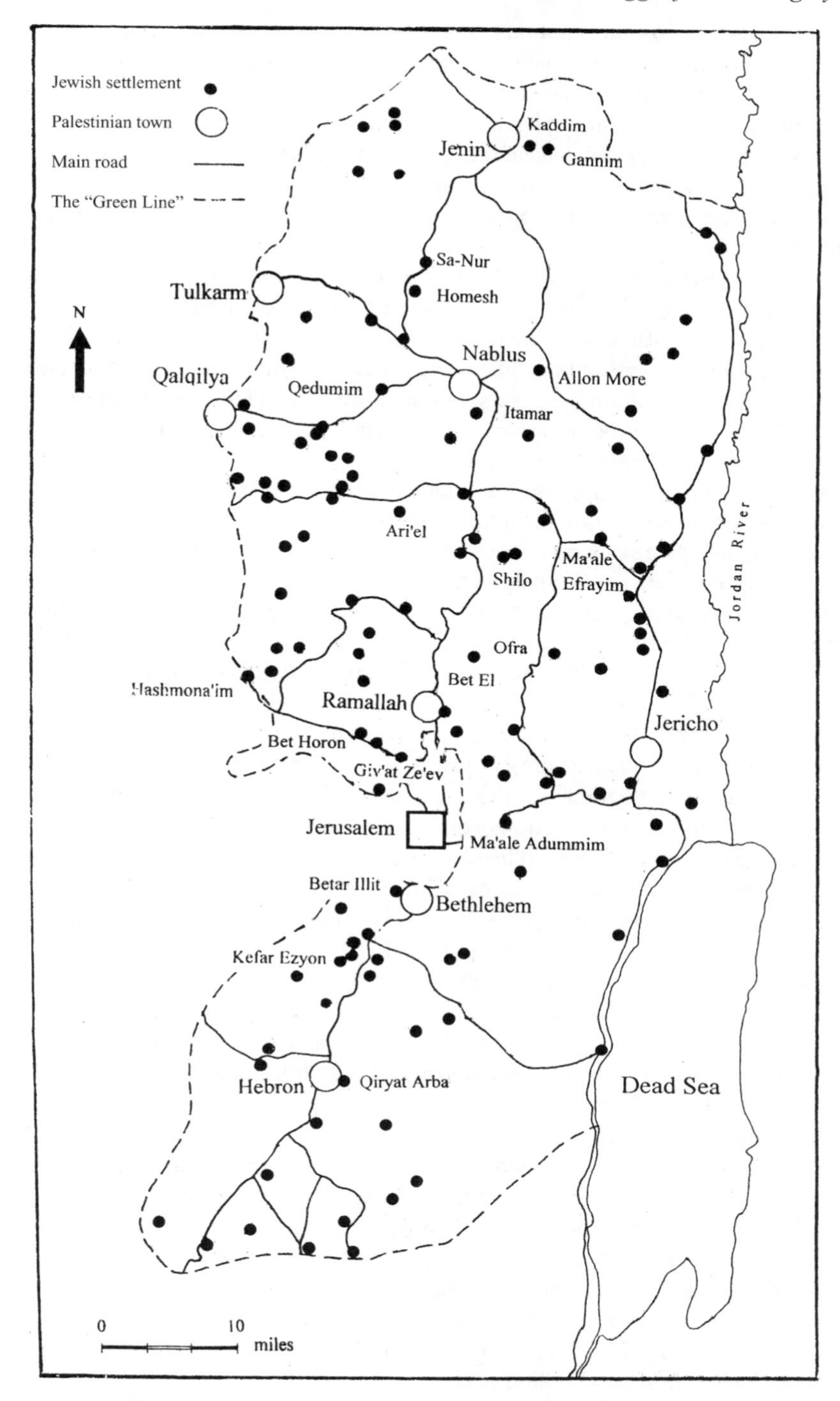

Fig. 2.10 Jewish settlements in the West Bank

As well as these two concentrations there exist in Judea and Samaria three smaller ones, but these are less problematic from the point of view of political activities, because of their rural and suburban character. One of them is the Rehan bloc in northwest Samaria, which had to be evacuated in 2005 according to Prime Minister Sharon's disengagement plan, and another is the strip of settlements in the southern Hebron Mountains. Two other concentrations of settlers with less political and territorial involvement in their Arab surroundings are those of the Ezyon bloc and the Jordan Valley.

Besides all these there exists a concentration of Jewish settlers near the municipal border of Jerusalem, with strong economic and social relationship to the city, although they reside officially in the territory of the West Bank. The future of these suburban settlements should be connected politically with the destiny of Greater Jerusalem. Their population creates a suburban frame around the city, from Giv'at Ze'ev and Har Adar in the northwest, with their 10,000 inhabitants, to Ma'ale Adummim in the east with 32,000 people.

Various government ministries, particularly the Ministries of Defense and Housing, began in 2004 implementing Prime Minister Ariel Sharon's policy of strengthening the large settlement blocs, although the geographic boundaries of the blocs have been somewhat limited. Extensive construction is under way only in the settlements straddling the seam line and the very large urban blocs as Ma'ale Adummim and Betar Illit, for example. In most of the West Bank settlements, new building plans are being ratified, and whatever construction is taking place began a few years ago.

Every week, council heads discover that areas that had been included in the master plans for their settlements are now outside the building zones drawn according to aerial photographs by the defense establishment, in accordance with the commitment to the U.S. to refrain from construction beyond the existing built-up areas. Also every week, council heads are informed of new freezes, delays, and suspensions of approved plans and transfers of funds to the settlement. The defense establishment is holding up approval of about 160 construction plans in the settlements, mainly those outside the large blocs.

At the end of the fourth year of the Intifada Al-Aksa, Israel appears to be losing the battle of the narrative that has been the backdrop of the conflict since its beginning. Israel's claim that this is a just war of defense against ruthless terror from peace rejectionists is being worn down by the decline in attacks. The relative quiet on the Israeli side against the daily casualties on the Palestinian side strengthens their claim that they are fighting for their freedom from occupation. The consensus that held inside Israel when it was under fire has been broken, and the debate over the purpose of the war has been renewed. At the center of the debate is the question of how many settlements must close. The rightist parties want to keep all the settlements, some are ready for vague concessions but not now, and some of the lefties parties would make do with giving up all but a few settlements. In the middle is Ariel Sharon, who proposes giving up some settlements so that others will survive. He is trying to revive the distinction made by the Labor government between settlement blocs and isolated settlements.

The problem is that the domestic debate does not interest the international community, which regards all the settlements as a crime. Those who scorned the international community's position and relied on the belief that America is with Israel, and that there is nothing to worry about, were devastated by blows from the International Court of Justice in The Hague, which rejected all of Israel's actions in the territories as violations of law. Prime Minister Sharon understood the danger and portrayed his disengagement plan as a last-ditch battle against the pressure to drive Israel back to the 1967 borders as a deal to save the West Bank at the small expense of Gaza.

The conclusions which could be drawn are that the number of settlers threatened with possible evacuation from Judea and Samaria in the future is much less than declared; most of the settlers' families have a large number of children, so that the potential adult militant body is not greater than a few thousand people; their dispersal in the region and their small number in most of the settlements reduces their deterrent force. Gradual evacuation of the settlers, when it is decided upon, should be done at first in the problematic sites, then in the two concentrations on the mountain crest, so that the militant core will be neutralized, and the threat to future continuity of a peace process may be removed.

The struggle for land

One of the basic channels of the struggle over settlement is land, both as territory and as a source of livelihood. Since the land potential is absolute, each party wishes to take possession of as much of it as possible. The Arabs cling to their land because it is ancestral, and because to them it means existence, happiness, and honor. The Israelis have hoped to detach the Arabs from their land as a practical means of settling in the area, for reasons of religious tradition, ideology, security, and quality of life. The Palestinians also claim that they will not accept Jewish sovereignty over any part of the Land of Israel's territory. This indeed used to be the position of the Palestinian Liberation Organization and it remains today the declared position of Hamas.

Since the beginning of the occupation, Israel has taken control of hundreds of thousands of acres throughout the West Bank, with the primary objective of establishing settlements and providing reserves of land for their expansion. It has done this by means of a complex legal-bureaucratic mechanism whose central element is the declaration and registration of land as "State land". In addition, Israel uses three further methods to seize control of land: requisition for military needs; declaration of land as abandoned property; and the expropriation of land for public needs. In addition, Israel has also helped its Jewish citizens to purchase land on the free market for the purpose of establishing settlements. Despite the diverse methods used, they have all been perceived by the relevant bodies, the Israeli government, the settlers, and the Palestinians, as a single mechanism serving a single purpose, the establishment of civilian settlements on the occupied territories. The establishment of civilian settlements in the occupied territories is prohibited by the Fourth Geneva Convention and The Hague regulations. Exclusively using the seized lands to benefit the settlements, while prohibiting the Palestinian public from using them in any way, is forbidden and illegal in itself (B'tselem, 2002).

Regarding seizure of land for military purposes, humanitarian customary law obliges the occupying power to protect the property of residents of the occupied area and prohibits the occupier from expropriating it. However, an occupying power may take temporary possession of privately owned land and buildings belonging to the residents of the occupied area in order to house military forces and administrative units. Such seizure is by definition temporary. The occupying power does not acquire property rights in the requisitioned land and buildings, and is not entitled to sell them to others. Through 1968–79 Israeli military commanders issued dozens of orders for the requisition of private land in the West Bank, claiming that it was required for essential and urgent needs. In several cases Palestinian residents petitioned the High Court of Justice against the seizure of their land, claiming that the use of this land for the purpose of establishing settlements is contrary to the requirements of international law. At first the High Court rejected all these petitions and accepted the State's argument that the land seizure was legal because the settlements performed key defense and military functions, but later on in one case the High Court ordered the Israel Defense Forces to dismantle the settlement and to return the seized land to its owner. Toward the end of 2000 a new wave of land requisition through military orders began. Private lands were seized to construct new by-pass roads to replace old by-pass roads that were no longer safe. The new roads were intended to meet the needs of the settlers, who had suffered repeated attacks from the Palestinians while traveling on the roads (B'tselem, 2002).

The need to cope with the increasing number of High Court of Justice petitions led to pressure on the government from the settlers and right-wing parties to find another way to seize land in the West Bank. The solution was found through the manipulative use of the Ottoman law of 1858. By this method, approximately 40 per cent of the area of the West Bank was declared as State land. The Ottoman law stated that areas of empty land, such as mountains, rocky areas, rough terrain, or pastures, which are not owned by anyone on the basis of a deed, and are not designated for these purposes for any city or village dwellers, and are at such a distance from cities or villages that a person's voice cannot be heard at the closest settlement, are known as dead land. In Ottoman law any person who needs such land can, with official consent, cultivate it, except that the absolute owner is the Sultan. The meaning of this law is that any land that is uncultivated or uncultivable, and is not recognized private land, is State land. In view of the fact that 60 per cent of the land in Judea and Samaria is not cultivable, a large proportion of it in the unregistered areas could be considered State land.

The Ottoman law allows exception for a person who cultivates such land by permission, and indeed the Israelis allow certain rights on the land to residents who have cultivated a piece of land for at least ten years. Consequently, under conditions of non-registration in most of Judea and Samaria, it was possible, around the time of the occupation, to consider as potential State land all land except (1) land registered as private property and which can be proved to be such; (2) land cultivated for at least ten years, giving the farmer certain rights over it; and (3) land belonging to 1967 absentees managed under the abandoned property decree, and returnable in the condition it was in at the time of seizure, when the owners return (B'tselem, 2002).

The declaration of land in the West Bank as State land, issued shortly after the occupation began, was used through 1979 to seize control of land registered in the name of the Jordanian government, and amounted to a total of 131,750 acres (527,000 dunams) of such land. During the first five years of the occupation, an additional 40,000 acres (160,000 dunams) were eligible for the status of registered State land. Accordingly, through 1979, the Custodian for Government Property considered an area of 171,750 acres (687,000 dunams), constituting some 13 per cent of the total area of the West Bank, to constitute State land. In 1979 the Civil Administration in the West Bank initiated a project to map systematically all areas under cultivation, using aerial photographs taken periodically. This step led to the location and marking of lands that the sovereign was entitled to seize under Ottoman law and under the Jordan laws that absorbed this law. In these investigations the Custodian located approximately 375,000 acres (1.5 million dunams), or some 26 per cent of the area of the West Bank, that were considered to be State land. Approximately 200,000 acres (800,000 dunams) of land were declared as registered during the period 1980–84, but even at that stage the settlements had already been assured enormous reserves of land for the future. The declaration of hundreds of thousands of acres in the occupied territories as State land was made possible mainly because much land was not registered in the Land Registration Office. Although the Ottoman law required the registration of every plot of land, many residents during the period of Ottoman rule did not observe this provision. The reasons for this included a desire to preserve the collective ownership system; a desire to evade tax liability; and an attempt to avoid being drafted into the Turkish army. The records that survived from this period are vague, and do not permit the identification of a specific plot of land. By the time Israel occupied the West Bank, regulation proceedings had been completed for approximately one-third of the area, particularly in northern Samaria and the Jordan Valley (B'tselem, 2002). After the Six Day War an area of 1,469,500 acres (5,878,000 dunams) of land came under Israel's jurisdiction. Only 30 per cent of the West Bank had been registered during British rule before 1947, mainly to the north of the Jerusalem–Jericho line. Where registration had been carried out, Israel could operate only on State land; this term covered virtually all categories of land, except that owned by local residents.

As a result many Palestinians have discontinued or reduced their involvement in agriculture, in part as a result of the policies introduced by Israel in two spheres: water and the labor market. One of the main components of Israel's policy concerning water is to reject all applications submitted by Palestinians to receive permits to drill agricultural wells, which prevented development in that sphere. As for the labor market, Israel encouraged the integration of Palestinians in its own labor market. This became a highly attractive proposition because of the high salaries relative to those in the West Bank, and many Palestinians have been inclined therefore to abandon agriculture.

According to an order regarding abandoned property, any property whose owner and holder left the West Bank before, during, or after the 1967 war is defined as an abandoned property and allocated to the Custodian for Abandoned Property on behalf of the Israel Defense Forces commander in the region. The Custodian is entitled to take possession of the property and to manage it as he sees fit. He also may classify property as abandoned property in instances in which the owner or possessor of a property is unknown. In legal terms the Custodian for Abandoned Property becomes the trustee on behalf of the owner of the property who left the West Bank. The Custodian is responsible for protecting the property pending the owner's return. Moreover, on the return of the owner of the property defined as abandoned, the Custodian must return not only the property but also the profits he derived therefrom. As a general rule, Israel has forbidden the return of the refugees to the West Bank, and therefore has not had to face massive claims for the restitution of abandoned property (B'tselem, 2002).

Land expropriation in the West Bank, excluding East Jerusalem, is effected under the provision of a Jordanian law that delineates the phases required for the expropriation of land and the reviewing bodies. According to the law, a public body interested in expropriating private land must publish its intention in the official gazette. If no appeal is filed to the court by the owner of the land within 15 days, the application is discussed by the Ministerial Council, which examines whether the purpose declared by the initiating body is indeed in the public interest and decides whether to purchase the land or acquire rights of use for a defined period. Israel has amended this law to suit its needs twice, by means of military orders. The first amendment, in 1969, transferred the authorities of the Ministerial Council to the empowered authority on behalf of the commander of the region, which became head of the Civil Administration. In addition, the order abolished the requirement in Jordanian law to publish the decisions in the official gazette and deliver them to the owner of the land. The legal authority for discussing appeals against expropriations was changed by the order from the local court, as established in Jordanian law, to the military appeals committee (Fig. 2.11).

In practice, most of the notifications given to landowners are forwarded via the mukhtars. The status of the mukhtars is problematic, and they often preferred to refrain from giving out that information. Israel chose to undertake most expropriations only in urgent cases. Israel has used this law extensively as a tool for seizing control of land for the purpose of constructing an extensive network of roads serving the settlements, connecting one settlement to another and connecting the settlements to Israel and in most cases deliberately circumventing the Palestinian communities. These expropriations were upheld by the High Court, which accepted the State's argument that the need under review also met the transportation needs of the Palestinian population.

The legal tool used by Israel to seize control of land in East Jerusalem for the purpose of establishing settlements was a Mandatory Order from 1943 absorbed into Israeli legislation. This order is similar to the Jordanian law for acquisition of land for public needs as implemented in the remainder of the West Bank. The Mandatory Order empowers the Minister of Finance to issue expropriation orders for privately

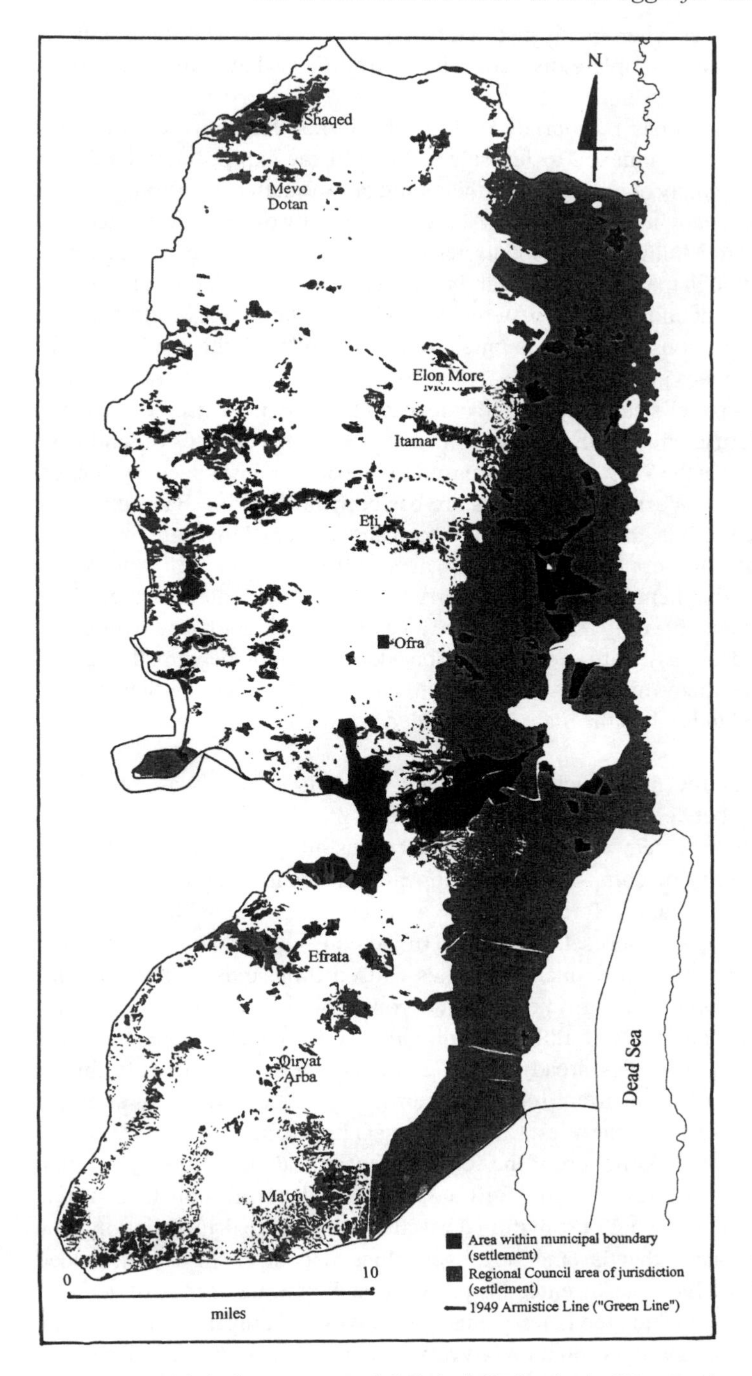

Fig. 2.11 Jewish built-up areas and their jurisdiction in the West Bank
Source: B'tselem, The Israeli Center for Human Rights in the Occupied Territories, 2002

owned land in cases when this is justified by a public need. This order grants the Minister of Finance complete discretion in determining what constitutes public purpose.

Since 1968, Israel has expropriated 6,125 acres (24,500 dunams) of land, over one-third of the land annexed to Jerusalem. Most of the expropriated land was, undoubtedly, privately owned by Palestinians and only a small proportion was State land or land owned by Jews prior to 1948. The vast majority of the expropriated land was used to establish Jewish settlements, termed neighborhoods in domestic Israeli discourse. Although the expropriated land was intended for Jewish population only, Israeli government and Ministry of Jerusalem officials claimed several times that the land expropriations were implemented for the benefit of all the residents of the city, Jews and Arabs alike.

In July 2004 Israel's cabinet adopted a decision to apply the Absentee Property Law to East Jerusalem, and thereby to confiscate thousands of acres of land from owners who live in the West Bank. The reason for the decision was security-related. Since, in practice, West Bank residents are barred from entering East Jerusalem because of the Intifada, the cabinet decided to enact an official measure that would prevent any use of these lands by their owners in the future as well, and would explicitly state that henceforth their property belongs to the State of Israel. Even though the owners live only a short distance away from their confiscated property, their names and addresses are known and no one doubts their ownership, the cabinet decided to label them "absentees" and apply the law that enabled the State to take over refugees' lands when the State was founded, a law which had never been used since then.

According to the law enacted in 1950, every person who was outside of Israeli territory between 29 November 1947 and September 1948 was considered "absentee", and his assets were transferred to the Custodian of Absentee Property, with no possibility of compensation or appeal. But even though the Absentee Property Law remained in force, successive Israeli governments decided not to apply it to annexed East Jerusalem, because of the injustice this would wreak. The decision to apply this Law once again has caused thousands of Palestinians, including many who live right next to their confiscated lands, to lose property overnight, worth hundreds of millions of dollars, and for which no one intends to compensate them. Israel has already seized land and property from the Palestinians during the years of occupation, reducing their living space in order to establish settlements in Jerusalem, the West Bank, and the Gaza Strip.

With the recent construction of the fence in the Jerusalem region, Palestinian landholders from Bethlehem and Beit Jala requested permission to continue working their fields, which are within Jerusalem's municipal jurisdiction. The State's response stated that the lands no longer belong to them, but have been handed over to the Custodian for Absentee Property. At stake are thousands of acres of agricultural land on which the Palestinians grew olives and grapes for many years. The Palestinian landholders and their lawyers term it "Land Grab", and also worry that nascent Housing Ministry plans will build on part of absentees' land.

Even in the last few years Israel has continued to expropriate territory in the West Bank under the guise of State lands to expand the settlements. At least some of these areas were appropriated with the direct approval of Prime Minister Ariel Sharon and Defense Minister Shaul Mofaz. Since the start of 2004, some 550 acres (2,200 dunams) of land in the West Bank have been declared State lands, such as the area between the Palestinian village Beit Ichsa and the Jewish settlement of Giv'at Ze'ev near Jerusalem.

The Sharon government made a commitment to the Bush administration in 2003 that the construction in the settlements beyond existing building zones would be placed on hold, and is now in negotiations with the U.S. administration over the territorial limits of the settlements. The Israeli promise to the U.S. includes a commitment not to expropriate territory for construction, but does not relate in any way to designating areas as "State lands". The "State lands" designated consistently served the governments of Israel in establishing and expanding settlements. In the late 1970s the Supreme Court forbade the expropriation of private Palestinian property for settlements.

There are currently 175,000 acres (700,000 dunams) – 13 per cent of the West Bank before 5 June 1967 – under different stages of "review". At the end of the "review" process it is possible to designate these lands "State lands". The majority of these tracts are in the southern Mount Hebron, in the area of Ezyon bloc, and on both sides of the Trans-Samaria highway.

Disputed waters

In contrast to the struggle for the land in Judea and Samaria, which does not exceed the bounds of the region, the struggle for water has a direct implication on the water potential of the State of Israel. The average consumption of water by Israel's population is about 1.4 billion cu. m (cubic meters) per year, and an additional 400 million cu. m of purified sewage and desalinized salt water. The total amount of water that the mountain aquifer supplies to the population is about 600 million cu. m per year, which is 40 per cent of the total amount of water which accumulates annually in the country by rain, while additional amounts of water are supplied from the Sea of Galilee and the coastal aquifer. From the water which accumulates in the mountain aquifer, Israel consumes about 500 million cu. m annually, while the allocation for the Palestinians is only about 100 million cu. m per year.

An underground aquifer, called the mountain aquifer, supplies about a third of Israel's water consumption, as well as most of the consumption of those residing in Judea and Samaria. The water that penetrates the surface in Judea and Samaria moves downward through the soil and rocks and reaches a groundwater reservoir, called an aquifer, which is a water-bearing rock formation. The groundwater reservoir beneath the Judea and Samarian Mountains constitutes the largest water source of the region, supplying 600 million cu. m per year. This is the best-quality water resource in the region. The aquifer has a storage area where the surface rocks are impermeable, and serve as a "roof" covering the groundwater reservoir. The storage area is located eastward and westward of the feeding area, beneath the margins of the Judea and Samarian Mountains and beneath the Coastal Plain. The vast majority of wells pumping water from the mountain aquifer are located at the storage area where the pumping rate is stable and pumping is cheapest. The western boundary of the aquifer is located on a line where the groundwater salinity exceeds 600 ppm (parts per million) chloride, which makes the water unsuitable for use. This western boundary is located beneath the Coastal Plain, at depths of 0.3–0.6 miles (0.5–1 km). The eastern boundary of the aquifer is located along the structural faults of the Jordan River Valley. When water infiltrates the aquifer at the feeding area, it flows in all directions following the hydrological gradient. The utilization and management of this important resource is, therefore, one of the major issues that must be addressed in any future peace talks between Israel and the Palestinians (Fig. 2.12).

The population of Israel consumes the mountain aquifer water for two main purposes: provision of domestic water consumption for the residents of Jerusalem, Tel Aviv, Be'ersheva and part of the Coastal Strip; and irrigation of agricultural land in the valleys of Yesreel, Jordan and Be'ersheva. The Palestinians consume the mountain aquifer water mainly for domestic and agricultural uses, and they claim that the water potential of the mountain aquifer should be apportioned differently, so that they should receive 500 million cu. m of water, and only 100 million cu. m of water should be allocated to Israel. They need the mountain aquifer water for several purposes: to increase their domestic consumption to 100 cu. m per person per year; for the transition from extensive to intensive agriculture; for development of new agricultural areas in the Judean and Samarian deserts; and for a certain amount of water that should be conveyed to the Gaza Strip, where a serious water crisis exists.

The Palestinians' claim is that the apportionment of the waters of this aquifer should follow its natural attributes. Accordingly, each of the two parties would be entitled to the amount of rainwater that falls on the respective feeding areas in the territory of each party. Thus, the claim goes, Palestinians should receive all the rainwater that falls on Palestinian soil (Gvirtzman, 1994).

The Palestinians' first demand seems to be quite reasonable, because it is unfair that an Israeli settler in the territories should get an amount of water three to four times higher than that a Palestinian resident gets for domestic use. Regarding their other demands, the Israelis suppose that their fulfillment may cause great harm to Israel in two ways: it may worsen the sweet water and endanger the population's health in the central part of the country. The allocation of the demanded amount of water to the Palestinians might force Israel to supply to its own population more water from alternative sources, together with a decrease of the mountain aquifer water quality. Therefore, on the one hand, it is impossible to continue with such an unequal apportionment of the mountain aquifer water, and, on the other hand, Israel refuses to respond to the Palestinians' demands for a more reasonable division of the water. In other words, water allocation should be determined on the basis of the location of the wells that would allocate the vast majority of the water to Israel.

In any political agreement between Israel and the Palestinian Authority that might be achieved in the future, it will be necessary to fulfill the equal human needs of all

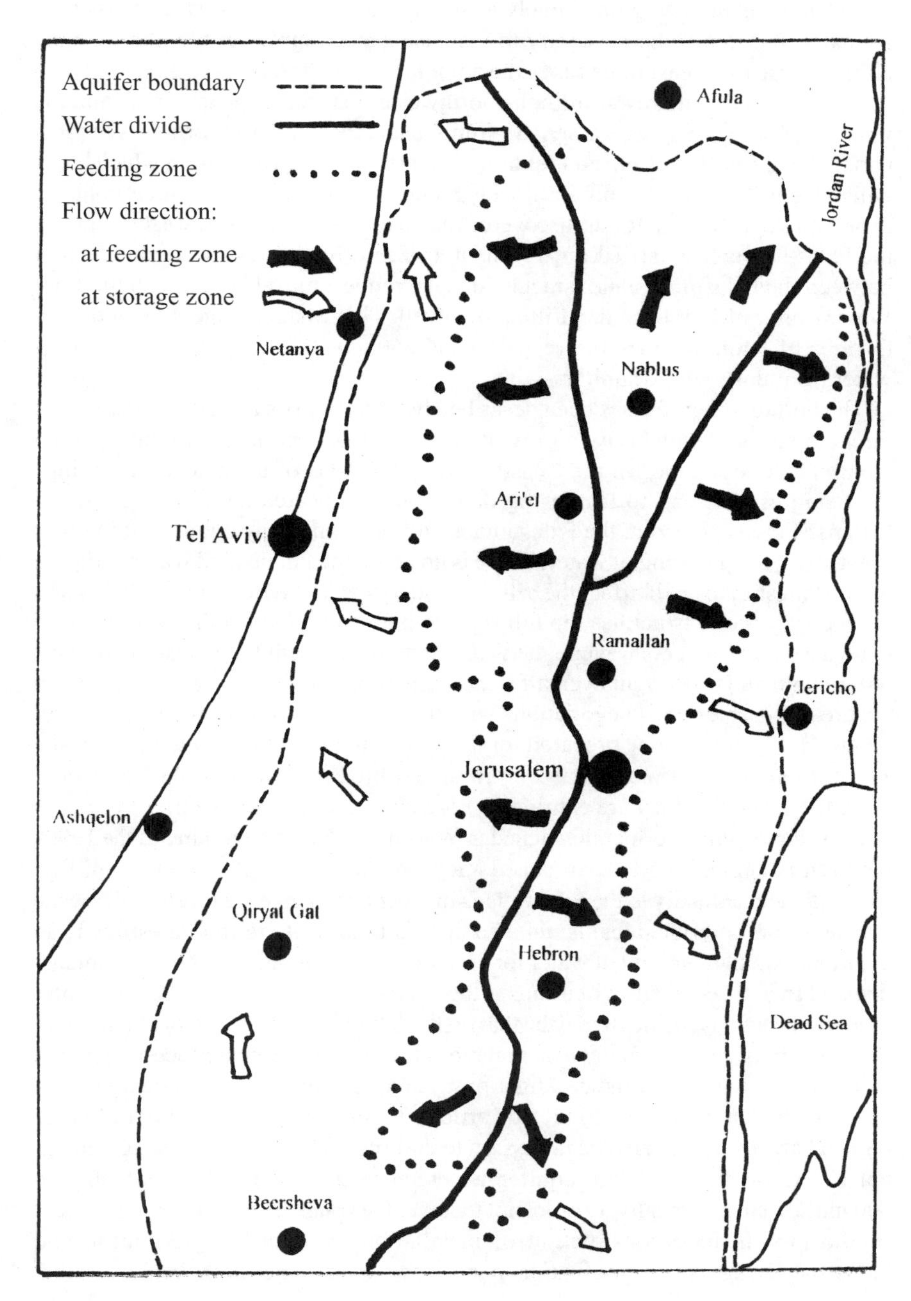

Fig. 2.12 Hydrology of the mountain aquifer

the inhabitants in the region, namely to supply 70–100 cu. m of water per person annually. It will also be necessary to increase water supply for the Palestinians' domestic use to at least three times the amount they get today.

The expected withdrawal from the northwestern Bank, in the area of Jenin, the villages of the Bet She'an Valley, the Gilbo'a, and the En Harod springs is in great part tied to the northwestern aquifer that is situated in the territory from which Israel will pull out. The Palestinians are already pumping water from that source, contrary to previous agreements. It was discovered that in the area of the northwestern aquifer the Palestinians had carried out 17 unauthorized drillings. The water agreement between the Palestinians and Israel held that a request must be filed with the Joint Water Committee prior to the drilling of a well. This was not done. In practice, in the area of Jenin there are between 150 and 260 unauthorized drillings, drawing water from this specific aquifer.

The northeast aquifer has been described by hydrologists as being under severe threat in terms of suitability to provide Israel with water, similar to the situation along the "Green Line" in the Coastal Strip. Hundreds of unauthorized drillings are being carried out, to increasing depths. It is expected that, once the Israel Defense Forces pulls out, the Palestinians will bring in heavy equipment in order to intensify the pumping of water. There is no doubt that intensified water pumping by the Palestinians will affect the villages and towns in the Bet She'an Valley and the industry there. Israel has the full right to put an end to unauthorized drillings that cause harm and contravene the water agreements with the Palestinians. This will remain an Israeli right even after the dismantling of the Jewish settlements in the area. The solution is negotiations with the new leadership on the water agreements. But Israel must be prepared for the Palestinians to point out that, out of the 130 million cu. m of water drawn from the northwestern aquifer, they take only 30 million, and that they are entitled to more under a new agreement.

In an agreement on principles signed in Washington at the beginning of the 1990s between Israel and the Palestinians, Israel promised to supply about 70 million cu. m of water annually to the Palestinians in order to equalize the levels of domestic consumption on both sides. Israel also agreed to allocate to the Palestinians an additional smaller amount of water for agricultural development. The Palestinians' demand to increase their agriculture at the expense of a decrease in Israel's water seems to be unreasonable. It may be that, in the future, it will be possible to improve the water division in the frame of negotiations toward a permanent peace agreement, that will be bound by juristic obligations. An agreement between Israel and the Palestinians will then have to include articles to prevent the possibility of hydrological hazards. It will also be necessary to enforce on the two sides an agreement not to exploit the mountain aquifer water more than its refilling potential of 600 million cu. m annually, in order not to lower the water level. Such an agreement should also include construction of installations for purifying domestic and industrial sewage water, originating in the towns and villages of the region, so that the ground water will not be polluted.

Israel's struggle for the right to use the mountain aquifer water for its own needs, seems to be reasonable to a certain degree, because the Palestinians, being without any supervision, may pump water from the aquifer in unlimited amounts, and even beyond the annual renewable amount of water, so that the water level of the aquifer might descend to below the "red line", without the ability to return to its average level. The party who dominates the water resources of the West Bank is able to dry out the Coastal Plain of Israel. The party who dominates the main mountain aquifer, the drilling of wells, and the water pumping in West Samaria and Jenin area may leave the agricultural area of the Coastal Strip without enough water for irrigation. It should also be indicated that in coming years the West Bank will suffer from a shortage of about 400 million cu. m of water annually. Permits for water pumping given by the Palestinian Authority, and the approval of more drillings of wells, will undoubtedly cause serious damage to the Coastal Plain water resources (Gvirtzman, 1994).

The vital water for the population in the region accumulates in the more saturated parts of the aquifer which are thick enough to allow water pumping from the wells. The less vital area is on the mountain crest and on the eastern slopes, where the soil layers are not saturated with water. Israel has, therefore, a special interest to safeguard the areas it occupied in the West Bank, where most of the saturated layers exist, namely, the western slopes of Samaria, the Gilbo'a Mountains, the mountainous surroundings of Jerusalem, and the Ezyon bloc. The western slopes of Samaria are most critical in this matter, because they supply significant amounts of water to the residents of the Coastal Plain for domestic consumption. When the Israeli governments decided in the 1970s to establish the first Jewish settlements in the region, they were aware of the importance of the water resources, and settlements such as Elqana, Newe Zuf, and others were established at that time partly to maintain control of the water resources. It may be assumed that, in negotiations with the Palestinians on a permanent peace agreement, Israel will have to surrender some of the rights claimed by the Palestinians, which will mean a decrease in Israel's amount of water potential from the mountain aquifer.

The hydrological situation in the Gaza Strip is quite different. The water dispute in this region between Israel and the Palestinians has its roots in a hydrological disaster that happened in the southern part of the Coastal Plain. Its results were a sharp decrease in the underground water level because of intensive pumping of water in the wells, which caused salinity and water pollution, so that in the future there is no chance of reconstructing the coastal aquifer in that area.

The underground water of the Gaza Strip flows on a clay layer in a light westward inclination toward the sea. The upper level of the groundwater is very close to the ground level which makes it very easy to pump and exploit water for all uses. The ground water is enclosed from all sides and has no connection with the coastal aquifer which lies to the north between Ashqelon and Ashdod. The water which feeds the Gaza aquifer originates from the rain which penetrates into the soil and is, as said, pumped from the many wells of the Strip (Gvirtzman, 1994).

The Palestinians blamed Israel for the hydrological disaster in the Gaza Strip because many wells had been drilled east of the "Green Line", and much water had been pumped from them, which prevented water from flowing to the Strip. The water situation that exists in the Gaza Strip has no direct connection with the water problems of Israel in the West Bank. It may be that decrease in the water potential of the Gaza Strip will reduce the home consumption to such a degree that Israel will be blamed as the occupying country. The water crisis of the Gaza Strip can be solved only by using alternative resources such as desalination of sea water or importing water from abroad.

The scarcity of water in the region makes water allocation one of the central issues to be resolved in the Arab–Israel conflict in general, and the Israeli–Palestinian conflict in particular. The actual needs of the communities that depend on the waters take precedence over the natural properties that exist in the basin, and, among these needs, priority is naturally given to past and existing uses, at the expense of potential uses. By indicating the relevant factors that may shape the potential uses of these waters, water allocation may slightly be modified in order to increase the Palestine domestic consumption to be equal to the consumption level usually found in Israel.

The Jewish–Palestinian demography

In any future agreement that might be achieved between Israel and the Palestinian Authority regarding the final borderlines, the results may be that certain parts of Judea and Samaria will be annexed to the sovereign State of Israel, including the Palestinian population that resides within them. If that is the case, the Israel government will have to decide how many Arabs to absorb and which parts of the West Bank will be left and remain under Palestinian sovereignty. In such circumstances the issue of the Arab demographic potential of the West Bank is going to be one of the most crucial problems for Israel. Regarding the demographic potential of the Arab population, four different areas should be considered: East Jerusalem; Judea and Samaria; the State of Israel within the "Green Line" boundaries; and the Jewish settlement blocs that are planned by Israel to be annexed in the future. The demographic reality in the region reveals that in each of these geographical areas there exists a mixing of Jewish and Arab population which has been involved since 1967 in a permanent demographic struggle for majority taking the form of a silent struggle by means of natural increase and internal immigration balance. One may therefore wonder, how many Arabs live in each of these geographical areas, what are the demographic components of the two populations, and what may be their demography in the next twenty years.

In Judea and Samaria, excluding East Jerusalem, there lived according to the Israel Defense Forces Census carried out in 1967, about 600,000 Arabs. In 2004 they numbered about two million, an increase of 3.3 times in thirty-eight years. The reason for that rapid increase was high birth rates of the Palestinian population and external immigration to the territories. The Jewish population in Judea and Samaria numbered in 2004 about 230,000 people, after more than three and a half decades of initiated settling in the region, but the results are that the Israelis did not achieve any demographic priority in the demography of the West Bank, not by means of birth rates and not even by attracting the settling of Jews in reunited Jerusalem and its surroundings. If we compare the demography between the Jewish and Arab population in the State of Israel within the "Green Line", we see that the Jewish population has increased from 2,383,000 people in1967 to about 5,260,000 in May 2005, an increase of 121 per cent, while the Arab population has increased in that period from 392,700 to about 1,350,000, an increase of 244 per cent. This proves that the Arab population increases at a high rate not only in the West Bank but even within the State of Israel under Jewish authority. With the assumption that the annual increase of the Jewish population in the State of Israel will be 2.47 per cent per annum with a limited Jewish immigration potential to the country, and that of the non-Jewish population will be 3.42 per cent per annum, the populations will be equal in number in another thirty to forty years. An even size of the Jewish population in Israel and the Palestinians in the territories, who number together with the Gaza Strip's population about four million, will be reached in another twenty years, and that of the Jews in Israel as against all the Arabs in Israel, the West Bank, and in the Gaza Strip in another ten years. From these facts it should be concluded that in order to keep a Jewish character in the State of Israel, the Jewish population increase has to be concentrated in the future only within the "Green Line" boundaries.

If certain areas of Judea and Samaria are annexed to Israel in the future, namely the so-called "consensus" settlement blocs where a majority of the Jewish population resides, where a relatively large number of settlements have been established during the last 38 years, it means that many Palestinian villages and their inhabitants will have also to be annexed to Israel's sovereign territory, which will increase the number of Palestinians under Israeli rule. If Israel's aspiration is to delineate Jewish settlement blocs with a reasonable territorial width, or settlement blocs with vital continuation between them, there will be no other way than to annex even more Palestinian inhabitants and villages that might increase the number of Palestinians under Israel's sovereignty by about 100,000. The Arab population which resides in these settlement blocs number about 2,500 people in the Jordan Valley, about 10,000 in the Ezyon bloc, about 18,000 in the Ari'el area, some 7,500 in the southwestern Hashmona'im bloc of Samaria, and about 60,000 in the Jerusalem vicinity, altogether about 100,000 people.

The Arabs who reside in these West Bank blocs, together with those who live in East Jerusalem and within the boundaries of the "Green Line", number about 1.3 million. This means that, by the territorial annexation of the Jewish settlement blocs in the West Bank, Israel may be thrown into a demographic problem of two main components, territory and population. The more territory Israel annexes, the more Arab population will have to be absorbed under its sovereignty, with all the political and economic consequences.

Public opinion regarding the Jewish demography in Judea and Samaria are divided and not unequivocal. A part of the public relates to it as positive facts while another part regards them as negative. According to the data of the Ministry of the Interior, a third of all the Jewish settlers in the West Bank live in the suburbs around Jerusalem. In western Samaria, adjacent to the "Green Line", there reside another 70,000, 35 per cent of all the settlers in the region. Among the seven Jewish regional councils, six in Judea and Samaria and one in the Gaza Strip, a relative population increase has occurred in the last four years. In the Benjamin Regional Council there was an increase of 10 per cent in the years 2000–1, while in the Ezyon Regional Council the increase was 4 per cent only. In all the other Regional Councils there was in the same period an increase of 0.8–1.6 per cent only. In the Megillot Regional Council there was even a decrease in the population. While the Regional Councils represent the main demographic trends in the area, it should be emphasized that Jewish population increase takes place mainly among those of western Samaria and in the Ezyon bloc. Among the Jewish towns in Judea and Samaria, those which showed a high increase were the extreme orthodox ones, such as Modi'in Illit with more than 24,300 inhabitants in 2003 and Betar Illit with 22,900 inhabitants in 2003. A decrease in the number of inhabitants occurred in Qiryat Arba, Ma'ale Efrayim and Immanu'el. Most of the demographic population increase takes place in three regions: in the surroundings of Jerusalem, in the Ezyon bloc, and in the Hashmona'im Bloc in southwestern Samaria.

Are there signs of abandonment of homes by settlers in Jewish settlements in Judea and Samaria? According to 2000 data, the total increase of the settlers in Judea and Samaria was 2.5 per cent only, as against 8–12 per cent in 1999, while half of the increase came from high birth rates. The rate of leaving the settlements was at that time about 5 per cent, as against 1 per cent previously. Most of the leavers were inhabitants who lived in hired houses or apartments, and who owned apartments in Israel that were rented temporarily to others till they decided on their permanent place of dwelling. Most of the leavers came from economically strong families who could afford to hire a house in the territories without selling their own home in Israel for the time being. In many of the settlements the population increase occurred because of the fact that orthodox people joined them, while most of the leavers were from the secular sector. The movement of newcomers to the ideological settlements originates mostly from the intensive activity of influential rabbis among the orthodox public, who call their members of the community to settle in the West Bank. The settlers who left their homes in the Jordan Valley did so because of economic reasons, the agricultural crisis that exists in the country and especially in the Valley, and because of the difficulty of getting foreign employees for agricultural work there. As we come closer to the "Green Line" boundary in the west, the rate of joiners and leavers is more or less even.

The Jewish settlement layout in Judea and Samaria is not immunized against political events that may occur in the future. Despite the strength that the settlers demonstrate in the territories, there are splits in their demography with a decrease in population in settlements, in governmental building of new houses, and in buying apartments, and a gradual increase in the abandonment of settlements, but also a population increase in some of the "ideological" settlements. The Jewish demography in Judea and Samaria proves that the influence of Jewish settlement in the territories is mostly selective and does not imprint its holding in the "Greater Land of Israel", while the Palestinian demography blows all the time down the neck of the Israelis.

Besides the Jewish–Palestinian demographic issue that will play an important role after the annexation of certain occupied territories to the sovereign State of Israel, the unsolved problem of the Palestinians' right to return to their homeland will continue to prevail and threaten Israel's demography. The former U.S. President Bill Clinton once declared that the Palestinians should be allowed to reside in Judea and Samaria wherever they want, and their right to return to the West Bank depends on the period of time they lived as refugees, their desire to return to the physical conditions they had in the past, and their readiness to return to the standard of living they were used to. The Israel establishment was quite embarrassed by that declaration and considered it as the United States' support for the right of return of the Palestinian refugees to the Land of Israel. While the Palestinian refugee issue is permanently on the geopolitical agenda in the region, and while it will have to be discussed fundamentally in negotiations toward a permanent agreement between the Israel and the Palestinians, it is worth clarifying the importance, and the spatial and demographic significance of it to the State of Israel.

During Israel's War of Independence in 1948 hundreds of thousand of Palestinians left their homes, escaped or were deported from their land and became refugees settled in the neighboring Arab countries. It may be assumed that after more than 57 years most of them became permanent citizens in these countries, although many of them still live in camps near towns in poor circumstances. The refugees see themselves as a people without a homeland, similar to the fate of many Jews in the world before the State of Israel was born. Their aspiration to return to their homeland Palestine has been declared and expressed by their leaders on many occasions and in many political forums. The spatial distribution of their camps is from the Gaza Strip in the west to the Hashemite Kingdom of Jordan to the east, Lebanon in the north, and Syria in the northeast. The refugees in their camps are considered as a Palestinian militant potential which is used by Arab leaders for political and nationalist purposes, without taking any initiative to improve their condition. The Arab countries never hurried to absorb them as citizens in their countries, assuming that absorption might weaken their aspiration to return to their homeland and reject the establishment of a Palestinian State in the future. As a result, hundreds of thousands of refugees still live today in camps, where their children are born, live, and die as refugees. Many of them survive only with the support of the U.N. Relief and Works Agency as secondary citizens in the Arab countries (PLO, Factfile, 2000).

The problem of the Palestinian refugees' right to return to the Land of Palestine seems to be a stumbling block in the negotiations between Israel and the Palestinian Authority regarding the achievement of a permanent agreement, and it is doubtful if it is possible to find a reasonable solution that will be accepted by both parties. The difficulty in finding a solution originates from the following facts: there exist many specific U.N. resolutions accepted over the years on the return of the Palestinians to their homeland which were not executed; the number of refugees and their descendants in the Arab countries is very high and reaches a few millions; the life condition of the Palestinians in these countries is temporary and unstable; the State of Israel is too small and too poor to be able to absorb the refugees and to compensate them for their suffering and for their abandoned property; while the Jews' property left in the Arab countries was confiscated when the mass immigration of Jews to Israel took place, and has never been compensated for.

Sometimes rumors are heard from politicians about the possibility of a gradual absorption of Palestinian refugees in small quotas in Israel in the framework of a permanent agreement. If so, it is important to relate to this problem and to its significance and complexity.

What is a refugee? The United Nations Relief and Works Agency for Palestinian Refugees in the Near East (UNRWA) defined a Palestinian refugee as any person whose normal place of residence was Palestine during the period 1 June 1946 to 15 May 1948 and who lost both home and means of livelihood as a result of the 1948 conflict. In the first session of the refugee working group in Ottawa 1992 the Joint Palestinian–Jordanian delegation provided another definition of the Palestinian refugees: those Palestinians and their descendents who were expelled or forced to leave their homes between November 1947 and January 1949 (the date of the Rhodes Armistice Agreement) from territory controlled by Israel on that date. This definition does not apply to camp dwellers, and certainly not only to those recognized refugees who enjoyed formal registration with UNRWA, since the latter never exercised jurisdiction over more than a segment of the total refugee problem. Such a definition includes all the 1967 and post-1949 displaced persons, the residents of border villages in the West Bank, who lost their agricultural lands in the War of 1948, and therefore the source of their livelihood, but remained in their villages, residents of the Gaza Strip refugee camps who were either relocated to the Rafah side of the Egyptian boundary or found themselves separated from their families as a result of border demarcation after the Camp David Agreement between Israel and Egypt.

How many refugees live in this region according to the above-mentioned estimates? For the years 1948–50 different estimates exist, calculated by Great Britain, the United States, the United Nations, Israel and the Palestinian Authority (Table 2.4).

What is the status of the refugees in the Arab countries? Refugee documents valid for five years have been provided in Egypt to three categories of Palestinians: those who in 1948–49 took refuge in the Gaza Strip, those who in 1948–49 took refuge elsewhere in Egypt, and non-refugees from the Gaza Strip. Since the late 1970s, and particularly following the 1990 Gulf crisis, the privileges the Palestinians had been enjoying in many sectors since 1948 have been gradually abolished. Such privileges concerned, for example, the renewal of re-entry visas free of charge, the right to register one's children in government schools, comparatively low tuition

Table 2.4 Palestinian refugees 1948–50 – estimates

Areas of arrival	*British*	*United States*	*United Nations*	*Israel*	*Palestinians*
Gaza	210,000	208,000	280,000	200,000	201,173
West Bank	320,000	–	190,000	200,000	363,689
Arab countries	280,000	667,000	256,000	–	284,324
Total	810,000	875,000	726,000	650,000	849,186

Source: The Palestinian Refugees 1948–2000, Factfile, Palestinian Liberation Organization, Jerusalem: April 2000.

fees for university graduates, free health services and social benefits. With regard to employment, only Palestinian refugees who are in possession of a refugee document are formally exempted from the requirement that native workers be given priority for employment. Otherwise, most laws and decrees regulating foreign labor in Egypt are applicable to the Palestinians.

Jordan is the only country to have granted full citizenship to all Palestinian refugees and their descendants. They have been considered fully fledged citizens of Jordan, formally enjoying the same rights and obligations as other Jordanians. Other Palestinian residents, such as the displaced Palestinians from the Gaza Strip who took refuge in Jordan after June 1967, have not been considered Jordanian citizens. They are not officially authorized to work and have a status that is inferior to that of the Jordanian Palestinians. In Lebanon, except for a group composed mainly of wealthy and skilled refugees who were offered nationality in the 1950s (about 30,000 people), the Lebanese authorities have constantly prevented the absorption of the Palestinian refugees, officially categorizing them as foreigners. Only those Palestinian refugees who took direct refuge in Lebanon in the wake of the 1947–49 exodus are considered legal residents. As to the Palestinians who immigrated to Lebanon after the War of 1967 or after the 1970–71 PLO–Jordanian dispute, they have not been granted identity papers and have thus been under constant threat of deportation. Syria, from the outset, has undertaken legal steps that have tended to place Palestinians on a par with its nationals in the economic and social fields. Palestinians residing in Syria since 1956 are considered as originally Syrian in all things covered by the law and legally valid regulations connected with the right to employment, commerce, and national service, while preserving their original nationality (PLO, Factfile, 2000).

Relevant U.N. resolutions regarding the Palestinian refugees provided some constructive steps for their right to return. The General Assembly Resolution 194 of December 1948 resolved that the refugees wishing to return to their homes and live at peace with their neighbors should be permitted to do so at the earliest practical date and that compensation should be paid for the property of those choosing not to return and for loss of or damage to property which, under principles of international law or in equity, should be made good by the governments or authorities responsible. The Security Council Resolution 242 of November 1967 emphasized the inadmissibility of the acquisition of territory by war and the need to work for a just and lasting peace in which every State in the area can live in security. The Security Council Resolution 338 of October 1987 called upon the parties concerned to start immediately after the ceasefire the implementation of Security Council Resolution 242 in all of its parts. A General Assembly Resolution of December 1980 indicated that the legitimate and inalienable rights of the Palestine people to return to their homes and property and to achieve self-determination, national independence, and sovereignty are endorsed by the Committee on the conviction that the full implementation of these rights will contribute decisively to a comprehensive and final settlement of the Middle East crisis.

To return to the figures of the Palestinian population in Judea and Samaria, it should be emphasized that they are quite different from those accepted in Israel, but the results of a population census carried out by the Palestinian Authority in 1998 revealed again the severity of Israel's demographic problem. If we accept the demographic data indicated by the Palestinians, the main trends of their demography in the years 1967–98 are remarkable (Table 2.5).

The weakness of the Jewish settlement in the West Bank in all its components is that it is under Palestinian demographic threat, not only in the territories but also in the sovereign territory of Israel. The State of Israel faces the demographic crisis but its establishment is under religiously motivated pressure and is not able to do too much against it. The governments of Israel did not make any important decision on the national level relating to this problem, except for one decision regarding the disengagement from the Gaza Strip which may be executed in 2005 and may improve the Jewish demographic situation. Israel should relate this situation more seriously to what may happen in the next 15 to 20 years (Table 2.6). The demographic clock works very quickly against Israel's interests, and it is therefore surprising that the Israel public behaves so indifferently toward the issue. It may be that the reason for this is the difficulty in accepting abstract statistical data, together with, so to speak, its racial significance. There is a trend among the public to disregard it because of the feeling that the whole process is slow. But after all, the main factors that really threaten the Jews are not so much the dramatic bloodsheds as the gradual demographic process which many want to disregard. The State of Israel will be able to exist as a Jewish State only if it includes in its boundaries a strong Jewish majority who live in a territory of which its size and boundaries enable it to realize its sovereignty and defense.

Table 2.5 Palestinian population census 1998

Region	*1967*	*1998*	*Increase (%)*
Jerusalem	–	113,837	
East Jerusalem	71,300	210,000	194.5
West Bank without East Jerusalem	595,900	1,848,818	210.2
Gaza Strip	389,700	1,020,913	161.9
Total	1,056,900	3,079,631	191.3

Source: *Ha'aretz* newspaper, 2004. The 1998 Jerusalem figures relate to undefined boundaries.

Table 2.6 Jews and Arabs in the Land of Israel

	2000	*2010*	*2020*
All the Land of Israel	9,319,000	11,698,999	14,353,000
Jews	5,170,000	5,980,000	6,697,000
Arabs in Israel	1,178,000	1,555,000	1,976,000
Arabs in the West Bank and Gaza	2,973,000	4,163,000	5,680,000
Percentage of Jews	55.4	51.1	46.6

Source: Central Bureau of Statistics estimate for the years 2010 and 2020.

The Central Bureau of Statistics reported in April 2005 that Israel's population will reach 9.3 million in 2025, an increase of 45 per cent compared to 6.4 million at the end of 2000. Seventy per cent, or 6.5 million, of Israel's residents in 2025 will be Jewish. The total average annual population growth rate in 2001–25 will be 1.5 per cent, compared to 1.8 per cent in 1995–2000. According to the forecast, the Jewish population will grow in 2001–25 by 1.1 per cent, or 60,000 people annually.

The Arab population in Israel is expected to reach 2.3 million, or 25 per cent of Israel's population, in 2025, compared to 19 per cent, or 1.2 million, today. The Arab population will increase at a rate of 45,000 per year, a growth rate of 2.7 per cent. The figures also presume that an Israeli woman's average number of births will decrease from 2.9 at the beginning of the period. Life expectancy will rise during this period by 2.6 years for both sexes, reaching 79.8 and 83.8 for men and women respectively. During this time, 543,000 people will immigrate to Israel, and the number of migrants leaving the country is expected to be 340,000.

The significance of the Jewish–Palestinian demography is that no signed agreement between Israel and the Palestinians will be permanent because it will be impossible to prevent disputes that may arise from a national, economic, or social background. The Land of Israel is small in comparison with other countries with a similar size of population. About 60 per cent of Israel is a semi-arid desert where it is hard to establish settlements, because of climate and shortage of water. About 42 per cent of Israel's territory is taken by military and security bodies. The rest of the country that remains for settlement is the northern half that extends from Be'ersheva upwards, which is already densely populated and where it is quite difficult to absorb hundreds of thousands of refugees without doing harm to the quality of people's lives.

A rapid increase of population in the "Greater Land of Israel", despite the birth rates of the Palestinian population, might also have a severe effect on the ecology in the country. The problem originates in two opposed factors: on the one hand there are in the Land of Israel population rates of increase typical of Third World countries, and on the other hand the Jewish population in Israel lives at a level of consumption typical of western countries with an increasing standard of living. The result is that Israel is getting very close to an extreme density in the Coastal Plain, for instance, where most of the Jewish population resides. This limited space for further development is already felt in many domains: the buckling of the water and communications systems, and so also the disposal and sewerage systems, the destruction of coastlines and disappearing of sand dunes as natural sites, the decrease in agricultural land, the disappearance of much of the open space, failures in physical planning decisions – and above all the deterioration in human relations.

When the Land of Israel between the Mediterranean Sea and the Jordan River supports about fifteen million people in the year 2020, there may be a decrease in fresh air, in drinking water, and in sources of energy. There is no doubt that such a large population in this small country will also create large problems of garbage disposal and sewerage. In these aspects Israel will have a common fate with the Palestinians. Without a serious attitude of the government towards the ecological problems in the region, Israel may turn into a Third World country with a direct effect on the safety of the community and its national security. Every leadership has to consider such problems and prepare itself properly for the year 2020 by a change in development priorities. Among them are to return to the population dispersion policy, to the development of the northern Negev and Galilee, to the construction of an appropriate infrastructure for a population of fifteen million, and to a strict enforcement of laws.

The possibility of reaching a permanent peace agreement with the Palestinians on the basis of the demographic situation in the region is not certain. Many factors play against it: the demographic components of the Palestinian people; the corruption that prevails in the Palestinian Authority; the Palestinians' aspiration for the right to return; the unsolved refugee problem; the Palestinian demographic changes that occur in reunited Jerusalem which do harm to the city's economic and social aspects; the demographic increase in the Jewish settlements; and the refusal of the settlers to be deported from the territories.

Worries about demography, meaning anxiety about an Arab majority, have in the last years taken over the shaping of Israel's national policy. On the right the slogan goes, "no Arabs, no terror", and they preach for mass expulsion. On the left they speak about "a Jewish majority between the Sea and the River" which means escaping the territories to save Zionism. Arab birth rates are higher than Jewish ones, immigration is at a trickle, and experts compete with gloomy forecasts whether the moment of the demographic tie will arrive in another five years or in fact it has happened without anyone noticing. The solution of withdrawal from the territories is no longer enough for the angry prophets of demography. They recommend surgery in which Israel also gets rid of the residents of Wadi Ara and the "Triangle" in the eastern Coastal Plain, lest the Arabs of these districts multiply and start demanding their national rights. The records of birth rates in the Palestinian Authority, the "Triangle", and Galilee, which once only interested statisticians, are now the basis for debate. Are the Arabs having fewer children, or did the Intifada actually spur the birth rate? Experts wonder how to develop family planning and social cutbacks that would encourage Jews to have more children and Arabs fewer.

Some Jewish demographers in the U.S. suppose that the figures concerning the future majority of the Arabs in the Land of Israel are wrong. They claim that the Palestinians are trying to inflate the number of residents in the territories in order to undercut Israel's image. The best way to deprive the Palestinians of this tactic, they suppose, is to challenge the accuracy of their exaggerated numbers. The public debate over the demographic problem is being conducted on the basis of mistaken data that inflate the number of Palestinians and diminish the scale of Jewish majority in the country. Their findings purport to undermine the conventional verities and show that there are many fewer Arabs in the territories than is generally thought. According to their calculation, there are not more than three million Arabs in the territories and not 3.8 million, which is the number that is usually accepted and is based on data of the Palestinian Authority's Central Bureau of Statistics. Cross-matching of figures issued by the Palestinian Health Ministry, which counts the number of births and deaths in the territories, with the data of Israel Border

Control, which monitor the entrances to and departures from the West Bank and the Gaza Strip, showed that the estimate of the Palestinian Authority was exaggerated. The birth rate in the West Bank and the Gaza Strip was lower than expected and the Palestinian balance of immigration has been negative in recent years, in contrast to the forecast. They also counted Palestinians who are residents of East Jerusalem, who also appear in the official statistics of Israeli residents. After these adjustments, the number of Palestinians in the territories is put at 3.06 million, which is hundreds of thousands lower than the accepted figures.

Objections to this study have been voiced by Professor Sergio DellaPergola, one of Israel's famous demographers. He estimated that the Jewish majority in the Land of Israel would reach an end around 2010. His conclusion was that the country should be divided on a demographic-ethnic basis, with exchanges of population areas: the Palestinians would get the Arab towns and villages in the "Triangle" area in return for the settlements adjacent to Jerusalem and those in western Samaria: Ma'ale Adummim in exchange for Umm al-Fahm. According to his calculations, there are 3.4 million Palestinians in the territories. He supposes that, even if we make the unreasonable assumption that the Arab fertility rate will fall immediately to the Jewish level, without taking immigration into account, there will be erosion in the Jewish majority. It will be lower, but in the end we reach the day of tie, and the day on which Jews will be a minority between the Sea and the River. It seems that both sides show in their reports that demographic forecasts tend to be proved wrong, especially in unstable areas such as the Land of Israel.

One of the reasonable alternatives to weaken the demographic problem is a complete disengagement from the Palestinians by an Israel unilateral initiative if no serious partner exists for such a bilateral move. Then a borderline should be demarcated in Jerusalem, territorial corridors should be delineated between the three parts of the Palestinian Authority, the West Bank, Samaria and Judea, and the Gaza Strip, small isolated settlements should be evacuated, and a separation should be made between the infrastructural systems that existed between Israel and the Palestinians during years of occupation. The benefit from an initiated unilateral disengagement will strengthen the existence of a Jewish and Zionist State in the Land of Israel and the retention of a massive Arab penetration into the Land of Israel. It is also necessary to care for the dominance of Israel's sovereignty in all the settlements in the same way as it exists in all the other settlements in Israel. It is necessary to encourage the policy of high-rise building in any place and region and to conduct a war to the bitter end on illegal building, while limiting the expansion of settlements into boundaries that makes it possible to administer them economically. If Israel will return to normal boundaries and will disengage itself from the burden of the large Palestinian population, its society will be able to renew the Zionist dream of absorption of Jews in a western and modern country. If the disengagement between Jews and Arabs fails, it is quite clear that an Arab majority will reduce Israel's Jewish character in the future.

Apartheid roads

In 2004 Israeli officials were requesting from the World Bank representatives, and via them the donor countries, funding for building a total of some 300 miles (500 km) of roads and some 16 by-passes, tunnels or bridges, and roads slated for upgrading or construction in the West Bank. Three roads came from a list of 30 that Israel told the World Bank it wants to see upgraded. Other roads for Palestinians – some new, some existing, some to be upgraded with tunnels and by-passes – will be added to the list that Israel expects the donor states to finance. The logic is clear here, too. The settlements are a given, a fact. The danger to the lives of the settlers and other Israel civilians on the joint roads is tangible, as has been proved by many drive-by shootings. But the freedom of movement for the Palestinians, as the World Bank has stated, is vital for economic recovery. The by-passes were intended to keep Palestinian and Israeli vehicles far apart by diverting the Palestinian vehicles to secondary roads. Israelis, that is Jews, will for the most part travel on a system of well-maintained highways. The Jewish settler logic of ethnic separation based on blatant discrimination in rights, living conditions, laws and the official attitude toward Jews and Palestinians has deepened over the years until it has become second nature for Israeli society. It is also not surprising that Israel expects the donor countries to finance these alternative roads and by-passes, which are aimed at ensuring the well-being of the settlements and their ability to develop and expand. The cost of the Israeli plan to build a new system of roads in the West Bank is about US$ 200 million. The plan was drafted in an effort to respond to demands for Israel to lift its prohibitions on movement within the West Bank. The map of alternative roads and passages for Palestinians only, which Israel asked the donor countries to finance, demonstrates that, after implementing the plan to disengage from Gaza and the northern West Bank, Israel plans to strengthen its hold on most of the territory of the West Bank and to leave the settlements intact (Fig. 2.13).

Since the year 2000, many of the roads in the West Bank have become the only roads carrying all the Palestinian traffic in their regions and between the regions in the area. Israel prohibits Palestinians from using the main inter-urban highways in the West Bank or it drastically limits their rights to use those roads, which are mainly for use of the settlers. In recent years, thousands of Palestinian vehicles have been daily directed to use the secondary roads, and banned from the highways.

Seemingly, it is a temporary innocent solution answering the need to protect the safety of Israel citizens because of the current reality. The creation of two separate road networks is a logical step, a part of a long-term systematic planning of the settlements that began almost as far back as 1967. Its purpose is to expand the borders of the State of Israel as much as possible, according to the spreading and strengthening of these settlements. The donor states, if they finance the work on the Palestinian roads Israel wants upgraded and improved, will be contributing to the temporary relief of many Palestinians. But they will be direct accessories to turning land available for farming and construction into unnecessary asphalt, further damaging the landscape and environment, and they will assist in consolidating a uniquely Israeli regime of separation and apartheid, making permanent the

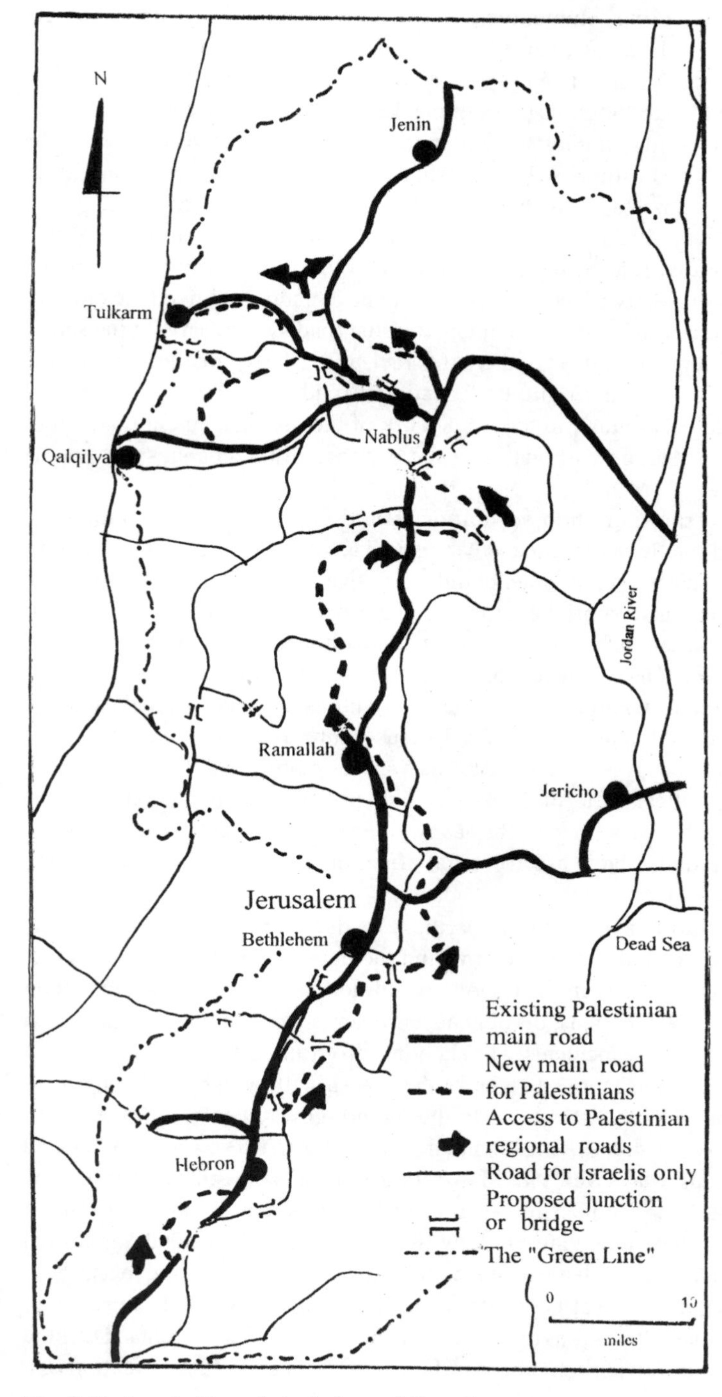

Fig. 2.13 Apartheid roads in Judea and Samaria

separation of neighboring communities divided on ethnic grounds, in an area where most of the land has been taken away for the benefit of a dominant minority.

Israel proposed a system of 16 by-passes, overpasses and tunnels, as a technical solution that could make possible the continued existence and expansion of all West Bank settlements by maintaining two separate transportation networks, one for the Israelis and one for Palestinians. The Palestinians would be promised a contiguous transportation system in a region corresponding to Area A and Area B (see p. 93), but this system would lack any economic logic. Besides the construction of two separate and parallel road systems it also lacks logic from a transportation and environmental perspective. The main roads that have naturally linked the cities of the West Bank for decades will become part of the road system serving the settlements, linking even the smallest of them to Israel, and will require the construction or upgrading of long and circuitous Palestinian roads. The by-passes Israel is proposing would ensure that, in the framework of the disengagement plan, all of the settlements would be sustainable at the expense of the chances of a viable Palestinian State.

The proposed transportation separation would enable Israel to continue to develop all of the settlements and to create Israeli territorial contiguity in the West Bank, while at the same time Israel could claim that it is fulfilling its promise to grant the Palestinians territorial contiguity. The proposed by-passes would divert Palestinian transportation from the existing main roads, which would be perpetuated as roads for Israelis only, to secondary roads, including some that would need to be built. These roads would be less efficient, circuitous and have limited capacity. The by-passes would enable the Israel Defense Forces to remove many of the checkpoints manned by soldiers today, as well as many roadblocks at village entrances. The political status of the by-passes is still not clear but Israel would be able to close them to Palestinian traffic at any given moment. There is no doubt that such a plan would also have a detrimental effect on the chances of reviving the Palestinian economy.

What lies behind Israel's plan of apartheid roads? The harmful results of the Israeli occupation in Judea and Samaria, and the many Palestinian terror attacks executed on Jewish settlers in the region, in addition to the frequent shootings on passengers who used the roads, brought a significant change in the way the Israeli army had to react to these incidents. The shootings from ambushes and from passing Arab vehicles was a substantial danger for the Jewish settlers, especially on access roads which connect the settlements to the main highway between Hebron and Jerusalem or between Jerusalem, Ramallah, and Nablus. These access roads and even parts of the highways were closed from time to time to prevent the Palestinians from conducting their routine life. As a result from this new situation the Israeli government approved the laying of many by-pass roads in Judea and Samaria in order to ensure access to settlements which were in security danger, and to use these roads for a wider and more effective dominance of areas that might be annexed to Israel after a permanent peace agreement is reached with the Palestinians. Over the years the process of Jewish settlement in Judea and Samaria and the creation of a

Plate 2.4 An apartheid road near the Jewish settlement Elqana

large number of settlements has been highly favored as a means of occupation, but it was realized that a secure Israeli road system in the region is no less important.

A Cabinet Minister of Israel once said that the time had come to use separate roads in Judea and Samaria for the Israelis and the Palestinians. In these words he expressed publicly for the first time a hidden idea that had prevailed among the security establishment since the outbreak of the first Intifada in 1987. Separated traffic is crucial, according to the security authorities, to prevent friction between the two peoples. Since then the Israel army has imposed strong restrictions on the Palestinian traffic in the West Bank, mainly to disrupt the road traffic and movement of potential terrorist groups which try to combat the settlers' life in the region. The closures which were imposed from time to time on Arab towns and villages indeed disrupted free movement on the roads, although assurance of total security to the Israelis was not within reach. Actually, more than half of the existing roads in the West Bank took the unofficial status of separated roads because both sides used them by themselves as such for their own reasons and security. The Palestinians do it also to by-pass the many military road blocks and check points which inhibit their traffic. The realization of the road separation idea, by creating one network for Israelis and another one for Palestinians, may change the original functions of some historical roads of the region, as for instance, the central main road between Jenin and Ramallah, of which parts are closed from time to time, so that traffic has to be diverted to other roads on dissected terrain on the mountain crest and with many curves.

The roads in Judea and Samaria have always been known to be constructed with regard to topography, to agricultural land, and to the rural and urban layout of settlements. The physical compact mountain crest made it possible to lay a longitudinal main road on the watershed of the Hebron–Jerusalem–Jenin mountain axis with some branches and junctions in Samaria, and a longitudinal road in the Jericho–Bet She'an axis at the Jordan Valley. In the Judean Mountains only a few lateral roads could be laid because of the existence of a desert in the east and the relatively high summits of Hebron in the west. In the morphological dissected Samarian Hills more lateral roads were built with more branches. But, generally, the road system in Judea and Samaria has not changed too much since historical times because the entire network has been developed gradually in a natural way according to the needs of the local rural Arab population.

The Jewish settlements in the West Bank were established on State land and on sites that have a political significance for the Israelis, and were connected by access roads to adjacent existing highways, even if it was necessary to break new alignments in high topography, in rocky areas or on steep slopes, even if the number of settlers that may use these roads was very low, and even if these long roads needed considerable investment of money. About 6.25 miles (10 km) of roads, for instance, were laid to connect the settlements of Kaddim and Gannim in northern Samaria to a main road, although they are home to about 160 and 150 people respectively, and although they are included in Sharon's disengagement plan for 2005; a road of 5 miles (8 km) was laid in a stony terrain with many curves to connect the 445 settlers of Ma'ale Levona to the Samarian main road; a road of 8.75 miles (14 km) was laid in the southern Hebron Mountains for the 296 settlers in Shim'a; more than 19 miles (30 km) of roads were laid between Teqo'a and the Dead Sea shores to connect 980 settlers with the isolated settlements of Ma'ale Amos and Mizpe Shalem; about 5.6 miles (9 km) of roads were laid for the 171 settlers of Eshkolot in the southern Hebron Mountains to connect them to the isolated settlement of Lahav.

The separation of roads is seen by the Israeli public as apartheid and as a move to create a different kind of territorial occupation in which certain areas of Judea and Samaria will remain under Israeli dominance in the future. Accordingly a new highway was planned a few years ago, one of the most important ones in the region and known as road No. 80, which may create a geographical and environmental change in the road network of the country. This planned highway has to be built east to the Judean Mountains on the Arad–Ma'ale Adummin axis with a 22-mile (35-km) connecting road to Teqo'a in the west. Because of its strategic importance the road should actually delimit the Palestinian Authority's domain in the east and create an unofficial borderline to the dispersion of Arab villages eastward. In its general functions this highway should be a southern continuation to the "Allon Highway" which was laid years ago at the western part of the Jordan Valley. This new planned highway has been approved by the government and carries much political significance for future road building in the region. In the past no such longitudinal road in a north–south direction has been planned, because of the rough dissected terrain, the many wadis that cross the desert, the steep slopes of the Judean Desert and its steep cliffs that rise along the western Dead Sea shore.

The dispersed layout of settlements needed in many cases high-cost by-pass roads which were built on appropriated land because of their proximity to Arab villages. The by-pass road of Jericho in the east, the road between Qiryat Arba and Hebron, the tunnel road between Jerusalem and the Ezyon bloc, the road north of Tulkarm, the road east of Nablus and the northern by-pass road of Jenin are evidence of all that. The Jewish settlements in the Jordan Valley needed the "Allon Highway" by-pass, and this necessitated the cross roads in the Samarian Hills, a cross road in the Judean Mountains and a Jerusalem–Ma'ale Adummim cross road in the east

This imposed network of roads could be characterized by lack of consideration for the existing historical road network in the region; by inappropriateness of topography; by construction in marginal areas for a small population; by land confiscation of Arab villages; by lack of a logical hierarchy of roads with defined traffic functions; and above all by the development of a new road system as a means of territorial dominance in the region. The octopus arms, which hold a grip on Palestinian population centers, connect to Israeli settlement blocs via broad highways allocated "for Jews only", while parallel roads are laid "for Palestinians only". Together, these road systems damage the landscape and destroy ecological habitats.

It may be assumed that a part of the roads which have been laid in the West Bank, and especially the peripheral access roads in northern and eastern Samaria, in the Judean Desert and in the southern Hebron Mountains, will not be useful enough because of the impoverishment of settlers in these problematic areas. Of low use are roads that are blocked from time to time for security reasons, such as the tunnel road near Jerusalem, the roads in western Samaria between Bet El and Dolev, the road between Qiryat Arba and Adora, the Efrata–Jerusalem by-pass near Bethlehem, the Atarot–Giv'at Ze'ev and Mevo Horon–Makkabim roads, etc. It seems that Israel's sovereignty in Judea and Samaria will be remarkable in the future more for domination of the region's road network to ensure free access to the main Jewish settlement concentrations in the Ari'el Bloc, the Ezyon bloc and the surroundings of Jerusalem than for settlement locations.

How is the daily routine traffic on the apartheid roads in the West Bank? Every day soldiers confiscate the identity cards of West Bank Palestinians even though this is prohibited by the law, even by military orders, except under very specific conditions. In the best cases, people are delayed for five, six, or seven hours, far more than for any reasonable check, and then they get their cards back at the end of the day. In the worst cases, the identity cards get lost in the shuffle between soldiers' shifts. Often the soldiers tell people to come tomorrow to some place where they will get their identity card back, at the district co-ordination office, which means another checkpoint. The West Bankers show up the next day and are greeted by apathetic shrugs. But the confiscation of documents, like the hours of delays at the checkpoints using security checks, is one of the most common harassment measures that define the Israeli to Palestinians: arbitrary, malicious, negligent, arrogant, brutal. And it is not only identity cards that the soldiers confiscate. Every few days there are more cases of cars being seized. The army has completed a legal process that allows soldiers to confiscate cars that get past checkpoints using prohibited routes through groves, valleys, and orchards.

At some checkpoints there are lines beyond which only pedestrians are allowed, up to the place where they are checked. There is a distance of a mile or so between the checkpoints of the West Bank and the "Green Line" where no private traffic is allowed. Taxi drivers exploit this situation and make good profits by ferrying passengers between these points. In practice, when many taxi drivers are competing for every passenger, they cross the line, but only by a few feet. Then soldiers sometimes consider that enough to delay drivers more than six hours, and then to order the confiscation of their taxis for a week. They know that hundreds of appeals by the Center for the Protection of the Individual on the matter of confiscated documents don't threaten them. They understand, without any orders, that instilling fear of harassment and complications such as lost time, livelihood, and money, in tens of thousands of Palestinians every day, is a weapon just as effective as the rifle they carry. They know that the little daily harassments are an integral part of their routine. That duty is to enforce the control of one nation over another.

The fact is that the checkpoints are not a product of the Intifada, they gave birth to it. They were born in 1991, two years before the Oslo Accords, and were greatly reinforced after these agreements were signed. The checkpoint system is not part of the Intifada, but it did grow and strengthen thanks to it. This system is also not going to end when the Intifada is over. The checkpoint system belongs entirely to the Israeli unwillingness to give up all the territory of the West Bank, including all the settlements. This system is aimed at ensuring Israeli control over the lives of the Palestinians. From this perspective, the settlements are not the reason for the checkpoints. The isolated settlements and the settlement blocs are the pretext for the checkpoints but they reveal their real function: we are present everywhere, we will split the Palestinian territory in every way, we will control them.

The Jewish settlers in Judea and Samaria are claiming that they don't get enough security on the roads that they use, while the army is doing the best to safeguard them, although it is difficult to protect all travellers on such a wide and branched network which includes more than 625 miles (1,000 km) of roads. But the public in Israel claims that there is no need to support these settlements by so many new roads, and, in order to ensure their security, it would be better if they remained in a few concentrated settlement blocs adjacent to the "Green Line", and so save enormous sums of government money which could be invested in more important projects.

It may be concluded that the traffic security of the Jewish population in the region is after all not safe enough, and, despite all the investments in by-pass road construction, roads are being totally abandoned by settlers or remain in low use. Those who expected them to be bridges for a solution of the political dispute between Israel and the Palestinians now find them hostile borderlines. The apartheid roads in the West Bank are more problematic to the Israelis than their real efficiency suggests because the whole fabric of the artificial Jewish settlement project in this region, which was quite alien to it and to its physical and geographical structure, cannot find a positive solution in the shape of a road network. The geographical inferiority of the Jewish settlements in Judea and Samaria has a direct influence on the degree of usefulness of these roads, which have to be seen as temporary roads at the best.

Peace patterns in an insurgency region

The West Bank might be considered an insurgent region lying adjacent to the official borderlines of the State of Israel. The people who live there want a country of their own in a territory currently dominated by a government in which they have no participation. To advance their cause, the Palestinians engage in various activities ranging from petitioning to terrorism. An insurgent region or State develops when a rebellious group secures and retains control of a territorial base of operations. The territory then becomes the basis for a State that performs most, if not all, governmental functions and services. The Palestinians in the West Bank claim a significant geographical area as a national homeland.

The terrorist attacks against Israel that have occurred in recent years because of the occupation of the territories, and the frustration and suppression of the Palestinians, have unfortunately given rise to violent confrontations between the Palestinian population and the Israel security forces in Judea, Samaria, and the Gaza Strip, which even run over the "Green Line". The late Yasser Arafat declared once that there is no chance of ending the dispute between the two peoples without accepting the national, political, territorial, and social legitimate demands of the Palestinian people.

What are the characteristics of an insurgency? Insurgency is an armed insurrection or rebellion against an establishment of government in a State. If the violent challenge by the insurgents is forcefully resisted by the incumbents, and it normally is, a civil war or internal war situation will result. Such outcomes lead to protracted violence between the parties. Insurgencies are normally aimed at one of two goals. Centripetal insurgencies seek to replace the incumbent regime with a system of government more conducive to the interests and inclination of the insurgents. Typical of this category are movements for the independence of colonial peoples and territories which seek via the insurgency to end formal colonial control. Centripetal insurgency is also a typical form of violent opposition to authoritarian regimes within States that are formally independent. In this sense the term is isomorphic with the idea of revolution, although not all revolutions take the form of insurgencies. The Hamas organization in the territories, for example, which did not take part in the Jerusalem uprising in 1987, became afterwards the most extreme insurgent organization in the Gaza Strip and carried out many violent and terrorist attacks on Israelis all over the country. Other political organizations in the territories followed Hamas and called their people to demonstrate in towns and villages and to express on any occasion their protest and frustration at the Israeli occupation. Centrifugal insurgencies, on the other hand, are aimed at secession from the incumbent State and the formation of a new entity. In the present situation centrifugal insurgencies are likely to be associated with expression of ethnic nationalism. Individuals and groups are recruited into insurgency movements by two principal appeals: to their sense of ethnic identity and to their political allegiance. These two appeals may fuse. Social groups that are recruited into insurgency movements include the intelligentsia and the rural peasantry.

Since insurgencies are protracted conflicts, external or third-party intervention is the norm. Third-party intervention tends towards one of three typologies. First, a third party may attempt to mediate between the insurgents and the incumbents. Diplomatically such intervention requires giving at least a *de facto* recognition to the insurgent movement. Second, intervention may occur because the external actor has been drawn into the violence as an ally or protector of one of the parties. If this intervention is made on the side of the insurgents, then they will look to the ally to provide them with a sanctuary or base area, safe and secure, from which operations against the *status quo* regime can be conducted. For the latter, on the other hand, the most important role an ally can play is to give diplomatic support and economic aid to assist in prosecuting their campaign against the insurgents. Third, an outside party can use an insurgent to penetrate the State concerned militarily and economically for its own interests. This can occur as a spillover from alliance links or it may be quite independent of the parties. As a result the target State becomes in effect a client or satellite, whatever the outcome of the civil war (Evans, 1998).

The deep and widespread causes of insurgency in the region of Judea and Samaria include the basic Arab hostility toward the Jews, who are considered an alien people, and toward the continuing presence of the State of Israel; ongoing demands for the right of Arabs living in refugee camps to return to their lands held before the 1949 armistice; and an internal, spontaneous expression of frustration regarding a perceived intractable discrimination.

To these root causes many specific complaints might be added, for example, overcrowding in the camps, the widening disparity in living conditions between Jews and Arabs, inadequate physical infrastructure in the occupied territories of Judea and Samaria, and the frustration of educated people who remain unemployed or have only low-paid and low-status jobs. Still other points include bureaucratic barriers and restriction in daily life under a hostile military administration and a feeling of helplessness resulting from the total economic dependence on Israel.

Although none of these actors alone would probably have provoked a reaction, together they provide a rationale for inciting strikes, demonstrations, disruptions, and disturbances in the region which carry over to the territory of the State of Israel. Arab leadership encourages the population to continue the insurgency day after day, local leaders exhort the Palestinians to make personal sacrifices by opposing Israeli administration, although such actions ultimately harm the inhabitants by promoting Israeli military responses. Residents of villages, towns, and entire zones strike on different days; Arabs who work in Israel are asked to disrupt building projects by being absent; merchants in business districts in the region are forced to limit shopping hours; Arabs are forced to boycott Israeli goods; Arabs are coerced into withholding tax payments and resigning jobs in the Israeli administration. The violence associated with the insurgency expands to include Arab attacks on soldiers, throwing stones and bombs at passing Israeli vehicles, or sometimes murder of Israelis when an opportunity is presented.

In reaction, Israel takes measures to require the Arab population to obey military orders and regulations. As a deterrent move, the administration limits supply of fuel to Arab filling stations, disconnects electricity and telephone services, interrupts, albeit only temporarily, traffic in certain Arab regions, or closes the river bridges connecting Judea and Samaria with Jordan. Administrative and economic pressure is jointly applied, and military actions are implemented, including the dispersion of demonstrators, massive arrests, and prolonged curfews. In extreme cases, houses of participants in the insurgency are demolished or bulldozed and selective deportations are carried out. Israel even punishes thousands of Palestinians who have not participated in terror by destroying their homes. Between September 2000 and the end of 2004 the Israel Defense Forces were responsible for the demolition of 4,100 homes in the territories; 628 housing units, which were home to 3,983 people, were demolished as a punishment measure. The military forces routinely destroy homes after every terrorist attack As soon as the name of the terrorist is known the family begins to pack its bags and to move in with neighbors or relatives. The military says the demolition is meant as a deterrent to other would-be terrorists, and that the intelligence information has shown that they have indeed been deterred by the thought that their family will be left without a roof over their heads. The military claims that it does not destroy homes on the basis of suspicion alone, but only after it has been determined beyond any doubt that the bomber lived in the home. It may be that it is the State's right to defend its citizens, and that action is forced by circumstances, but homes were destroyed also as a means of putting pressure on families to reveal the whereabouts of wanted men. Israel thus attempts to regain control in the region by weakening the resolve of the populace through intimidation and by forcing the people to reject the leaders of the insurgency. It nevertheless continues, and more Arabs join it. Still others passively support it as hostility to the application of force by the Israeli government increases.

After 38 years of Israeli rule in the West Bank, and four and a half years of the second Intifada of an active and violent Palestinian insurgency, which started in the year 2000, no political solution has yet been found. It seems that only a scheme with clearly delimited political, geographical, and demographical characteristics can promise fulfillment of the two peoples' aspirations and bring peace to the region.

Political developments which have recently occurred in the Middle Eastern arena, Israel's basic agreement to participate in bilateral and multilateral negotiation committees, and the change of power in Israel's government under the leadership of Prime Minister Ariel Sharon, head of the Likud Party (till November 2005), raised the problem of withdrawal from territories in exchange for peace, which has been under dispute between Israelis and Arabs and among Israelis themselves since 1967. While this subject has been discussed for a long time in a general or in a theoretical way, it seems that at the beginning of the 2000s the Israeli government will have to relate constructively in a more concrete manner, and introduce its clear and detailed position. Israel will have to decide at a certain stage which territories it is ready to give away in order to achieve true peace with the Palestinians and its neighboring countries and which territories it will not give up at any price.

Since the Jerusalem issue is meanwhile not included in any concrete agenda, and as the issue of the Golan Heights remains mainly a Syrian–Israeli problem, and since the Gaza Strip is seen as a region from which the government of Israel has withdrawn since August 2005, it emerges that the territorial problem in Judea and Samaria is the focus of the future peace negotiation between Israel and the Palestinians, and that by the result of that peace in the region will rise or fall. It is therefore worth demonstrating some geopolitical approaches to this problem with the emphasis on the spatial perspectives and the geographical pattern from the Israeli point of view which may solve insurgency in the region.

The geopolitical reality in the occupied territories which exists today emphasizes Israel's interests in the following domains: security, territory, water, demography, and accessibility. Their relative importance for the security of the State and as a subject to be discussed is still a bone of contention among the public. Each of these domains has a meaningful geographical impact on the future of the State of Israel. A return to the pre-1967 borderlines on the one hand or permanent total occupation of Judea and Samaria on the other hand are both too extreme proposals which might not lead to any positive solution when negotiations take place, so some other alternative patterns should be introduced. These should be related to possible scenarios of giving up some territories in exchange for peace with an emphasis on advantages and disadvantages for Israel's security and economy.

The planning system

The settlement map of Israel today is very different from what it was in the 1950s and 1960s, and is continually being further altered by the development of additional new settlements throughout the area, by the internal migration of population to them, and by new priorities of political development. No other period in the history of the State of Israel has witnessed such rapid and significant changes in the settlement map. The decade of the 1970s was especially crucial, for it was then that Israel's ties with the occupied territories were strengthened. A new map was drawn during that decade, influenced by the new political situation resulting from the Six Day War. Israel then gained control of territories of different economic, social, and demographic character, which for political and security reasons dictated a new settlement endeavor beyond its 1967 borders.

The planning system in the West Bank, which was implemented by the Civil Administration, has a decisive effect on the map of the West Bank. Like other mechanisms established in the occupied territories, the planning system operates along two separate tracks, one for the Jews and the other for Palestinians. While the system works vigorously to establish and expand settlements, it also acts diligently to prevent the expansion of Palestinian settlements.

In legal terms, the planning system in the West Bank operates on the basis of the Jordanian legislation applying in the area at the time of occupation, principally the City, Village, and Building Planning Law. The Jordanian Planning Law was changed by Israel by means of a military order, issued in 1971 and amended several times over the years. The order introduced far-reaching changes in the planning system in the West Bank. These changes reflected almost exclusively the interests of the Israeli Administration and the settlers, while minimizing Palestinian representation on the Planning Committees and Palestinian influence in planning matters. With signing the Interim Accords in 1995, and following the redeployment of the Israel Defense Forces in the years that followed, planning powers in Areas A and B (see p. 93) were transferred to the Palestinian Authority. The planning powers relating to Area C, which since 2000 accounts for some 60 per cent of the West Bank, were not affected (B'tselem, 2002).

One of the principal changes that Israel made to the Jordanian law was the transfer of all the power granted in Jordanian law to the Minister of the Interior to the Commander of Israel Defense Forces in the region. In addition, Israel eliminated the district planning committees and the planning authorities of the village council. These authorities were transferred to the Central Planning Bureau. Over the years, the main tool used by Israel to restrict building by the Palestinian population outside the borders of the municipalities was simply to refrain from planning. As a result, until the transfer of authority to the Palestinian Authority, two regional plans prepared in the 1940s by the British Mandate continue to apply, one to the north of the West Bank and the other in the south. The Mandatory outline plans were already a completely unreasonable basis for urban planning in the initial years of the occupation, and they are even more so today. One of the principal reasons for this is the discrepancy, which has widened over the years, between the population on which the Mandatory plans were based and the current one.

In the early 1990s, the Central Planning Bureau of the Civil Administration prepared Special Partial Outline Plans for some 400 villages in the West Bank. These plans were supposed to fill the role of the detailed plans required by Jordanian law. However, instead of permitting the development of the villages, these plans effectively constituted demarcation plans. Aerial photographs were taken of each village, and a schematic line was then added around the settled area. Construction was prohibited on land outside this line. According to the perception of these demarcation plans, construction in Palestinian villages is supposed to take place by filling of vacant areas within demarcated areas through high-rise construction and a gradual increase in the population density.

The use of the outline plans as a tool for restricting Palestinian building, and for promoting the building of the settlements, is also widespread in East Jerusalem. Immediately after the annexation of East Jerusalem, in 1967, and contrary to the remainder of the West Bank, all the Jordanian outline plans applying in the area were nullified, and a planning vacuum was created and has only gradually been filled. The most striking feature of these outline plans is the extraordinary amount of land, approximately 40 per cent, defined as open landscape, in which any form of development is prohibited. The plans approved through the end of 1999 show that only 11 per cent of the area of East Jerusalem, excluding the expropriated land, is available to the Palestinian population for building (B'tselem, 2002).

The legal and institutional system responsible for planning in Palestinian areas is also responsible for planning in the settlements. The criteria applied in these two cases are opposed. In institutional terms, the outline plans for the settlements are discussed and approved by the subcommittee for settlement operating under the auspices of the Supreme Planning Council. The Israeli administration defines the Jewish local authorities in the West Bank as Special Planning Committees, empowered to prepare and submit to the Supreme Planning Council detailed outline plans and local-general outline plans, and to grant building permits to residents on the basis of plans. Not a single Palestinian village council has ever been defined as a planning committee for the purpose of this law.

The Jewish local authorities, in their function as the local and District Planning Committee for the settlements, operate in co-ordination and co-operation with the various institutions of the military and governmental system, in a constant process of expansion and growth. The Jewish local authorities prepare their outline plans in co-operation with the settling body responsible for establishing the settlements – the Ministry of Housing and Construction or the Settlement Division of the World Zionist Organization; these bodies continue to support the settlement after establishment.

In practice, the ability of Palestinian residents to object effectively to the outline plans for the settlements is extremely limited. The main reason for this is that most of the grounds that might lead the objections committee to accept an objection to the outline plan for a settlement are already resolved before the plan is deposited for public review. The question of land ownership, for example, is settled during the process of seizure of land. Any potential conflict between the outline plan for the settlement and the development needs and aspirations of the Palestinian communities is resolved by the Israeli planning system through the demarcation plan approved by Israel in the 1990s, as well as by the restrictive land-zoning provisions established in the Mandatory outline plans.

Between 1967 and 1977, the ruling Labor Party implemented the old ideology of the Labor movement, which, as before 1948, had posited settlement on an agricultural basis. This ideology was also applied to the West Bank, which in turn necessitated the identification of fertile and arable land. By way of solution, the government either declared the land as belonging to absentees, and leased it to settlers, or seized it for security purposes. Likud's rise to power in 1977 heralded a change in the concept of settlement across the "Green Line", that is the pre-June 1967 armistice line, to one favoring settlement in all parts of the West Bank. In 1979 Israel's Supreme Court issued a ruling that confiscation for military purposes could not be used for the establishment of a permanent civilian settlement. This in turn pushed the government in the direction of the Ottoman law. Rocky areas and unused lands were pinpointed through aerial photography and declared as State land. As two-thirds of the lands were unregistered, and 60 per cent were defined as uncultivable, a great deal of land was available for urban settlement on relatively small areas, with no need for an agricultural hinterland. Most of the Likud settlements were thus located on State land without impinging on privately owned Arab land, and without expropriation for military needs (B'tselem, 2002).

To counter Jewish aspirations for control of the land in the West Bank, Palestinians resorted to a series of means. This included the unsupervised extension of village areas by scattering buildings; construction in isolated spots unconnected with villages; and resumption of cultivation of abandoned fields. They seized State land and established *faits accomplis,* in the hope of arresting the steady diminution of land with every new Jewish settlement. These activities were especially obvious around Jerusalem and along arterial roads, and enjoyed political encouragement and financial support from the outside.

The map of the West Bank and the implications of the settlement policy

The map of the West Bank which was created, as said above, following the occupation of 1967 reflects the radical transformation of the area that has resulted over the years. The establishment of dozens of settlements that extend over enormous areas and are connected to each other, and to Israel, by means of an extensive network of roads, the character of the settlements as Israeli enclaves, separated from and closed to the Palestinian population, are an important source of the infringement of the Palestinians' human rights.

Four different areas may be indicated in the map of the West Bank today, as longitudinal strips of land stretching from north to south, excluding the Jerusalem area, which constitutes a separate group. The eastern strip includes the Jordan Valley and the northern shores of the Dead Sea, as well as the eastern slopes of the mountain range that runs along the entire West Bank from north to south; the mountain strip is the area on or adjacent to the peaks of the mountain range which is also known as the watershed line or the mountain-range area; the western hills strip includes the western slopes of the mountain range, and extends to the "Green Line" to the west; and the Jerusalem metropolis is an area which extends across a wide radius around West Jerusalem. Although in purely geographical terms this area lies mainly in the mountain strip, it has unique characteristics that demand separate attention.

The map of the West Bank also indicates the division of powers between Israel and the Palestinian Authority following the implementation of the signed Oslo Accords. In Area A the Palestinian Authority is responsible for most internal affairs, including building and security; in Area B the Israel Defense Forces hold security control and are entitled to enter freely while the Palestinian Authority holds control in civilian matters; in Area C Israel controls security matters, planning, and construction (B'tselem, 2002).

The eastern strip of the West Bank is bordered by Jordan to the east, the "Green Line" in the vicinity of Bet She'an in the north, and the "Green Line" north of En Gedi to the south. The western boundary of this area is less sharply defined, but may be characterized as the point where the arid climate typical of this strip gives way to the semi-arid climate, at or around the 1,200 ft (400 m.) altitude level. Owing to the climatic conditions, only a limited number of Palestinian communities developed in this area, and the Palestinian population there is relatively sparse. No permanent Palestinian communities exist in the Judean Desert and Dead Sea area (Fig. 2.14).

The Jordan Valley was the first area in which settlements were established, on the basis of the outline plan sketched by the "Allon" plan, because this plan recommended avoiding settlement in areas densely populated by Palestinians. An additional reason was that a significant proportion of land in this area was already registered as State land under the Jordanian administration, so that the process of seizure was easier. The limited scope of Palestinian farming in this area also facilitated Israel's declaration of additional land as State land after 1979, both in the Jordan Valley and on the shores of the Dead Sea and the eastern slopes of the

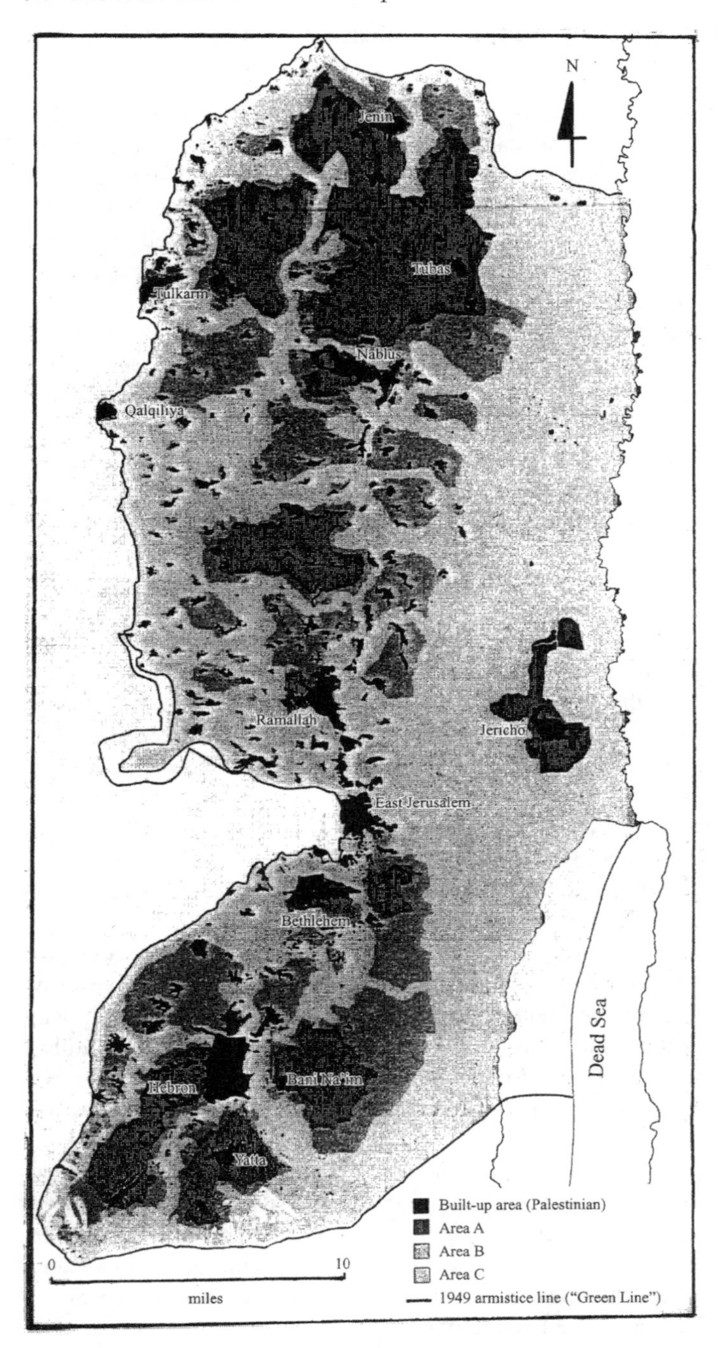

Fig. 2.14 The division of the West Bank into A, B, and C areas
Source: B'tselem, The Israeli Center for Human Rights in the Occupied Territories, 2002

mountain range. As a result, most of the land reserves held by Israel in the West Bank and registered in the name of the Custodian for Government and Abandoned Property is situated in this strip. Control of these land reserves has enabled Israel to establish settlements in the Jordan Valley and Dead Sea areas according to the co-operative settlement model. These settlements depend mainly on agriculture, with the exception of one urban settlement – Ma'ale Efrayim.

Most of the settlements in the eastern strip were established to the north of Jericho. In terms of geographical distribution, these settlements may be divided into two parallel strings extending along the north–south axis, one along the Jordan Valley road, and the other further to the west. The areas of jurisdiction of most of the settlements in this strip extend across areas many times bigger than the built-up area of the settlement. However, and in contrast to the other areas, the outline plans for the settlements in this strip define most of these areas as agricultural land and only a small portion is zoned for construction. In this strip, the main infringement of Palestinian human rights relates to the restriction of opportunities for economic development and for agriculture, in particular (B'tselem, 2002).

As proved by the settlements located along the Jordan Valley, the land in this area permits the development of diverse branches of agriculture through the use of irrigation technology. The reason that Palestinian agriculture did not develop in this area prior to 1967 on a more significant scale is the lack of knowhow and resources that would enable exploitation of the underground basins. The reliance of the Jordan Valley settlements on agriculture denies Palestinian residents the opportunity to enjoy a large proportion of the water resources in the region. The water consumption of the population of the Jewish settlements in the Jordan Valley is equivalent to 75 per cent of the water consumption of the entire Palestinian population of the West Bank for domestic and urban use.

An enclave handed over to the control of the Palestinian Authority in 1994 includes the city of Jericho and the Auja area. The two sections with their approximately 20,000 inhabitants are linked by a narrow corridor surrounded by Israel Defense Forces bases preventing any urban sprawl beyond the boundaries of the enclave. In total, the municipal boundaries of the settlements in the eastern strip encompass approximately 19,000 acres (76,000 dunams), of which 20 per cent comprise developed areas inhabited by the 6,000 Jewish residents.

The mountain strip extends along the entire length of the West Bank in the peaks of the mountain range along the watershed line. The northern and southern borders of the strip are the "Green Line". The eastern and western borders are not clear and may be set around the 1,200 ft (400 m) elevation contour. The strip includes the six largest and most populous Palestinian cities in the West Bank – Jenin, Nablus, Ramallah, East Jerusalem, Bethlehem, and Hebron – which are surrounded by dozens of towns and small and medium-sized villages. During the first decade of the occupation, the governments refrained from establishing settlements in this area. The wave of settlement in the area thus began after the rise to power of the Likud Party, and particularly after 1979. Most of the settlements were established by the Settlement Division of the World Zionist Organization, and were transferred to the management of Gush Emunim, which was responsible for populating them with settlers. The community settlement is by far the most common form of settlement in the mountain strip. Most of the settlements do not farm the land, and most of the residents work in urban centers inside Israel. This is due to the topographical conditions and to the dense Palestinian population in this area, which prevented Israel from seizing control of extensive patches of land and allocating them for agriculture.

The settlements in the mountain strip are arranged in two parallel strings. The first and central string extends across the length of the West Bank, alongside and parallel to the main road connecting the six main cities. The second string of settlements is situated to the east of the watershed, along the "Allon Highway". The dispersion of settlements along the main road reflects Israel's objective to control the main transport artery of the Palestinian population by creating blockages preventing the expansion of Palestinian construction toward the road, and to prevent the growing together of Palestinian communities located on different sides of the road. In most cases, these settlements are isolated and occupy relatively short stretches of the road. In several places, however, Israel has managed to create a bloc of settlements controlling a more significant section of the main road. Because of the location of these settlements on or adjacent to the main road, the Oslo Accords stated that most of the roads would continue to be under direct Israeli control. The presence of Israeli citizens at various points of dispersion along a long stretch passing through densely populated Palestinian areas has led to significant military presence to protect these citizens.

During periods of rising violence against settlers, Israel has responded by imposing harsh restrictions on the freedom of movement of the Palestinian population along this key artery. Shortly after the outbreak of the Al-Aksa Intifada in 2000, Israel blocked the access roads from Palestinian communities in the mountain area to the main road, either by means of physical roadblocks or by establishing checkpoints staffed by soldiers that prevented the passage of Palestinian vehicles. Moreover, some of the settlements along the main road block the urban development of the six main Palestinian cities in some directions. Bethlehem and East Jerusalem are affected mainly by the settlements in the Jerusalem metropolis. The city of Hebron is blocked to the east by the settlement of Qiryat Arba. Within the heart of Hebron there are a number of scattered Jewish settlements with a total population of a few hundred. The settlements in the heart of Hebron severely damage not only the urban development of the city but also the ability of the residents to live a normal life. The development of Ramallah and Al-Bira to the northeast is completely blocked by the settlement of Bet El and a large military base on the south of the settlement, which houses the headquarters of the Civil Administration. The urban area of the city of Nablus, which includes eight villages and two refugee camps that are completely contiguous with the city, is surrounded on almost all sides by settlements that block the area's development.

The impact of the settlements along the eastern chain of the mountain strip on the Palestinian population is less immediate than in the case of the settlements along the main road, because the former lie to the east of the Palestinian population centers. The main impact lies there in seizure of land which, were it not for the settlements, could have been used for the development of the Palestinian economy and the urban development to the east of the population centers on the mountain ridge. The seizure by Israel of extensive land in this area exploits the sparse Palestinian communities and topographic conditions that have made it difficult for Palestinians to engage in significant agricultural activities in these areas (B'tselem, 2002).

The strip of the western hills lies along the north–south axis, between the mountain strip and the "Green Line", varying in width from 6.25 to 12.5 miles (10 to 20 km). In geographic terms, this area is characterized by slopes descending toward the Coastal Plain. The two Palestinian cities in this strip, Tulkarm and Qalqilya, are both situated in the north of the strip. However, the entire strip includes many medium-sized towns from north to south, as well as dozens of smaller villages. This strip includes the most fertile land in the West Bank, and accordingly it has been the site of the development of Palestinian agriculture. Most of the Jewish settlements in the western hills were established in the 1980s as a result of the "Sharon Plan".

The main characteristic of the western hills area north of Jerusalem that attracts Israelis, and has led to a relatively rapid growth rate, is its proximity to the main urban centers of Israel's Coastal Plain. This area was defined by Israeli development bodies as the "high demand area" because of the short travel times of 20 to 30 minutes to employment centers inside Israel. In the area south of Jerusalem, only isolated Jewish settlements have been established. The main forms of settlement in this strip are urban and regular rural settlements. The main form of dispersion in the western hills runs from east to west, along latitudinal roads that mainly connect the central mountain road. A further characteristic in several parts of the strip is the creation of contiguous border settlements, forming contiguous urban areas or blocs, controlled by the settlements. In other parts of the strip the areas of jurisdiction of the settlements are not contiguous, and are interrupted by the Palestinian communities defined as Area B, as well as agricultural land defined as Area C. At the center of the strip lies the town of Ari'el which was home in 2004 to about 20,000 people.

Apart from limiting the possibilities for urban and economic development through the seizure of land, the main impact on the Palestinians of the settlements in this strip is the disruption of the territorial contiguity of the Palestinian communities situated along the strip. Following the transfer of powers to the Palestinian Authority under the Oslo Accords, this situation has resulted in the creation of over fifty enclaves of Area B, and a smaller number of enclaves defined as Area A, all of which are surrounded by Area C, which continues to be under full Israeli control. This phenomenon is less pronounced to the south of Jerusalem, owing to the smaller number of settlements in this area, but is still evident (B'tselem, 2002).

A further ramification resulting from the location of some of the settlements in this strip, literally on the "Green Line", is the blurring of this line as a recognized border between the sovereign territory of the State of Israel and the West Bank. In certain areas, the "Green Line" runs within an urban area extending to either side. This phenomenon is even more pronounced in the Jerusalem area.

The fourth region in the West Bank is the city of Jerusalem and its surroundings. Since 1967 Israel has acted vigorously to establish new physical situations within an extended circle with West Jerusalem and its center. The result of these activities has been the creation of a large metropolis extending along three geographical strips: from the outskirts of Ramallah to the north to the bloc of settlements to the southwest of Bethlehem in the south, and from Ma'ale Adummim to the east to Bet Shemesh, which is in Israel proper, to the west. The Jerusalem metropolis was established with the declared purpose of serving its Jewish residents. The idea of planning the Jerusalem area as a metropolis was embodied in 1994 in a master plan prepared for the government by the Jerusalem Institute for Israel Studies, which proposes guidelines for development for the area through the year 2010.

Municipal Jerusalem includes approximately 17,500 acres (70,000 dunams) of the West Bank, which had been annexed to the municipality of Jerusalem pursuant to a decision of the Knesset in 1967, and in which Israeli law was imposed on an official basis. Approximately 9 per cent, 1,500 acres (6,000 dunams), of this area formed part of Jordanian East Jerusalem, while the remaining 91 per cent belonged to 28 villages in this area. Settlements there are perceived by most of the Jewish public in Israel, and by the government, as constituting an integral part of the State of Israel, and their development has continued on an intensive level since the beginning of the occupation. One-third of the area annexed to Jerusalem in 1967 was expropriated during the years that followed, and was used to establish 12 settlements around the city. Several settlements create full contiguity with West Jerusalem, while all the others are interspersed with Palestinian areas, with the elimination of any signs of the "Green Line" through contiguous urban development (B'tselem, 2002).

The main harm to the Palestinian population inherent in the establishment of the settlements in municipal Jerusalem is the massive expropriation of land, most of which constituted private Palestinian property. The settlements around Jerusalem significantly restrict the capacity for urban development in the Palestinian neighborhoods and villages annexed to Jerusalem. The outline plans approved for the Palestinian neighborhoods in the annexed area through the end of 1999 show that approximately 11 per cent of the area remaining after the expropriation is available for Palestinian construction, and approximately 40 per cent of the planned areas within these neighborhoods are defined as "open landscape areas", where construction of any kind is prohibited. In some cases, the settlements in municipal Jerusalem create divisions between Palestinian areas and prevent their normal expansion and the creation of territorial contiguity.

An additional problem is the physical severance of the Palestinian areas of municipal Jerusalem from the remainder of the West Bank, as a result of the general closure imposed by Israel in the West Bank in 1993. Since then, Palestinians without a special permit have been prohibited from entering Jerusalem. This measure has severely impaired the right of freedom of movement because it disrupts travel between the southern and northern portions of the West Bank.

Greater Jerusalem includes four blocs of settlements that are thoroughly connected to municipal Jerusalem and to the west of the city. The main component is the presence of a complex and sophisticated network of roads making possible rapid travel between all parts of the metropolis and the center. This network enables the western portion of the city to function as an employment base and a center for various services for the Jewish residents of the entire metropolis. One of the settlement blocs is situated on the northwest of the area of jurisdiction of Jerusalem. A second bloc of settlements lies to the northeast of the border of the city. The principal influence of these two blocs in the north of the metropolis is to create a barrier severing the surrounding Palestinian villages. The third bloc of settlements is situated to the east of the eastern border of Jerusalem. Its principal component is the settlement of Ma'ale Adummim, the largest settlement in the West Bank outside municipal Jerusalem. This bloc severs the territorial connection between the south of the West Bank and the north. The fourth bloc is situated in the southern part of the metropolis, to the west and south of Bethlehem, and includes mainly the Ezyon bloc with its 16 settlements. However, this bloc functions as part of the metropolis thanks to the tunnel road which permits rapid travel to and from Jerusalem while avoiding Palestinian-populated areas.

In total, the municipal boundaries of the settlements in the Jerusalem metropolis include some 32,500 acres (130,000 dunams), and the population of these settlements numbers approximately a quarter of a million. Contrary to other areas, most of the land of which Israel has seized control over the years in the Jerusalem metropolis has been attached to one of the settlements.

It may be concluded that the manner of dispersion of the settlements over most of the areas of the West Bank creates obstacles preventing the maintenance of meaningful contiguity between the Palestinian communities. This phenomenon removes the possibility of establishing an independent and viable Palestinian State. Entry into the vast areas over which Israel has seized control over the years, which were added to the areas of jurisdiction of the regional councils, is denied to the Palestinian residents after a military order was issued declaring the land a closed military area. This prohibition restricts the possibilities available to Palestinians for economic development in general, and for agriculture in particular. The location of some of the settlements around Palestinian cities and towns, and sometimes adjacent thereto, restricts the possibilities for the urban development of the Palestinian communities, and in some cases prevents such possibilities almost completely. The location of some of the settlements along key roads that, prior to the establishment of the settlements, served the Palestinian population, has led to the imposition by Israel of strict restrictions on the freedom of movement of this population, with the goal of ensuring the security and freedom of movement of the settlers.

For all these grandiose visions and tireless toil, Israel's settlement ability in the occupied territories seems to be highly limited, both economically and demographically. The exorbitant investments in the territories have exhausted resources that could have otherwise been directed to development areas within the "Green Line". After 38 years of occupation, approximately 230,000 Jews live in the West Bank, as opposed to more than a million Palestinians; the gap between Jewish political and territorial aspirations and the actual reality thus remains very wide indeed, if not unbridgeable. Not least, the fact that a mere 5 per cent of Israel's

Jewish population have settled in the territories affords a vivid illustration, if such were needed, of public reluctance to participate in this endeavor.

The Israeli–Palestinian Declaration of September1993 has effectively brought the Jewish settlements in the occupied territories to their political and territorial end. Now they will have to play their last card following Israel's withdrawal from the territories and the establishment of a Palestinian autonomy, by ensuring some improvements for the future. In 1993 the Labor government froze further construction of houses in the settlements and prohibited the establishment of new ones; the settlers responded by adding infrastructure within the confines of their settlements and securing their commuting routes to "Green Line" areas. Yet as the bilateral negotiations between Israel and the PLO unfold, the feeling that they may not stay in their places of residence indefinitely seems to be dawning on most settlers. Many houses in the settlements remain empty, as no Israelis would consider moving to the territories in these uncertain times. Even more indicative of the growing anxiety within the Jewish community in the territories is the formation of the settlers' organizations with a view to negotiating fair compensation in the event of evacuation. The most recent events have apparently invalidated the widespread assumption among politicians and scholars alike of the irreversibility of the settlement fabric in the West Bank. As the implementation of the first stage of the autonomy agreement in Gaza and Jericho approached, some Jewish settlers in these areas, having lost faith in Israel's political and military authorities, began barricading their settlements against the eventuality of Israeli withdrawal – this probably being their last desperate act before disappearing from the stage.

It may be safely assumed that in the future fewer and fewer roads will be protected by the Israel Defense Forces so that the way of life in many settlements may be further restricted. Only clusters of settlements adjacent to the Tel Aviv agglomeration or to Jerusalem will have a realistic chance of survival, while all the rest, mainly the remote and small settlements, will disappear over time. After all, even a quick glance at the West Bank settlement map reveals that only in 20 to 30 Jewish settlements, out of 140, does the population exceed the one thousand mark. Most of all the others comprise no more than a few hundred people each.

The Jewish population in the West Bank has been too widely spread, in line with past governments' policy of large distribution of settlements so as to capture as much land as possible. Only a few urban or semi-urban concentrations of settlements in the region are likely to play a role in the future redelineation of boundaries. Foremost among them are the towns of Ari'el, Ma'ale Adummim, Elqana, Efrata, and Qiryat Arba.

Undoubtedly the settlers will have to fight for their survival in a region increasingly governed by Palestinian autonomy. Some of them, those whose first homes in Israel are still available, will leave very soon. Others will leave when provided with alternative housing inside Israel itself, while a small group of extremists, the most ideological kernel among the settlers, will remain under Palestinian rule and continue to claim the rights of Jews to settle in all parts of Greater Israel. For how long these die-hard settlers will be able to last as a small island in a hostile ocean, and under what circumstances, remains to be seen.

Various government ministries, particularly the Defense and Housing Ministries began in 2004 implementing a policy to strengthen the large settlement blocs, although the geographic boundaries of the blocs have been limited. Extensive construction was under way only in the settlements straddling the seam line and the very large urban blocs as Ma'ale Adummim and Betar Illit. In most of the West Bank settlements, no new building plans were being ratified, and whatever construction was taking place had begun two years or more earlier. Areas that had been included in the master plans for the settlements were then outside the building zones that were drawn according to aerial photographs by the defense establishment, in accordance with the agreement with the U.S. to refrain from construction beyond the existing built-up areas. New freezes, delays, and suspensions of approved plans and transfers of funds to the settlements were also made. It may be that even the large settlement blocs, intended to expand, will not be able to expand beyond the existing built-up area.

Patterns toward peace

The Israeli debate about the solution to the Israeli–Palestinian conflict moves between two poles. One, adopted by most of the public, is based on the "two States for two peoples" idea with a variety of positions regarding the territorial solution ranging from a return to the "Green Line" to an evacuation of no more than 40 per cent of the territories. The other pole is the position held by the settlers and their representatives to the right of the Prime Minister, who are trying to master the "Greater Land of Israel" and want to push the Palestinians eastward, whether through a long-term process based on the current polices or as a result of a war, which from their perspective is inevitable.

The debate between the supporters of the two alternatives is over the principle, and does not take place on the same level between them. Most of the first group would also be happy to live in a State of Israel that goes from the Sea to the Jordan River if it could manage to maintain a Jewish majority, a democratic regime, and economic prosperity, and be a member in good standing of the family of nations. But this public is aware at various levels of the limits of Israel's ability to have its cake and eat it too, and wants to implement the Zionist dream now on only part of the Land of Israel. The settlers on the right, on the other hand, believe that continuing the Zionist dream requires more time to fulfill the divine promise, and that the Land of Israel belongs only to the people of Israel. They explain that the demographic issue will be solved through divine intervention, without too much enthusiasm for democratic values. If the different features sketched out by the two alternatives are similar in essence and different only with regard to the amount of time and effort involved, then the question must be asked, what is the price of a mistake by the alternative sides, and what is the probability of either being actualized?

The failure of the alternative based on partition of the land along 1967 lines, in addition to losing 23 per cent of the land of the Jewish forefathers, could be expressed in the creation of a small and poor Palestinian State suffering from anarchy, instability, and lack of governmental uniformity, and exporting local terror and criminal activity against Israel as the preferred manner of dealing with the frustration and despair of its citizenry. The State of Israel will have to continue fighting the Palestinians, parallel to its economic support for the Palestinian State. On the other hand, insistence on the dream of the "Greater Land of Israel" could, because of the absence of Palestinian emigration eastward and the impossibility of separation on demographic grounds that exist nowadays, be turned into a nightmare where the State of Israel maintains an apartheid regime, with the Jews rejecting the demand by a majority of the Arabs for equal civil rights.

The failure of the Oslo Accords to reach a permanent solution turned into a belief in Israel that there is no enthusiasm on the Palestinian side for the first alternative, and by default led to the perpetuation of the current situation, which serves the expansion of the settlement enterprise in the West Bank, the heart of the second alternative. The fact that the price of the mistake of the settlers' alternative is obviously greater than the other alternative requires most of Israeli society to start to work on behalf of the partition idea, while there is a partner in the form of Mahmoud Abbas, and to reunite around the strategic choice made by Israel's first Prime Minister David Ben-Gurion, who preferred a Jewish State to a "Greater Land of Israel".

What are Israel's basic needs to achieve peace in the region? One of the most important patterns of thought regarding a peace settlement in this region indicates that, in order to secure the State of Israel from Jordan, a massive defense line is needed along the eastern flanks of the Samaria and Judea Mountains opposite the Jordan River and the Dead Sea. In 1969 the Deputy Prime Minister Yigal Allon expressed his agreement with that view and pointed out, as mentioned above, that the western edge of the Jordan Valley should be based on a series of suitable topographic strongholds making the greatest effort to avoid the inclusion of any large Arab population. The defense line must be based on a topographical system constituting a permanent obstacle for the deployment of motorized force and a base of counter-offensive by the Israelis. It must provide the State with a reasonable strategic depth and ensure an early warning system. The area which fulfills such needs lies adjacent to the mountainous rural Arab settlement line in Samaria and Judea and may form a buffer zone between the Arab population in the hill country and the Jewish one in the Valley.

Another Israeli territorial peace pattern indicates the need for holding Jewish agricultural areas that were settled in the past. These form a continuous agricultural settlement region based on land cultivation as an expression of Jewish taking roots in the region, similar to the typical Zionist pioneering in the Land of Israel before the establishment of the State. Actually, there exist only two areas where such a kind of settlement has occurred, namely the Jordan Valley and the Ezyon bloc.

As the characteristics of the Jordan Valley have been described above, it remains to outline the importance of the Ezyon bloc, which lies in the Hebron Mountains, 12.5 miles (20 km) south of Jerusalem, and where 16 new settlements have been established since 1967, in which about 35,000 inhabitants reside today. Since 1920 this region, purchased by a Jewish contributor, has been a target for Jewish rural settlement in the hill country of the Land of Israel. Three trials were made between 1927 and 1947 to settle this area, in which four kibbutzim were established, based economically on hill farming. During the 1948 war the area was occupied by the Jordanians and the four kibbutzim were abandoned. In a fourth trial, made after 1967, the Jewish settlement in this region was renewed by young people whose parents had fallen in defense of the bloc in 1948. New kibbutzim were established and many other villages with the town of Efrata as a regional service center.

Against the background of these historical events, it may be assumed that the deep Israeli emotional attachment to these two regions, one as a settlement plan representing the most important innovation in Israel's strategic and settlement conception, and the other as a symbol of restoring the Hebron Mountains to pristine splendor, amount to a national consensus to hold them forever.

A third Israeli territorial peace pattern regarding Judea and Samaria takes into account the importance of its underground water. The mountainous north–south backbone in Israel, as mentioned above, is a natural catchment area where underground water in aquifers is collected in basins. The mountain aquifer of Samaria and Judea is the most important one for Israel because its water feeds the Yarqon and Taninim springs at the western foothills and a few others which are the main local resources along Israel's Coastal Plain. The total water potential of the mountain aquifer is 600 million cu. m per year. The western and northeastern aquifers are over-utilized and yield an annual total of 475 million cu. m per year: they supply about a quarter of Israel's annual water consumption. Over-utilization has resulted in a drop in the water table. Over-pumping affects water quality, causing increased salinity. Continuous over-pumping could also make the underground water sink below the "red line" which decreases the usefulness of the aquifers. Israel is concerned about the future utilization of these water resources. Their occupation and control by hostile forces are a risk to Israel because they could be polluted by over-pumping or by exposing them to sewage. In that case the demand for the continuous holding of western Samaria and Judea by the Israelis could obviously be justified.

A fourth Israeli territorial peace pattern for maintaining Israel's sovereignty in this region concerns longitudinal and lateral axes of communication. Such axes should be built generally in a gridiron form in order to connect the predominantly Jewish population which is dispersed in small settlements and strongholds all over the area, safeguarding territorial interests. Three such longitudinal axes, one along the Jordan Valley, one on the hill country, and a third one along the western flanks of the hills, together with six lateral ones, which will be under Israeli domain, may fulfill minimal security needs on the basis of linear accessibility, if no other territorial solutions are accepted.

By a communications axis is meant a territorial strip of land, a few hundred feet wide, used for traffic, transportation, and commuting through the region; in these strips no further Arab building will be permitted. These axes may or may not coincide with existing roads that run through Arab territory, but should by-pass towns, refugee camps, institutions, and local civilian installations as much as possible. The success of the existing lateral Samarian and Judean new roads which have been constructed in recent years supports such a pattern, which can provide security to the Jewish settlements without occupying too much land.

A fifth territorial peace pattern regards the Jewish settlements. The Six Day War significantly influenced the settlement geography of Israel. The greatest changes occurred in places from which the Arabs fled. After the war various groups of people who believed in a hard-line attitude to the Arab States and in the retention of all the newly incorporated territories, came to prominence in Israel's political life. Quantitatively the process of settlement by these groups took the form of an exponential growth, with the year 1978 being the turning point. It started as a return of Jewish inhabitants to their pre-1948 homes in settlements or neighborhoods evacuated in the 1948 war, such as the Jewish Quarter in Old Jerusalem, the Ezyon bloc, and Hebron. Other more subtle forms followed later.

A squatter pattern for this region indicates that several Jewish urban centers which were created after 1967 justify holding urban territories. The biggest concentration of urban settlements exists along the eastern part of the Coastal Plain. This was once in high demand for Jewish settlements because it was defined as within 30 minutes' commuting distance from the outer ring of Tel Aviv, and within 20 minutes' commuting distance from Jerusalem or other towns in the Coastal Plain. It extends geographically 6.25–9.4 miles (10–15 km) east of the former "Green Line". It has adequate roads connecting it with the large cities and bringing it physically closer to the population of the Coastal Plain. Its attractiveness caused an unexpected increase in its urban centers such as Ari'el with 20,000 inhabitants, Qarne Shomron with 6,500, Immanu'el with 4,000, Elqana with 3,500, Alfe Menashe with 5,500, and some other suburbs with one to two thousand inhabitants each.

Other new urban concentrations exist around Jerusalem, such as Har Adar, Giv'at Ze'ev, Pesagot, and Ma'ale Adummim east of Jerusalem with 32,000 inhabitants. In the Judean Mountains there is the town of Betar Illit with 17,000 inhabitants and Qiryat Arba near Hebron with 6,500 inhabitants. In all these Jewish urban centers there reside today more than 100,000 people, who make up more than half of the Jewish settlers in Judea and Samaria.

A most significant expansion process was the post-1978 wave of settlement which exploited the greater spatial-economic potentialities of the West Bank, namely its close proximity to the metropolitan region of Tel Aviv and the city of Jerusalem. Apart from Jewish immigration from abroad, the migration flows originated in three major regions: the Tel Aviv metropolitan area, the city of Jerusalem, and Israel's periphery in Galilee and the Negev. More migrants from the Tel Aviv area moved to settlements in the western Samaria region, while most migrants from Jerusalem moved to a group of settlements around Jerusalem. The Haifa area contributed its part to the settlement in northern Samaria, and the Israeli periphery contributed mostly to western Samaria or the Jerusalem area.

Jewish colonization of the West Bank was mostly part of the metropolitan expansion of Tel Aviv and Jerusalem. The development eastwards started mainly after 1977 as a consequence of the massive and rapid construction of new settlements on the western fringes in the hills of Samaria. These settlements were constructed as suburbs, devoid of a local economic base, as part of a declared government policy, to attract settlers of the occupied territories. This was implemented by a large-scale investment in land purchasing, by the construction of infrastructure and housing projects, and by declaring the whole of the occupied territories a development area. This implied high government subsidies for housing and generous loans to private construction companies and for investment by industries.

Settler population in the territories grew by more than 12,000 in the year 2003, an increase of about 5 per cent in the territories. Some 74 per cent of the 230,000 settlers in Judea and Samaria live in areas which are due to remain under Israeli sovereignty in a final-status agreement, according to the maps published under the various proposed peace arrangements. Some 53 per cent, about 121,900, live in the Greater Jerusalem area and about 48,300, 21 per cent, live in western Samaria. The remaining 59,800 inhabitants live in areas which are supposedly to be left in Palestinian hands. Two-thirds of the overall growth in 2003–4 can be attributed to the high (3.5 per cent) annual fertility rate among the settlers, only one-third of whom actually moved to settlements in that year. Of the 140 legal settlements, 129 grew in size, but only 64 of these had more than the natural birth increase. Most of the settlements that increased were ones with a strong ideological core.

A sixth and minimal territorial pattern indicates some needed border revisions along the "Green Line". Required revisions would affect the former Latrun enclave, the surroundings of Jerusalem, the surroundings of Qalqilya, northern Samaria, and the northern part of the Jerusalem Corridor. The common factor to all these sections is that over the years many Jewish settlements and suburbs have been established there which are now strongly linked to both sides of the former "Green Line".

What are the Palestinians' basic claims against Israel's peace patterns? It is obvious from a study of Israel's approaches to the possibility of relinquishing territories in exchange for peace that the Palestinians' standpoints concerning land, autonomy, and sovereignty in Judea and Samaria will lead them to refuse most if not all of them at the first stage.

In reply to the Israeli claims, as mentioned above, Palestinians may justly claim that they own and cultivate half a million acres of land in northern and southern Samaria, in the hill country and its western flanks, where plantations of fruit and olives are dominant. They also need, no less than the Israelis, a free network of roads in this region without building restrictions, to strengthen their connections between Judea, Samaria, and Jerusalem, and with the Gaza Strip in the west and with Jericho in the east.

Regarding water resources it should be indicated that the Arabs own in this region 335 wells which supply 800 million cu. m of water per year and 300 springs which supply 40–60 million cu. m. Most of this water is used for agriculture. Through Israel's intensified water consumption they may lose their potential amount of water which is needed for agriculture. Water has been a touchy geopolitical issue in the Middle East. Israel faces a steadily worsening water shortfall and its neighbors face even worse. In the absence of any significant likelihood that peace will solve the problem of water distribution, an ever increasing possibility exists that force may be used to determine who has water and who is deprived of it. Israel is currently estimated to use its water resources 15 per cent faster than they can be replenished. Without creating new resources of water, and with equal and proportional distribution, the problem will remain unsolved. New resources could be created by circulation of drainage water, and by introducing advanced methods in agriculture which will decrease consumption.

Israel's special water problem lies in the urgent need to recycle sewerage water which has become more salty and polluted over the years. Both Israel and the Palestinians should therefore invest all their knowledge and energy in purification of sewerage water, so that the water problem for agriculture will be less severe. In Israeli urban and industrial sectors the average demand is 100 cu. m per person per year, as against 35 in the West Bank. In the next few decades the Palestinians' demand for water will increase and become equal to that of the Israelis. The present water resources in Israel, including underground water, the Jordan basin catchment area, and recycled water, provide about 2 million cu. m annually, which is not enough for future consumption. The resources will not increase amounts of water significantly, so that other artificial and sophisticated methods should be introduced.

Concerning the Israeli squatter patterns of settlement, Palestinians may also claim that Arab urban concentrations have existed in Judea and Samaria for a long time. In this region there even exist about 450 Arab settlements which maintain a spatial dominance all over the region.

In a direct negotiation process no side will be able to receive all it wishes and therefore compromise will be needed on the basis of these territorial patterns. It could also be assumed that no single pattern will be dominant throughout the negotiation process and that some variations of them may be accepted. However, there is no doubt that a comprehensive approach to these patterns on the basis of "territories in exchange for peace" will make possible a rational selection of priorities for each side on the road toward the achievement of an agreement, its stages of implementation, and the testing of each side's seriousness and intention for peace and for the normalization of the region.

These basic patterns may also provide politicians and decision-makers with guidelines to enable Israel's gradual withdrawal from the West Bank or at least for an interim agreement if needed. After 38 years of Israeli rule in the territories and more than four and a half years of the second violent Palestinian uprising, no workable political solution has yet been proposed. Only a scheme with clearly limited political, geographical, demographic, and military characteristics can promise fulfillment of the two peoples' aspirations and bring peace to the region. It seems that the foundations of a peace achieved with the Palestinians and the neighboring countries lie in both sides' attitude to the insurgent region of Judea and Samaria.

The opportunity that has been created with Yasser Arafat's death cries out for swift, courageous, and intelligent exploitation. The Palestinian leadership that is being formed is in need of concrete achievements and is ready for changes that were impossible during Arafat's era. In order to end the war and to change the atmosphere, there is need for a practical plan of action with a good chance of success. The simplest thing to do, a step the success of which will bring about a substantial change in the situation, is a co-operative and co-ordinated implementation of the results of Israel's exit from the Gaza Strip and northern Samaria and the handing over of the Gaza Strip to a responsible and functioning Palestinian government.

There are many reasons why this step has a chance. The disengagement plan had widespread support among the Israeli public. From the Palestinian point of view, the plan was a kind of initial precedent for a full Israeli withdrawal from an area that was filled with settlements, and there was no opposition to it among the Palestinians. The international community provided political and economic support for a plan of evacuating Gaza that was not declared to be the last withdrawal; the success of the plan will show the Palestinian government's ability to govern effectively in a territory handed over to its control; a co-ordinated Israeli disengagement from Gaza has a good chance of stopping terrorism originating from Gaza; such a co-ordinated implementation is likely to lead to a significant improvement in the standard of living in Gaza, which has deteriorated drastically. This plan did not touch the sensitive issues of a final status agreement. It spelled out mutual arrangements, both economic and security-related, that benefit both parties – a Palestinian operation to end terrorism, accompanied by an end to the belligerent operations of the Israel Defense Forces; at the same time, gradual and significant lifting of restrictions on Palestinian movement and commerce, development of infrastructure, agriculture, and industry in the Gaza Strip by a combination of foreign investors and the Palestinian business sector; and using the areas of the evacuated settlements to establish building initiatives for the benefit of the inhabitants of the Gaza Strip.

The separation fence

Many years passed before Israel realized that the conception of abolishing the "Green Line" was basically wrong. Not only was there no justification in disregarding the "Green Line", there was a vital need to return to it unequivocally by strengthening it as a security borderline between Israel and the Palestinian Authority. The events that have occurred in the last decade, the Intifada and the many terrorist attacks on Israeli targets and on innocent citizens, have proved undoubtedly that Israel needs a solid borderline on its east side, and that the population cannot be a "living fence" between the two entities and be a victim to a false conception which professes an open borderline between Israel and the Palestinians. Such a conception may fit European countries or states in North America, but not countries in the Middle East, where those who want to survive have to protect themselves and fortify their homes.

In the light of Israel's security situation, and a future peace agreement with the Palestinians, a definite territorial separation is needed between the two peoples by an efficient fence, with control points and border passes along it, between Israel and Lebanon, Egypt, Jordan, and the Gaza Strip. There is no reason why such a fence should not be constructed along the "Green Line", not because it might completely prevent terror attacks but because a sovereign State, which strives for cultural homogeneity, needs a borderline. There is less significance in where exactly the fence will be set out, because every line agreed upon between the Israelis and the Palestinians could be afterward recognized by the international bodies, as happened with the "Green Line" in 1949. Such a fence will even have an additional importance to Israel, one of the only countries in the world to exist without defined borderlines for many years. Israel hesitated too long in building a separation fence. The building of such a fence seems to be very complicated politically and physically and even very costly, but things of this kind have happened in the world.

In 2002 Israel started to construct a separation fence east of the "Green Line" in the West Bank, including in it Jewish towns such as Ari'el, Qedumim, Immanu'el, and Jewish settlements which are located around them. The construction of such a fence needed land appropriation at variance with the U.S. government's understanding that such steps would not be taken in the foreseeable future, and that the separation fence project in these West Bank areas would be deferred. Prime Minister Ariel Sharon promised his government members at that time, that the separation fence would be completed before the withdrawal from the Gaza Strip in 2005, but this did not happen. The idea of a separation fence gained broad public support because it promises to reduce the number of terrorist attacks inside Israel (Fig. 2.15).

The lands that were appropriated are the southern part of what Israeli security officials refer to as the "fingernails zone" – the term alludes to stretches of the separation fence that will enclose large Jewish settlements in the West Bank. Fingernails planned for construction included the area around the town of Qedumim in the north, around Immanu'el and Qarne Shomron in the center of this West Bank region, and Ari'el in the south. According to plans, these fingernails will in the future be expanded into what Israeli officials call "fingers" – meaning that the separation fence will be continued up to the "Green Line" border. It turns out that those fingernails are planned on privately owned Palestinian land. While at first it seemed that Ari'el would be temporarily fenced in close to the settlement as a temporary security solution, over time the fingers have thickened and multiplied and turned into a kind of first stage toward linking up the separation fence in the future. The fingernails plan is meant to delay as much as possible any future discussion of the settlements in the Ari'el bloc. The plan to build the separation fence from Ari'el to Qedumim would eventually lead to the annexation of 58.6 sq. miles (150 sq. km) of the West Bank territory to Israel's territory. American officials originally demanded that Israel should abandon plans to build the separation fence in these areas of the West Bank. All the harassment of the Palestinians in this interim period, harming their source of livelihood, their lands, homes, and freedom of movement, will only sow more hatred. Ultimately, no separation fence route will be able to defend Israel from that hatred.

On May 2005 the Israeli High Court of Justice canceled, for security reasons, its interim order to freeze the construction of three sections of the fingernails zone east, north, and south of Ari'el which was given in February as a result of Arab farmers' plea from the villages Salfit and Haris against the fence route. Government representatives have promised that the new sections of the fence will include gates and checkpoints to enable the farmers to cultivate their lands beyond the fence on

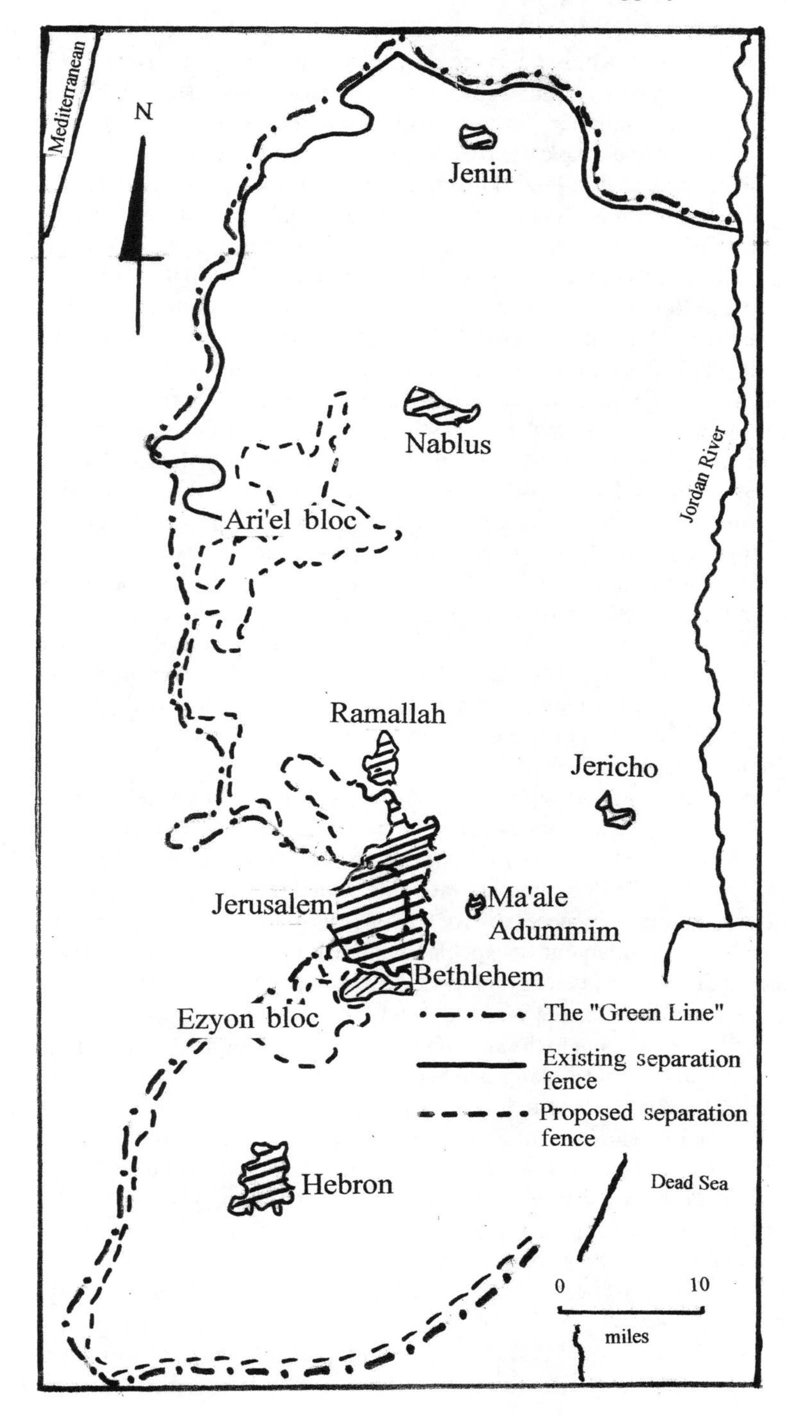

Fig. 2.15 The separation fence alignment in Judea and Samaria

the Israeli side, and that the olive trees that will be cut down will be replanted in an alternative zone. Farmers whose lands are confiscated because of the fence will be compensated for the damage. If the Arab farmers' plea is accepted in the High Court at a further stage, the situation in the area will return to its previous position.

Defense Ministry officials have tried to co-ordinate construction of the fingernails with settlers from the area, but Jewish residents have voiced opposition to the plan to build the separation fence around their settlement. Also, legal obstacles impeded the construction of the fence in some places. In addition, dozens of Palestinian villages will be affected by the construction of the separation fence in these stretches of the West Bank. Residents of some of these villages will be caught in enclaves. In the area between Modi'in and Jerusalem, construction of the fence will cause much suffering to the Palestinian population. There are eight villages that the fence will turn into an enclave and affect some 10,500 acres (42,000 dunams) of their land. The problem in this area arose with the construction of a road which links Modi'in with northern Jerusalem. This road was built to the north and parallel to what was once known as the Jerusalem Corridor, along the route of an ancient thoroughfare that led to Jerusalem. For the entire length of the road to be within the boundaries of the fence, together with adjacent settlements, there was a need to isolate or annex to Israel those villages south of the road. These villages are home to some 35,000 people and are linked for the most part to the Ramallah district, where many of the residents work and study, and from where they get important services. The Palestinians know that expropriated land will never be returned to its owners, even if not even an inch of the separation fence is ever built. The fence will promote development in the Jewish settlements, whereas it will cut off and destroy life in local Palestinian villages.

In a country where nearly everything is controversial, it is no wonder that there are Israelis who are suggesting that the fence should be dismantled. That being said, it must be understood that the security rationale is not the primary case for the fence. Far more important is the demographic rationale, which has already entered the political lexicon. The security necessity for the fence will diminish if an agreement is reached with a Palestinian entity capable of imposing its will in the territories under its jurisdiction. But the demographic necessity for the fence will remain valid, and, with population growth in the West Bank, it is fair to assume that its population will be more or less equivalent to the size of the Jewish population, especially if the return of refugees to the Palestinian State becomes possible.

Meanwhile, at a distance of a few miles from the backward Third World Palestinian State will be an industrial western welfare-state country that provides a high standard of living and whose citizens hold valuable assets. Such wealth will render incursions into Israel as a endless source of attraction. The agricultural robberies of the 1950s and car theft after 1967, and the invasion of 150,000 illegal residents since then, will be a mere preview of coming attractions that can be expected as the gap widens between the standards of living in the Palestinian State and Israel in coming years.

If an effective fence does not divide the two neighbors, life in Israel will not be livable, and a fast process of abandonment will begin. Whoever claims that there is no need for such a fence is in fact suggesting that Israel should commit suicide as a western Jewish State, and is preventing the establishment of a bi-national Middle Eastern State.

The disputes surrounding the separation fence have been not ones of principle with regard to the very construction of the barrier, but rather over its route. The Palestinian public did not want the fence on any route, and neither was the Palestinian Authority very enthusiastic regarding the principle of erecting walls and fences between Israel and the territories.

Between 1967 and 1993 there were no fences and not a single roadblock between Israel and the territories, and the residents there were able to move totally freely throughout the country. They took advantage of it for the purpose of employment and commerce. On the backdrop of this came the official Palestinian position that Israel has the right to build fences and walls anywhere it chooses, but only within the borders of the State. The State of Israel did not accept this approach, and neither did the High Court of Justice, which ruled that the State of Israel has the right to build a security fence, but that security considerations must also take into account the effect the fence has on the Palestinian public. The defense establishment had to do some engineering juggling to meet the Court's stipulations, and changed the route of the fence so that the residents of these villages had free access to their lands and maintained their vital links with Ramallah.

Israel's Council for Peace and Security was also a party to the petition against the construction of the fence along the route planned by the Defense Ministry. The Council has proposed an alternative route for the fence to shorten the barrier by some 94 miles (150 km) and cut around NIS 1.5 billion from the cost. In that case it was the first time that the Supreme Court justices were able to consider a professional opinion based on security considerations against that of the defense establishment.

Twelve major changes were made in the fence's route following the High Court ruling. The changes move the fence about 3.1 miles (5 km) and will cost some NIS 25–35 million. The section of the fence running from Elqana to Jerusalem was slated for completion by the end of 2005. The 8,500 acres (34,000 dunams) of the West Bank originally slated to be included inside this section of the fence had been reduced by about 4,750 acres (19,000 dunams) owing to the Court's ruling. Of the remaining 3,750 acres (15,000 dunams), only 1,500 acres (6,000 dunams) are private Palestinian land; the rest is State land. About a hundred miles of the fence will be built either along the "Green Line" or inside Israel. A portion of the Modi'in–Jerusalem main road will remain outside the separation fence. The planners had been compelled to leave the section from Bet Horon to the Makkabim checkpoint outside the fence by High Court Justice ruling, which declared an 18.75-mile (30-km) portion of the fence illegal because of the harm it caused to local Palestinians. This section of the road will be bordered with concrete slabs to protect the cars that use it from gunfire.

The new map, which was drawn up after the High Court of Justice rejected a portion of the existing route, will bring the barrier closer to the "Green Line", and will put an end to the vision of the "greater fence" climbing deeply into the West

Bank and including most of the settlers. Such are the reversals of political fortune: the same Ariel Sharon who dedicated his life to blurring the "Green Line", and wiping it off maps and documents is now resurrecting it on the ground with bulldozers, reinforced concrete, and barbed wire, making it much more obvious than before 1967.

Almost a year has gone by since the cabinet approved the earlier route. In that time only a minute part of the fence has gone up. It turned out that even unilateral moves, under the heading "security and not political", as it were, are not implemented in a vacuum. The planners of the project admitted that they were working under pressure of the suicide attacks, and paid no attention to the Palestinian quality of life along the fence. This lack of attention, dictated from above, trapped the fence in the legal system. It exacted the high security price of an unprotected border, the high political price of international condemnation, and the high economic price of double and unnecessary work, which will reach its grotesque climax with the dismantling of sections already constructed.

From its early days, the fence has been surrounded by double-speak and false promises, the purpose of which was to try to hide its real essence as a border marker, and to show activity where there was one. The political zigzagging has left the planners at a loss. How should they bring the Ezyon bloc into the fence, with its Palestinian villages and fields, when the High Court has prohibited harming the Palestinians? And if the Ezyon bloc is taken out of the fence, what will the National Religious Party do? Those who have been part of this project have lost. So has Sharon, who hesitated until he agreed to the project and then complicated it, as well as the legal minds who prepared the dubious route and after their fall in the High Court galloped back to the "Green Line". Experience shows that massive construction does not automatically turn an area into an integral part of Israel. This attempt at sleight of hand is going on in discussions with the Americans, the Palestinians, the settlers, and the Israeli public. The argument that the fence going up in the West Bank is only for security and is not a political fence is one type of fraud. The argument that the Americans will allow Israel to annex the Ari'el bloc is another sort of fraudulent self-deception. There is no sign that President Bush and his government agreed to even a hint of continued construction in the territories or to annexing Ari'el.

Much has already been said about the wall and the fence under construction inside Jerusalem, what is termed the "Jerusalem envelope". But what has been done in the Arab neighborhoods between Jerusalem and Ramallah was unlike anything else, first because this was a crowded urban area with some quarter of a million residents, and second because the presence in the region of numerous Jewish neighborhoods and settlements has prompted those planning the route of the walls and fences to perform juggling tricks that boggle the imagination. If the plan of surrounding Jerusalem by a separation fence is implemented, the lives of the Arab residents throughout the area are destined to change to such a degree that it will be nearly impossible to live there. The lives of hundreds of thousands of Jewish people are already determined by a decision that is considered one of Israel's more enlightened ones; to be separated from the Palestinians unilaterally. Even now,

Plate 2.5 The separation wall in Jerusalem

approximately 400,000 Palestinians in the metropolitan area of Jerusalem, out of about 700,000, need services of the city from outside the fence.

The history of the area where the fence is going up is well known. After the Six Day War, when East Jerusalem was annexed to Israel and its borders expanded, the government decided to include the small Atarot airport within Jerusalem's city limits. The presumption behind this move, primarily touted by then Mayor Teddy Kollek, was that Israel's capital needed an airport. To implement this idea, a sort of long finger of land pointing northward allowed the airport to be included within Jerusalem's jurisdiction.

During the subsequent 38 years, the Arab population in East Jerusalem has almost quadrupled, from about 65,000 to 230,000. The Arab neighborhoods could not absorb the new population, particularly because construction permits were not issued for them, and that is why thousands of Arab Jerusalemites built their homes in new neighborhoods that developed outside the city limits, that is in West Bank territory but adjacent to Jerusalem. At the same time, large Jewish neighborhoods such as Pisgat Ze'ev and Newe Ya'aqov were built in the open spaces within the northern borders of the city, and a series of settlements beyond, reaching all the way to the Ramallah district's eastern boundary.

For over 20 years there were no closures or roadblocks, and residents did not require transit permits as Jews and Arabs, Israelis and Palestinians moved around freely throughout the terrain. The northwestern neighborhoods of Jerusalem became a crowded urban space containing businesses, banks, schools, factories, restaurants, and entertainment venues. The route of the separation fence in these neighborhoods does not exactly correspond to the municipal border. In many instances, the fence route deviates from the border for a myriad of reasons, most of which have to do with topographic conditions of the road system and housing density.

There are the Arab neighborhoods outside the wall and the fences which are actually the northern neighborhoods of Jerusalem: Ar-Ram, the largest one, which has about 60,000 inhabitants; Anata and its surroundings with some 30,000 residents; Shu'afat refugee camp is home to some 30,000 people; the villages to the northeast, Hizma and Jaba, which have a population of 8,000; the neighborhoods to the north, Kefar Aqeb and Samiramis, have around 20,000 residents; Qalandiya refugee camp has some 30,000 residents; Bir Naballah neighborhood and the villages in its vicinity have 35,000 residents. Thus, in the entire region outside the fence and the separation wall, there are over 200,000 residents.

The existing route of the envelope fence has been marked almost parallel to the municipal boundaries of the city, and has left behind it thousands of Palestinians who possess legal Israeli identity cards that give them the right, according to Israeli regulations, to work within the city. These inhabitants, who once decided to live in the suburbs of the city, have now to evacuate their homes and to immigrate to East Jerusalem, and to rent their houses at low rates to Palestinians from the West Bank. The result is that the number of the Palestinians in Jerusalem and adjacent to the municipal boundaries is increasing, a phenomenon which does not fall into line with Israel's policy of keeping the demographic balance between the two peoples stable. The growth of the Palestinian population in Jerusalem, and mainly in the Old

City, increased the population density there, and reduced the quality of life in that urban area. It also increased the demands for public services which the municipality is unable to provide. The envelope fence in Jerusalem disconnected many Palestinian neighborhoods, their roads to the city, and the inhabitants' places of employment. Besides the humanitarian harm which the fence does to the population, it has raised the level of hatred for the Israelis and the potential for insurgency.

In 2005 East Palestinians were denied freedom of movement into Ramallah. By then, the separation wall in the area, a series of cement plates, was completed. The Qalandiya checkpoint was moved off the Jerusalem–Ramallah road and upgraded into a terminal. The Qalandiya checkpoint is not on the "Green Line" between Israel and the West Bank, but inside the West Bank on the Jerusalem–Ramallah road, in a narrow strip north of Jerusalem that was annexed to Israel in 1967. The neighborhood of Er-Ram, south of the checkpoint and east of the roads, is in the West Bank, as are the villages to the west – Bir Naballah, Al-Jib, Biddu, and others. The Atarot industrial zone, also west of the road, was annexed to Israel.

North of the checkpoint, the road to Ramallah is Israeli territory, as are those parts of the Qalandiya village west of the road and some of the houses in the Qalandiya refugee camp, east of the road. So is the village of Kafr Aqab, whose residents pay city taxes to Jerusalem and theoretically are supposed to get services from the city The barrier now cuts the Er-Ram–Qalandiya road, and surrounds all of Qalandiya. A series of tunnels is supposed to be built to serve the villagers in the area who want to reach Qalandiya. Israelis and settlers will take a raised highway that is meant to connect the settlement of Giv'at Ze'ev, which is west to Ramallah, to the settlements to the east of the Palestinian city, such as Bet El, Ofra, and Ma'ale Adummim.

The construction of the security fence in the Jerusalem area will change some functions of the checkpoint. Holders of Israeli identity cards who want to go through the checkpoint will be required to have permits to enter Area A. So far the order regarding entry to Ramallah has not been applied to Palestinians from East Jerusalem. Residents of East Jerusalem with blue identity cards who want to enter Ramallah will be required to have permits to enter Area A like all Israeli citizens

Before the work on the envelope fence around Jerusalem is finished three different alternatives to the route of this fence have been proposed to the Prime Minister Ariel Sharon and to the military bodies that are engaged in its construction. The many problems that this fence has made for the civilian population need, according to the Jerusalem Institute of Israel Studies, a deeper consideration on all its aspects (Fig. 2.16).

The first alternative for the fence route that has been proposed by the Jerusalem Institute of Israel Studies is called a demographic view, aiming to disengage the Israelis and the Palestinians in Jerusalem. This proposal actually returns the city to a great extent to the arrangement between 1948 and 1967 when the city was divided through fences and posts between Israel and Jordan. This alternative proposes to take out from the current municipal area a few neighborhoods and villages that were not included before 1967 in the municipal area of Jerusalem, as for instance Sur Bahir, Um Tuba, Beit Hanina, and Shu'afat. The advantages of this alternative

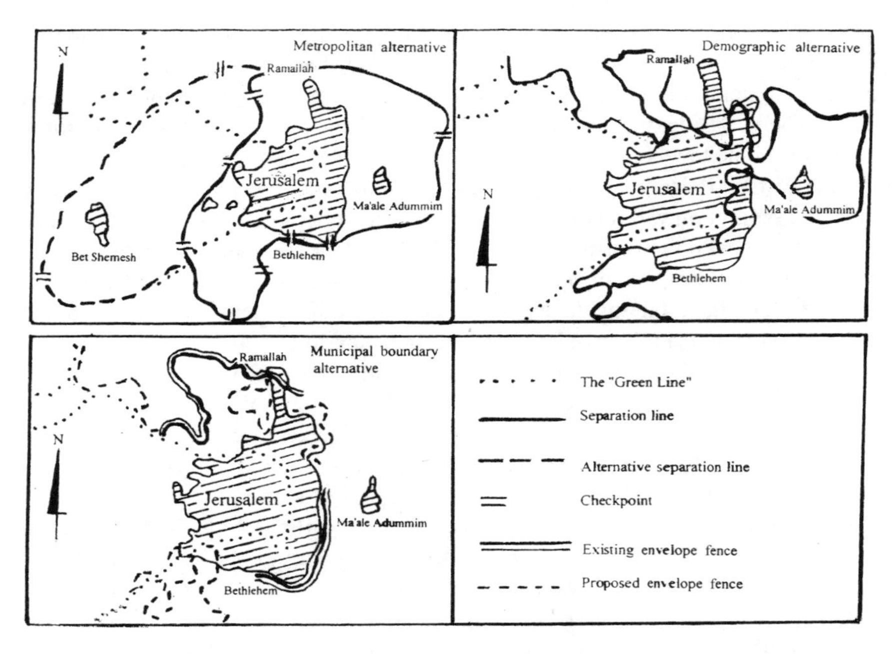

Fig. 2.16 Alternatives for the envelope fence alignment in Jerusalem

are: improvement of the security for the Jewish inhabitants; relatively little harm to the life fabric of the two peoples; a rapid improvement of the demographic balance because only 40,000 Palestinians will remain in the city as against more that 200,000 today; and financial saving of governmental and municipal budgets. The disadvantages of this alternative are that the division of the city will not be easily accepted by parts of the Israeli public; it will be a unilateral step without any political value in exchange; the division of the city may be difficult for the Palestinians who relate to Jerusalem as an open city for all citizens.

The second alternative, with the view of improving the fabric of life in the area, proposes to add to Jerusalem a few villages and even parts of Abu Dis and Al-Eizeriya because their inhabitants have strong economic relationships with the city. The advantages of this alternative are: reducing the harm for many Palestinian families who live beyond the fence; reducing conflict between the Palestinians and the military forces at passing checkpoints; and benefiting the villages by economic relationships with Jerusalem and the metropolitan area that will function as a whole region. The disadvantages of this alternative are that about one to two hundred thousand Palestinians will be added to Israeli territory; this greater population size may increase the danger of attacks; the economic burden of governmental and municipal budgets will be heavier and may reduce the provision to the population of social services and facilities such as roads, hospitals etc.

The third alternative relates to the metropolitan area of Jerusalem including the city in its municipal boundaries as a separated entity, something similar to Washington D.C. The envelope fence will in that case encircle a large area to ensure defense and security, on one hand, and that a group of settlements will be able to function economically and socially, on the other hand; the fence will include the town of Ma'ale Adummim and its satellites in the east, the municipal boundaries of Bethlehem in the south, road No. 443 and the southern boundary of Ramallah in the north, and the Mevasseret Ziyyon–Betar Illit axis in the west. The advantages of this alternative are that more Jewish settlements will be included in the metropolitan area, which will grow by 120,000 inhabitants; Jerusalem will get more land for building houses; many physical and topographic obstacles will be included in the security fence; there will be free traffic in the whole area that may strengthen the economic situation of Jerusalem. The disadvantages of this alternative are: a possible worsening of security because of the many Palestinian settlements that will be added to the metropolitan area; the fact that adding more Palestinians to the population of Jerusalem is against the government policy which strives to maximize disengagement between Israelis and Palestinians; an increase of the governmental and municipal budgets may reduce the provision of economic, physical, and social services for the Palestinians to be included within the fence route; Palestinians claim that Israel aims to annex parts of the Judean Desert, and that a corridor will be needed for connection with the northern and southern parts of the West Bank. After all, it is very difficult to align a good route for a fence that separates two peoples in such a complicated location as Jerusalem.

After Palestinian suicide bombers from the Hebron area carried out a terrorist attack in 2004 at Be'ersheva that killed 16 people, the Israel Defense Forces began to work on the southern section of the separation fence. Work has started on a 25-mile (40-km) stretch of fence southwest of Hebron. The bombing has put pressure on the government to speed up the construction of the fence, which has been delayed by a series of legal challenges. The specific segment under construction is part of the stretch of the fence that is supposed eventually to surround the Hebron Mountains to the southwest and southeast. There have been no significant objections raised to the construction of the fence in the area close to the "Green Line", but there are a number of sections of the fence in the Hebron Mountains that have yet to be planned, and the original route of the fence in this area would encroach on the West Bank, so as to include some Jewish settlements, as well as additional areas in which Palestinians live.

The new route of the separation fence proposed by the defense establishment will annex 100,000 acres (400,000 dunams) of West Bank lands as opposed to the 225,000 acres (900,000 dunams) that were to have been annexed according to the previous plan. The new route was planned after the High Court of Justice mandated changes that were in keeping with the principle of proportionality. In the main, the new route follows the alternative proposal suggested by the Council for Peace and Security. The new routing will return 25,000 acres (100,000 dunams) of Palestinian land in the area of the Jerusalem Corridor. The Palestinian residents of the communities of Beit Surik, Biddu, Beit Anan, and Qatanna will now not be separated as originally planned from their agricultural lands, which cover an estimated area of some 5,000 acres (20,000 dunams).

The decision that the Israeli government made in February 2005 on building the separation fence from the center of the country to the Judean Desert was the most important of Ariel Sharon's tenure. More than any other, this is the step that will define the "Sharon legacy" in shaping the country's borders, the political facts he will leave behind. Setting the fence route will mark Israel's eastern border – the border that will separate it in future from the Palestinian State that is slated to arise in the West Bank. The new route will annex to Israel between 7 to 8 per cent of the West Bank, with the major settlement blocs – the "Jerusalem envelope", the Ezyon bloc, Ma'ale Adummim and Ari'el – where most settlers live. In the major settlement blocs live about 57 per cent of all the settlers of Judea and Samaria, numbering about 143,000 out of approximately 230,000. The government stated that the fence is a temporary security measure to prevent attacks and does not embody a political or other border. The fence route approved by the cabinet marked the change in Israel's war goals vis-à-vis the Palestinians – from the policy of guarding every inch until the enemy gives in, to a rearguard battle to save the blocs of settlements, to annex Ma'ale Adummim, Ari'el, and Efrata.

But thus the separation fence is becoming an Israeli symbol. It embodies everything that is not right there, and it is no less symbolic of the Land of Israel in the way that it stabs into the heart of a fascinating past and into intoxicating but corrupted beauty. It is the model of the landscape of Israeli politics: stuck, sometimes arrogant, mistaken and angry, lacking a clear purpose, foreign to the environment, slicing through a beautiful land and destroying it. It is true that the fence has reduced theft and crime, and will perhaps reduce acts of terror, but against this hope there stands the intrusive act of urban destruction that is standing in the way of a solution, The wall is a continuation of the occupation by other means, and can be expected to be permanently fixed. Jerusalem, at any rate, did not need to be a part of this territorial perversion. It could have remained as an experimental site for real alternatives of Israel–Palestinian closeness, without the injustice of concrete and razor wire.

The High Court ruling regarding the separation fence

A panel of 15 judges at the U.N.'s International Court of Justice in The Hague decided in July 2004 that the construction of the separation fence in the West Bank is a violation of international law and called Israel to end the building of that barrier, and demanded that the sections which had been built on Arab land should be razed, and that the civilians suffering as a result of the building should be compensated. Building the separation fence, which the Court called a "wall", following the term coined by the U.N. assembly, is legal, the Israeli Court said, in that it creates a political precedent for the future border between Israel and the future State of Palestine. Building the wall creates a *fait accompli* constituting a *de facto* annexation. The International Court rejected Israel's claims that the fence is temporary and the citing of the right to self-defense, which is recognized by the U.N. charter. Former Minister of Justice Yosef Lapid said on that occasion that Israel will not follow the International Court of Law ruling on the fence, but will abide by the ruling of the Israel High Court of Justice, which ordered the Defense Ministry to reroute a 18.75-mile (30-km) stretch of the separation fence northwest of Jerusalem.

Israel has reached a stage where issues connected with the territories, which have received the stamp of legality from Israel's Supreme Court until the last ruling of the High Court of Justice, have been disqualified when they came before the International Court of Justice in The Hague. For 38 years, Israeli politicians and legal experts have lived in something of a legal bubble that has enabled the State to enjoy both worlds. On the one hand, the rule in the territories continued to be based on force and powers of military command in occupied territory. On the other hand, the authorities ignored the restrictions imposed on an occupying power, anchored in the Fourth Geneva Convention, against moving part of the population of the occupying power into the occupied territories, as well as the prohibition of confiscating private property and the obligation to hold property as a trustee. One of the justices in the International High Court wrote that the Israeli settlements in the territories are not in keeping with the Geneva Convention, and the parts of the wall being built to defend the settlements are themselves not legal.

The legal bubble led to the situation where the fence was built along a route part of which was not authorized by Israel's High Court of Justice, while all the parts of the fence which run through the territories were invalidated in the advisory opinion of the International Court in The Hague. The decision-makers in Israel have been accustomed to seeing the territories as a place where they have far-reaching authority to confiscate lands without legal process, to close entire areas and demand that their residents must get papers allowing them to live in their own homes, to uproot orchards, to destroy apartment buildings, to prevent children from having access to the schools, and all of this for the needs of the army.

Supreme Court President Aharon Barak's views were that the Court's main role is defending society's fundamental values and protecting democracy, a system in which human rights lie at the center. He warned that the Court must not refrain from deciding sensitive public issues, since that would reduce the possibility of defending democracy. According to this approach, the fact that a government agency has the authority to come to a decision does not mean that it also has the authority to decide whether that decision is legal.

Israel's image took a beating from the International Court of Justice at The Hague. For some time it seemed that Israel would be able to stop the ruling from becoming a binding U.N. resolution, but, in the long run, the judges' decision in The Hague damaged Israel's legitimacy and portrayed it as a criminal State that had been acting contrary to international law in the territories for 38 years. Israel's argument, that the West Bank is controversial territory, that the settlements are legal, and that it is waging a just defensive war against Palestinian terrorism, has been totally rejected. The judges ruled unanimously that Israel is an occupying power, that the settlements are in violation of international law, and that building the fence beyond the "Green Line" is prohibited.

Many stumbling blocks stand in the way of the southern half of the West Bank security fence. Since the High Court of Justice ruling decreed that the fence must avoid causing humanitarian harm to the Palestinians, the Defense Minister's planners have gone back to the drawing board to sketch a route that both provides security and avoids costly legal wrangles. The Ezyon bloc, for instance, is the most heavily populated settlement area on the western side of the fence in the southern West Bank, and poses the greatest challenge for the planners. The barrier encircling the Ezyon bloc of settlements southwest of Bethlehem is now the thorniest section of the 125-mile (200-km) southern fence. Prime Minister Ariel Sharon wanted to present a balanced plan under which Israel brings the fence closer to the "Green Line" in the Hebron Mountains and also includes within the fence all the settlements in the Ezyon bloc. The original route of the fence in the Ezyon bloc, approved by the cabinet in October 2003, included within the barrier an enclave of four Palestinian villages with a total of 17,000 residents. Following the June 2004 High Court of Justice ruling that rejected the proposed segment of the fence because of the harm it would cause the Palestinians, it was decided to re-examine the route so as not to forcibly annex the Palestinian villages to Israel.

Following the ruling of the International Court of Justice in The Hague concerning the route of Israel's separation fence, a team of jurists appointed by the Attorney General, recommended thoroughly examining the possibility and formally applying in the territories the 1949 Geneva Convention, which governs the treatment of civilians in occupied territory. Currently, the accepted approach is that the Convention's rules for protecting civilians in territory under "belligerent occupation" do not directly obligate Israel, since the treaty constitutes covenantal rather than customary international law, and the Knesset has never adopted it through legislation. This is also the approach taken by the Israel High Court of Justice even though the cabinet ratified the treaty in 1951.

If the team's recommendation is accepted, it would represent a change in the consistent policy of all previous governments which has been not to apply the Geneva Convention to the West Bank and Gaza. Israel's position is that there was no recognized sovereign in these areas before 1967, so they are not "occupied territory" as defined in the Convention. Israel has agreed to apply the Convention's humanitarian provisions *de facto*, but has always stressed that it does not constitute formal acceptance of the Convention's applicability. In particular, Israel rejects the claim that the settlements violate the convention, which forbids the transfer of civilians into occupied territory. The team also suggested that the government change its approach to the Convention, and to the International Court. It also argued that Israeli officials should refrain from attacking the court, and that the fence route must demonstrate sensitivity to the Court's ruling. Israel's refusal to apply the Convention formally to the territories stemmed mainly from the fear that it would restrict the establishment of settlements and other aspects of Israeli control over these areas. Thus it confined itself to repeatedly pledging to uphold the Convention's humanitarian provisions.

The Israeli High Court ruling in 2004 on the separation fence stated that the military commander's authority in the territories stems from The Hague Regulations, which reflect customary international law and the Geneva Convention. It stated that the question of the Convention's formal applicability is irrelevant, since the State agrees that the humanitarian provisions apply. It then examined the right to seize private land for military needs in light of international law, including the Convention, and its finding that the fence's route violates the right of local residents rested in part on this treaty. The International Court of Justice, in its opinion on the fence, cited an earlier High Court ruling, which said that the army's actions in the territories are governed by The Hague Regulations and the Geneva Convention. It therefore declared that Israel's Court considers the Convention applicable to the West Bank. The Court ruled that it, too, views the Convention as applicable to "Palestinian territory". The Court ignored Israel's stated position. When Jordan annexed the West Bank in 1950, only Britain and Pakistan recognized the annexation.

The team proclaimed that, in the light of the Court's ruling, Israel should reconsider the way in which the army and other Israeli agencies operate in the territories. The fence should be built as close as possible to the "Green Line", taking into account security needs and the need to minimize harm to Palestinians. Where settlements abut the "Green Line", the fence should lie as close as possible to the outermost houses of these settlements. The team also recommended adjusting the "permit regime" instituted for Palestinians living near the fence, in accordance with the principles of international law.

Israel's Attorney General warned that the decision on the separation fence by the International Court of Justice in The Hague could lead to anti-Israel actions in international forums that could include sanctions. It is difficult to overestimate the negative ramifications that the Court's decisions will have on Israel in various spheres, even on issues beyond the separation fence. The Attorney General recommended that, at the earliest possible opportunity, Prime Minister Ariel Sharon should adjust the decisions about the separation fence's route and arrangements in the borderline areas, so as to meet the principles fixed by the Israeli High Court of Justice, and that the corrected route of the fence be anchored in a new cabinet decision that would send a message to the world that Israel is upholding international law according to the decisions of its own courts.

In July 2004, as mentioned above, 14 of the 15 The Hague judges ruled that construction of the separation fence in the West Bank violated international law and constituted illegal annexation. The Court said Israel could not justify the fence by claiming self-defense and should stop construction immediately, dismantle existing sections and compensate Palestinians harmed by its construction. An Israel team found at the time that the ruling created a new reality for Israel and could accelerate international forums' actions against Israel. The State prosecution informed the High Court on February 2005 that the opinion of the International Court of Justice at The Hague on the separation fence was irrelevant. The prosecution said that it was based on partial, outdated information and should therefore be disregarded. The International Court examined a very different fence route from the one currently planned, and even more changes were submitted for cabinet approval. The High Court Justice asked for the State's response to The Hague opinion in 2004 while hearing a detailed petition regarding some villages, a petition that has become a fundamental examination of the separation fence. Israel's position is that The Hague opinion has no relevance to the High Court hearing for a number of reasons. First, when The Hague heard the matter, it was already looking at the wrong route. As Israel did not attend the hearing, the Palestinian side presented a route it claimed to have downloaded from the fence administration's website. Second, since The Hague published its opinion, there have been several substantial changes to the route, in part as a result of decisions by the High Court itself. The State's third argument was based on an expected cabinet decision changing the route of several sections of the fence that have not yet been constructed. The discussion will not include the fence route in the Ezyon bloc area, which will be considered separately. The expected decision will change the route and bring it closer to the "Green Line". Fourth, The Hague Court's opinion was regarded as superficial and deficient, in that the Court totally ignored the terrorist attacks that made it imperative to set up the fence, the considerations that led to planning its route, and the State's duty to protect its citizens. Fifth, the lack of factual infrastructure and the superficiality of the analysis constituted a substantial blow to the legal validity of the International Court's adamant findings and the legitimacy of its conclusions. Sixth, The Hague Court's ruling took the form of an advisory opinion that is not legally binding and does not have relevance to the discussion on the petitions against the fence. Altogether, the State's response noted that Israel will leave 8 per cent of the West Bank on the Israeli side of the fence. The Israeli calculation did not include the East Jerusalem municipal area. The State reiterated its position that the fence is a temporary security measure aimed at combating terrorist attacks, and does not in itself attempt to define the future border of the State of Israel.

While engaging the military jargon of humanitarian passes in the West Bank (allowing Palestinians to cross barriers for, e.g., medical and maternity care), Israel is turning fertile Palestinian territories into wasteland. While it talks incessantly of temporality, the fence is demarcating the border between Israel and the State of prison compounds, and between the compounds and the settlements. The constructed fence is continuing in its energetic destruction, but it seems that the fence will never be completed, because even after it is finished it will perpetuate the policy of annexation, usurpation, and severance. It will continue to cause disasters all around it.

It may be concluded that Israel created in the occupied territories of Judea and Samaria a regime of separation based on discrimination, applying two separate systems of law in the same area and basing rights of individuals on their nationality. Under this regime, Israel has stolen hundreds of thousands of acres of land from the Palestinians. Israel has used this land to establish dozens of settlements in the West Bank and to populate them with hundreds of thousands of Israeli citizens. The manner of dispersion of settlements over extensive areas of the West Bank creates numerous violations of the Palestinians' legal rights. The drastic change that Israel has made in the map of the West Bank prevents any real possibility for the establishment of an independent viable Palestinian State. The settlers, on the contrary, benefit from all rights available to Israeli citizens living within the "Green Line", and in some cases are even granted additional rights. The great effort that Israel has invested in the settlement enterprise, in financial, legal, and bureaucratic terms, has turned the settlements into civilian enclaves in an area under military rule, with the settlers given preferential status. The responsibility for the infringement of human rights created by the existence of the settlements rests with all the Israel governments since the occupation began. It is the government that initiated the establishment of the settlements, provided political, organizational, and economic support, and encouraged their continual expansion.

3 Jerusalem – reunited but divided

Background

The world has always had a great interest in Jerusalem, its holy places for Christians, Muslims, and Jews, its physical appearance, and its population. Over the ages, this universal concern, which was coupled with a desire to preserve and beautify the city, has bred a variety of planning perspectives. Jerusalem existed for many centuries as a typical Middle Eastern city on the fringe of the desert, densely built-up with small houses, surrounded by walls, with people living in a congested manner along narrow twisted lanes, and being dependent on local limited water resources. Nearly 400 years of the Ottoman regime in Palestine from the sixteenth century did not improve the economic and physical situation of Jerusalem. The Turks treated Palestine as a peripheral buffer zone in the south of their empire, opposite to the Suez Canal and Egypt, which was ruled by the British. This fact had an impact on their lax attitude to the planning of Jerusalem. The British were the first to make any significant progress in the basic planning and constructing of Jerusalem. The Israelis and the Arabs after 1948 only tried to modify the British planning of the town according to their political purposes, but with not too much success.

Jerusalem is located on the crest of the Judean Mountains. It is bisected by a north–south watershed, so that from Jerusalem the mountains slope down to the Judean Plain in the west and to the Judean Desert in the east. Jerusalem is built on a group of hills and valleys. While the hills are designated for residential construction, the valleys serve as open space and communications areas. The most typical structural features are in the Old City – the ancient center of Jerusalem. The Old City forms the core of the eastern section, containing most of the holy places.

The uneven topography of the Jerusalem region profoundly affected the settlement and growth pattern of the city. Hillocks and isolated interfluves alternate with winding valleys and scattered basins. These lower-lying areas originally were used for agriculture and for access, and on the steeper slopes were wasteland, forested parks, cemeteries, and public open space. The high elevations became the locations of residential neighborhoods and independent villages that were subsequently absorbed by the expanding city. The mosaic of residential clusters separated by agriculture, or open or institutional zones, emerged as the standard pattern of settlement in the late twentieth century.

The long-established neighborhoods beyond the Old City developed through years of accretion. Instead of displaying the conventions of modern city planning, they often reflect the personalities of their founders and original inhabitants who generally had a common origin and who formed a close-knit social group. In contrast with the modern practice of neighborhoods or towns, planned by central government authority, which are settled by heterogeneous inhabitants who want to undergo social education to adapt to new surroundings and neighbors, these old communities began with residents of relatively similar background, experience, and orientation. Settlements of this type were associated with each major religion.

More than thirty such residential neighborhoods had emerged in Jerusalem prior to the Second World War. The Jewish settlements were mostly west of the Old City. A further impetus to the proliferation of distinctive residential neighborhoods emerged solely in the Jewish community. Jews often refrain from mixing with their neighbors, a tradition that reflected centuries of discrimination in widely scattered areas. Most Jews who arrived after 1918 were not as bound by the conservative religious traditions, and conflict and tension soon arose between orthodox and liberal groups. With continued population growth, crowding and congestion in the Jewish settlements eventually led to the planning and the erection of neighborhoods in western architectural styles prevalent in the1920s and the 1930s. However, the established neighborhoods were largely unaffected by new trends. Gradually long-term residents who were less bound by conservative religious interpretation migrated into the western parts of the city, and the buildings thus evacuated in the old quarters were taken by the expanding orthodox Jewish communities.

The neighborhoods of East Jerusalem are more likely than those in other districts to be outgrowths of independent villages that coalesced. These neighborhoods tend to be traditional in orientation and not patterned in layout. As with other parts of the Muslim world they share rigid ideas about neighborhood form and housing to ensure maximum privacy of women and to deflect traffic from private spaces.

The city boundaries have changed many times in the course of history. Biblical Jerusalem lay entirely to the east of the watershed, on the eastern slope of the mountain ridge. From the end of the nineteenth century till the end of the British Mandate regime in 1947 the city moved westwards, so as to include numerous residential quarters in addition to the walled city. Then the 1948 war led to a far-reaching modification of the city boundaries through the arbitrary division of Jerusalem. The Israeli–Jordanian armistice lines, marking the former battlefront, ran right through the middle. The Old City and the quarters lying to the northeast and south of this line were ultimately annexed by Jordan, with a sovereign Israeli enclave on Mount Scopus. On the Jewish side the city boundaries naturally moved further to the west comprising an area of 9,250 acres (37,000 dunams), as the armistice lines checked all expansions to the north, south, and east (Fig. 3.1). After the war in 1967 the city boundaries have been changed again. Today they include Mount Scopus and the Mount of Olives in the east, Beit Safafa and Gilo in the south, and the Atarot industrial zone in the north, as well as the Old City and the entire western part of Jerusalem that had developed in the intervening 19 years. The city thus extends over an area of 31,500 acres (126,000 dunams). Since the eastern and

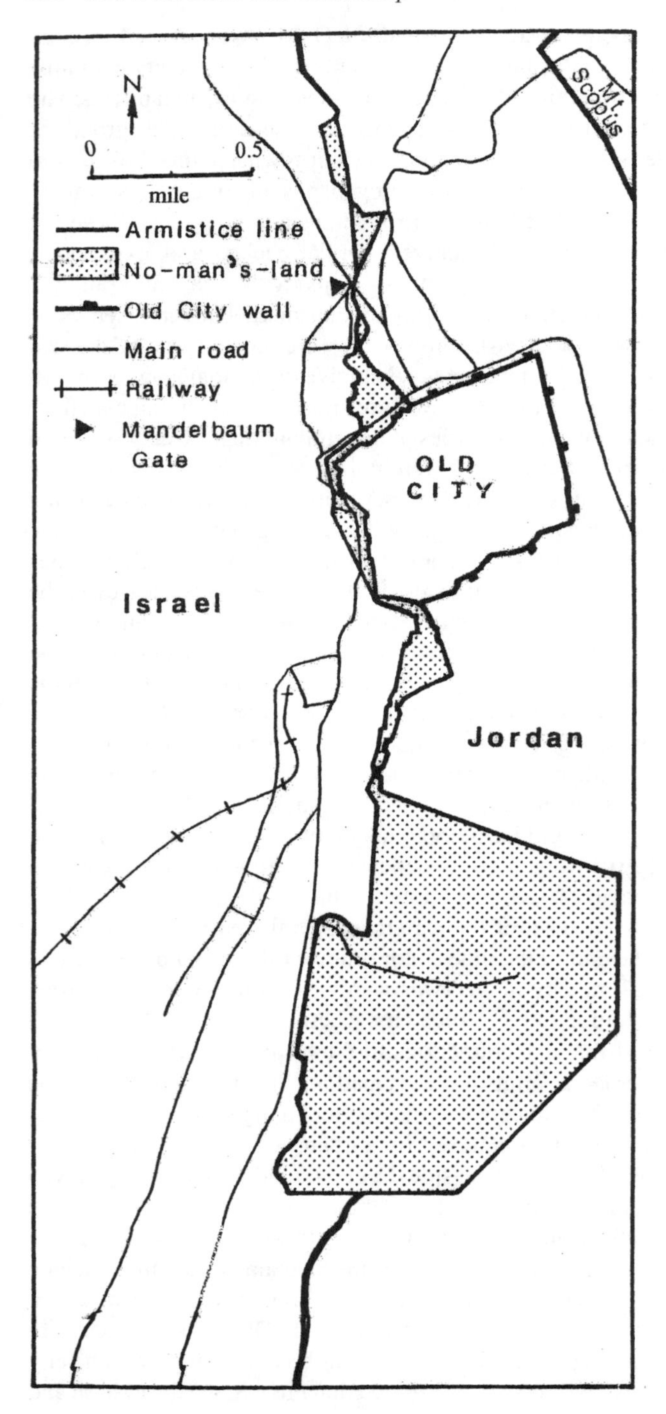

Fig. 3.1 A section of the Israeli–Jordanian armistice line 1948–67

western sections were totally separated from each other over the 19 years, the development of the city could not be co-ordinated. Many new neighborhoods sprang up in the Israeli part, existing neighborhoods continued to expand, and the city kept spreading to the west. In the eastern section the main expansion was towards the east and north, with a considerable growth of the villages lying on the outskirts of the city, which were gradually converted into suburbs.

Planning perspectives of the British

British town planning was essentially a political, social, cultural, professional, and technical response to a blend of circumstances which marked the years at the turn of the century. Town planning was essentially a reactive development, while it aimed at the future. Its immediate concern was a response to the past and present.

Proper planning began only after the British conquest of Jerusalem by General Edmund Allenby. On 9 December 1917 he announced the military's intention to prepare and maintain the places holy to the three religions, and in 1918 he commissioned an engineer from Alexandria, by the name of William McLean, to draw up the first town plan for the city. The British had a strong motivation in preserving the exclusiveness of Jerusalem, although the war in those days was still going on. As European conquerors they gave immediate orders to reconstruct and plan the town. As no topographic map was available, McLean's outline plan was of little value, but the building regulations issued at his instigation by the military governor of Jerusalem, Ronald Stors, remain relevant to this day. The main provisions were: preservation of the skyline of the eastern mountain range; a 35 ft (11 m) limit on the height of buildings; a ban on industrial construction within the city; a ban on all construction around the Old City walls; limited construction on Mount Scopus, on the Mount of Olives and in the Valley of Qidron; and the exclusive use of stone for the construction of roofs which in all public buildings had to be dome-shaped (Efrat, 1993).

The crown of British activity in Jerusalem at that time was the care and preservation of its beauty, renewal, and its planning as a modern city. That was expressed, *inter alia*, by the renovation of ancient sites, by planting trees along main roads and in public open spaces, by clearing gathered waste in the streets and by reconstruction of parts of the ancient walls. The initiator of all these activities was the Pro-Jerusalem Society founded by Ronald Stors. The Society included representatives of all the religious communities of Jerusalem and delegates of public and governmental bodies. The aim of the Pro-Jerusalem Society was to preserve the Old City and its surroundings; to develop handicrafts and light industry in the city; to plan the northern part of Jerusalem outside the walls; to initiate a reformation in the town's leadership; to establish a new planning council; to take care of the archaeological sites; and to establish a super-national committee for the preservation of the town as a whole.

These provisions, designed to preserve the special character of the Jerusalem, caused the city to develop mainly to the west and southwest, in view of the restrictions imposed on construction in the Old City and its immediate neighborhoods.

McLean's object, rather than to solve local problems, was to lay down general town planning guidelines. The Old City was regarded as the architectural, but not as the functional, core of the city, and was separated from the newer sections by green belts. McLean wanted Jerusalem to grow to the north, the west, and the south, with only little development in the eastern part, where he was aware of the climatic and topographical limitations. He also adopted the principle of urban dispersal, and proposed two main axes along main roads, the one to the northwest and the other to the southeast of the Old City. His guidelines were followed in most of the subsequent town plans (Fig. 3.2).

Patrick Geddes, a Scottish biologist, sociologist, landscape designer, and planner, and a generalist in an age of speciality, prepared a plan in 1919 in which the Old City was regarded as a separate entity, and the Mount of Olives and the holy sites were planned as open spaces so as to preserve their ancient character. The main stress was laid on the northwards and eastwards expansion of the city, and McLean's

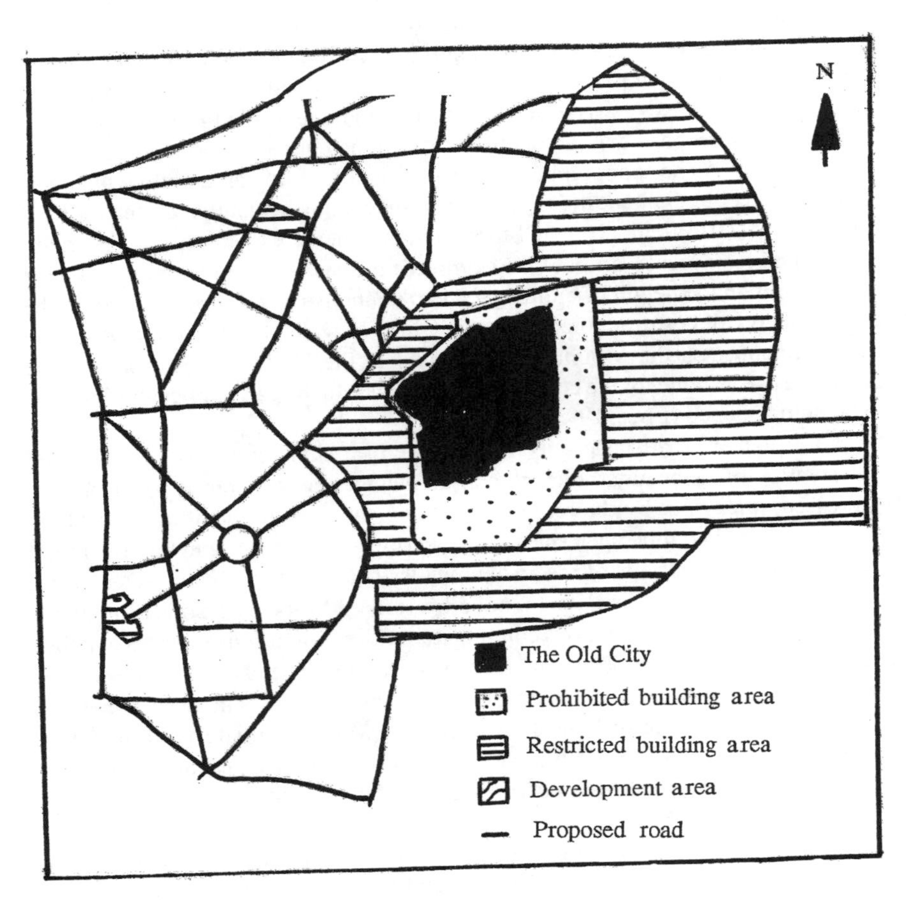

Fig. 3.2 City plan of Jerusalem prepared by W. McLean 1918

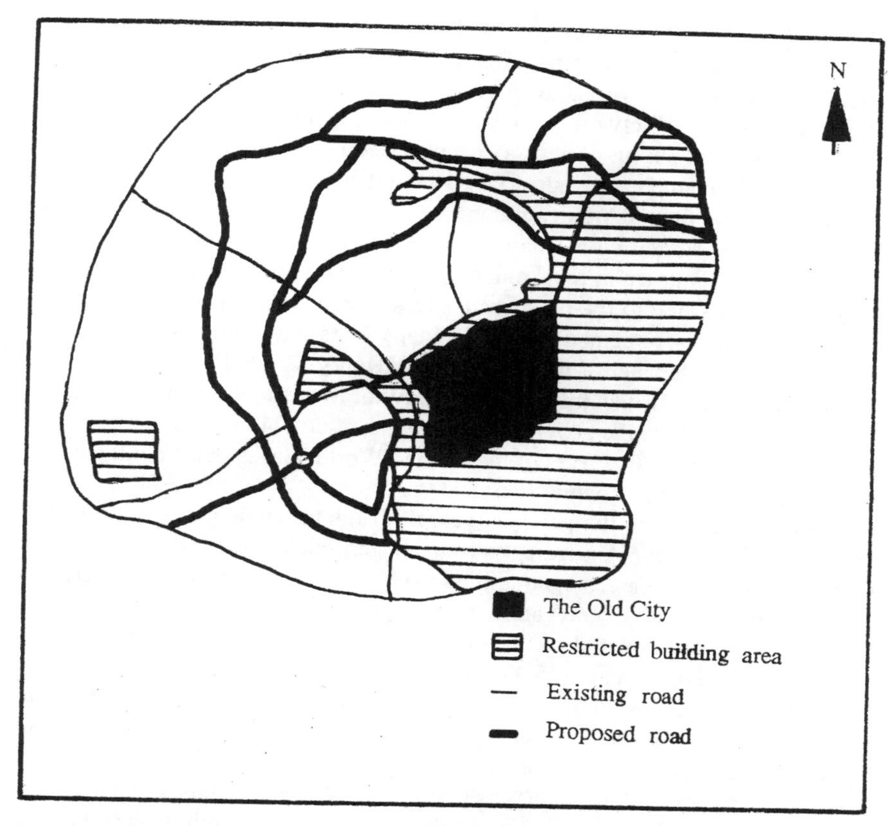

Fig. 3.3 City plan of Jerusalem prepared by P. Geddes 1919

two axes, conceived of as a counterweight to the Old City, were abandoned. Instead, a civic center was provided for on the longitudinal axis of Jaffa Road, Jerusalem's main street, while the Hebrew University was located on Mount Scopus, east of the Old City (Fig. 3.3).

In 1922 Clifford Ashby drew a more detailed plan. He was an architect who preached the idea of an integrated approach to life, praising art against the dullness of nineteenth-century mechanization. Being the secretary of the Pro-Jerusalem Society and advisor to the governor of Jerusalem, he was involved in the planning problems of the city. By him, for the first time, the city boundaries were fixed; and the planning space was subdivided by land uses and building regulations into four main zones – the Old City, open spaces and parks in the valleys, industry and crafts near the main traffic arteries, and residential areas. An attempt was made to follow the rapid development of the new neighborhoods outside the visual space of the Old City and the fast growth of commerce, workshops, and industry in Jerusalem.

In 1930 the British architect and town planner Clifford Holliday published another outline plan, based mainly on land uses and building regulations. In this case an attempt was made for the first time to incorporate Jerusalem in a county-wide plan. The roads were classified, with a ring road surrounding the city and linking it to the national road network. The scheme was an important step forward in regulative town planning of Jerusalem, by dividing the area into well-defined residential, commercial, and industrial zones and taking into account the needs of the growing Jewish and Arab communities in different quarters of the city. The scheme introduced zoning regulations for these areas, and established density control, both by fixing a minimum range in the size of building plots, and by limiting the extent of building to the main roads. This plan, which was largely based on former perspectives, remained in force for many years and determined the shape of the city until 1944, when it was replaced by Henry Kendall's outline scheme. Kendall served as a British town planning advisor to the government of Palestine and continued to serve the government of Jordan after 1947 in the same role. His plan was drawn up in the years of the Second World War under the influence of Abercrombie's *Greater London Plan 1944*.

In Kendall's scheme the perspectives of all the previous plans came to full expression and fruition. According to Kendall, Jerusalem was destined to become a major communication center straddling two main intersecting traffic arteries, as well as an administrative center and a meeting ground for British, Jews, and Arabs. Kendall's plan area covered 10,040 acres (40,160 dunams), against the existing municipal area of 6,250 acres (25,000 dunams), and contained a population of about 100,000. His object was to plan the city as a capital with administrative, political, and scientific-educational, rather than industrial functions. The existing road network remained the basis for the new scheme, but great emphasis was laid on by-pass roads. The light industry zones were surrounded by green belts, and parks were extended. A clear distinction was made between the different religious and ethnic communities, with most of the Jewish quarters in the west and most of the Arab neighborhoods in the south and east in order to prevent potential spatial conflicts. The concept of neighborhood units was also further developed. In spite of that, there was little chance for this scheme to extend an influence on Jerusalem development at the end of the 1940s because of the rising tension in the country between Arabs, Jews, and British (Fig. 3.4).

From this series of outline plans we may realize that during the British Mandate period satisfactory provisions were made to ensure an adequate architectural design, to conserve the landscape and topography of the city, and to maintain its ancient and holy sites. The Old City was regarded as the principal architectural element, which also influenced the planning of the new parts of the town. Use was made of the fact that the topography of Jerusalem lends itself to the construction of neighborhood units, and much weight was given to the height of the buildings to preserve its particular character. Strict requirements were imposed, and care was taken not to break up the skyline. In addition to the requirement that buildings should be properly set into the hillside, there was a stringent regulation that they should all be made of stone so as to present a solid and dignified appearance.

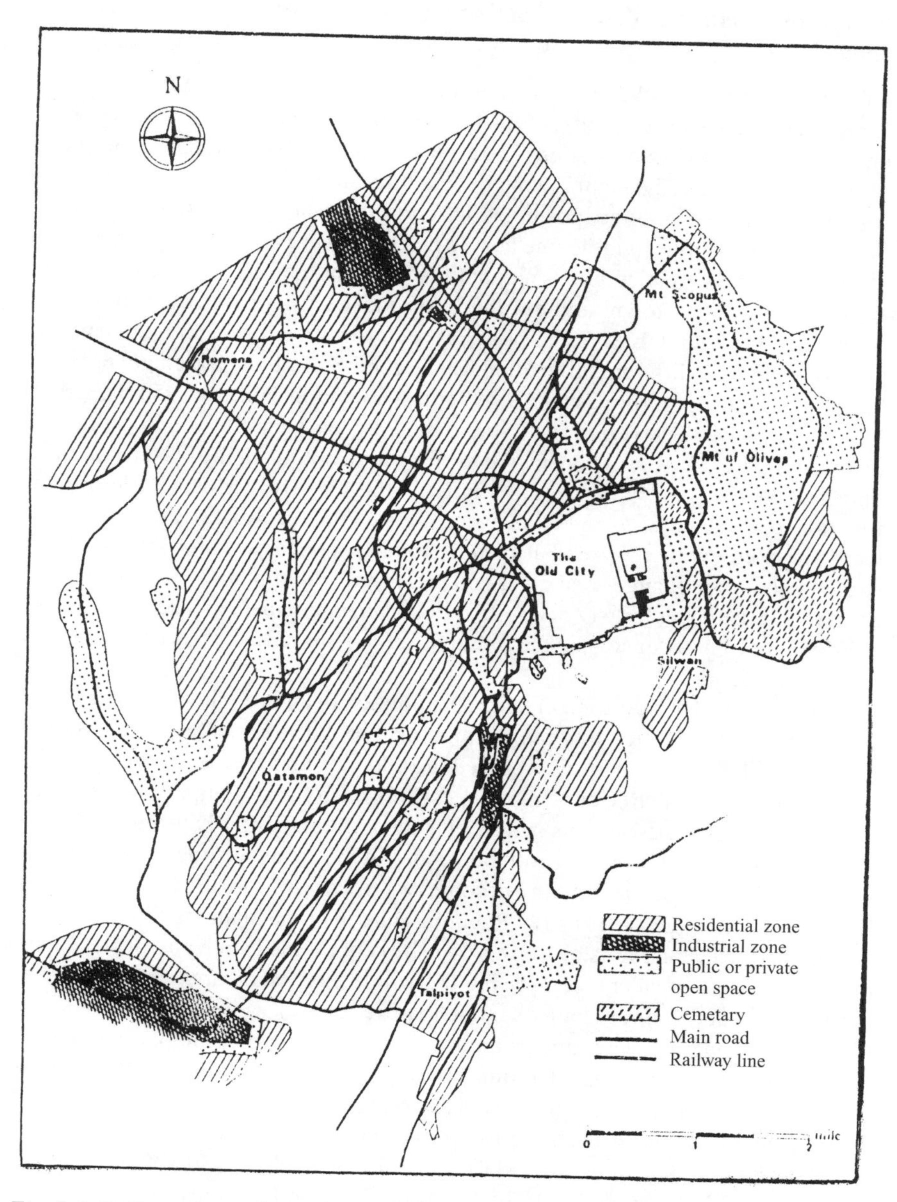

Fig. 3.4 Outline scheme designed by H. Kendall 1944

Planning prospects of the Israelis in West Jerusalem since 1967

After the Israel–Arab War of 1948 and the establishment of the State of Israel, Jerusalem became a border city, divided between Jews and Arabs, who were both opposed to its internationalization. The armistice line in 1949 confirmed the vision of the city and created a neutral zone to be administered by the U.N. between the Jordanian and Israeli military positions. That no-man's land comprised seven areas, but along most of this dividing line hostile positions were immediately adjacent to each other. The armistice line separated the Old City and its commercial center from the rest of the town, and cut the basic ideas of British town planning of Jerusalem into two halves. Each political sector in the city underwent separate development with different orientation. By December 1949 the Israeli government began to shift offices from Tel Aviv to Jerusalem and in January 1950 the Israeli Parliament (Knesset) averred that the city had always been the Israeli capital. In many circles this move was considered to be a contravention of the U.N. resolutions that had decreed the international status of the city. Nevertheless, Jerusalem functioned as the *de facto* capital of Israel. During the time of division, two plans were prepared, while the Kendall Plan of 1944 remained valid for the Jordanian sector with minor changes and amendments. From a total planned area of 10,040 acres (40,160 dunams), 6,412 acres (25,648 dunams) remained in the Israeli sector, 3,395 acres (13,580 dunams) in the Jordanian sector, and 232.5 acres (930 dunams) as no-man's land.

From 1948 to 1967 Jerusalem became a politically and religiously divided city (Fig. 3.5). The armistice line ran through occupied land, residential areas, and roadways. The Jordanian army occupied the Old City and East Jerusalem, and the Israeli army controlled Mount Zion, West Jerusalem, and an important enclave on Mount Scopus. Despite this irrational state of affairs, or perhaps because of it, unconventional steps were taken on both sides of the armistice line to promote the development of what had virtually become two towns. In 1949 the Israeli architect Heintz Rau, director of the District Planning Bureau of the Planning Division, then attached to the Prime Minister's Office, worked out for the Israeli authorities a new master plan for Jerusalem, comprising the whole city, on an area plan of 14,920 acres (59,680 dunams), as against a municipal area of 8,375 acres (33,550 dunams). Planning boundaries were always bigger than the official municipal boundaries because they took into consideration the surroundings of the city and its future political development. This plan was later on adopted by the Jerusalem District town planner as an outline scheme for the western part of the city, on an area plan of 9,250 acres (37,000 dunams) and for a population of about 250,000 inhabitants, and was officially approved in 1959. It was based on shifting the center of gravity westwards from the Old City by setting up a new artificial urban node (Fig. 3.6).

In the past, according to British planning perspectives, the city spread to the west, mainly because the eastern mountain range from Mount Scopus to Gethsemane was declared public open space and put out of bounds for construction. Now that the western part was cut off from the central business district of the Old City and

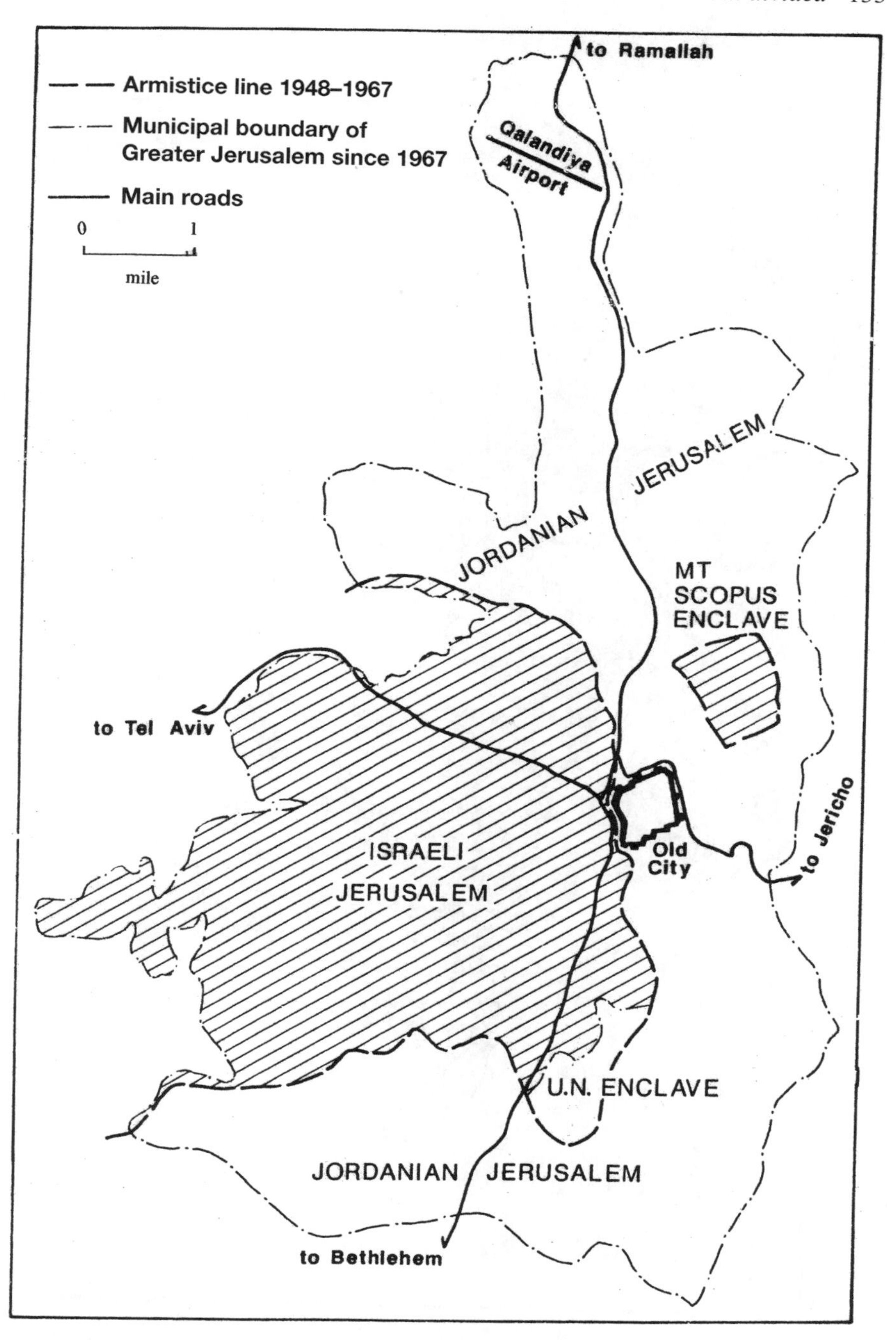

Fig. 3.5 Boundaries of divided Jerusalem since 1948 and "Greater Jerusalem" after 1967

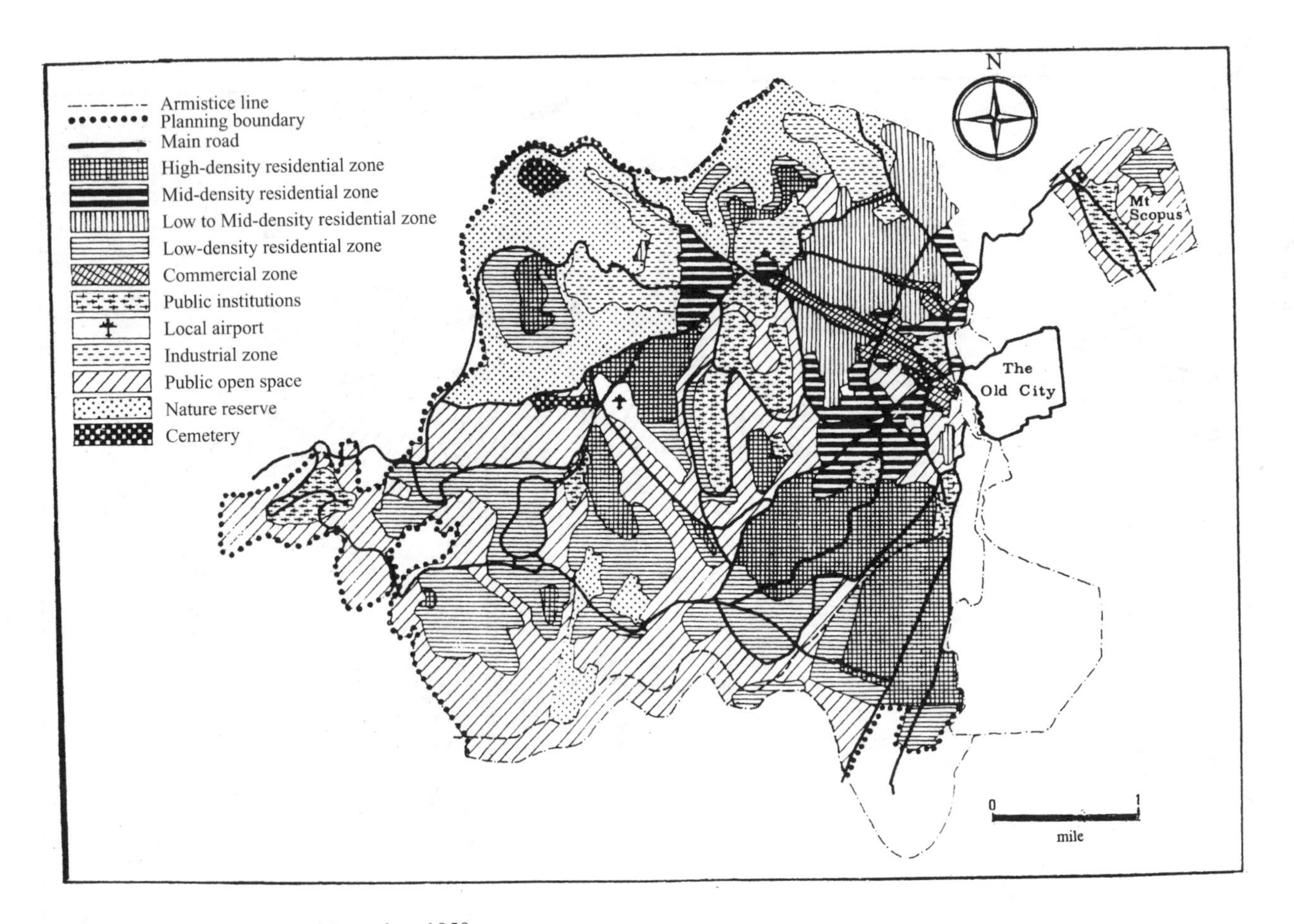

Fig. 3.6 Outline scheme of Jerusalem 1959

its environs, this direction remained the only outlet for expansion. At the same time the Jewish sector had become a national capital and as such had to accommodate a reasonable number of inhabitants, public institutions, parks, and public spaces. The size of the city was, moreover, determined by security considerations. As a border city it had to be big enough to be able to defend itself. The population target for 1985 was thus set at 250,000. It was also necessary to set up industries to give employment to those incapable of administrative work. In line with the city's international functions, a central site was allocated to public buildings and institutions.

Nevertheless, however much effort was put into the plan it could not overcome the fact that the bisected city was not a sound, well-integrated organism. While in the western section detailed town plans and strict building regulations, introduced during the British Mandate period, were enforced, a much more lax attitude was adopted in the older Jewish sections, and this tended to aggravate the dichotomy. The new detailed plans for the western section also took insufficient account of the possible reintegration of the city, especially as far as the communication arteries were concerned. Owing to the shift from east to west, the connection with the Old City, a principal element in all former British town plans, was severed. The new urban node, with its various public buildings, was located in the central space. Thus the planning perspectives adopted in West Jerusalem were a direct result of the unnatural conditions imposed on the city. Since the commercial center was displaced to the west, Jerusalem had to develop in an oxbow shape, with the central business district at the top of the residential neighborhoods along the two flanks, the old residential quarters near the border in the east and the new residential quarters in the west. According to the new outline scheme, the city was supposed to develop along the western spurs of the Judean Mounts towards the so-called "Jerusalem Corridor", an area highly unsuitable for urban development adjoining the terrain set aside for this purpose in the pre-1948 British plan.

It was not an easy task for the Israeli planners during the first decade of statehood to undertake planning according to the British Mandate perspectives because the new political situation in the city upset the apple-cart. Changes occurred in the boundaries, in trends of development, in environmental interrelationships, in economic functions, and in demography. No wonder that the Israeli master plan and outline scheme of the 1950s were quite artificial in their perspectives with small likelihood of implementation. Heintz Rau tried in his 1949 master plan to apply basic British town planning concepts and ideas. They led to a bifocal symmetrical urban development, so that some city elements were positioned in pairs: the Old City against the Government Conclave; the cemetery on the Mount of Olives mirrored by the cemetery and the National Pantheon on Mount Herzl; extensive open area in the west that found an echo in the big nature reserve on the slopes of the eastern ridges; and the new University campus – a reflection of the University on Mount Scopus. There could be no greater harm to Jerusalem than the bisecting of the city along the seam between the Old City and the new sectors in the west. This fact almost put to an end urban and architectural features which were created and formed by the British over many years. The Israeli planners had, therefore, to struggle between the urban and historical values of the city, and political and military factors which dictated the new situation, with a hostile borderline running through the city.

The altered status of the city, its exposed position, its enlarged size, the presence of a large minority group, and continued objection from the United Nations to unilateral Israeli control were the new context that planners faced. Though never formally articulated, a series of planning objectives evolved to govern the early decisions of Israeli planners. The first task, with such symbolic and political significance as to become paramount, was the reconstruction of the Jewish Quarter in the Old City. The quarter had suffered considerable damage during the 1948 fighting. The relatively few Arabs who had occupied the quarter from 1949 to 1967 had to be resettled, and the entire area was rebuilt with modern residences and services, but the ancient street alignment and structural forms were retained. The rebuilding offered the opportunities for extensive archaeological investigations and to restore and to preserve facilities that had almost disappeared centuries ago (Efrat and Noble, 1988).

A second objective involved the occupation and the exploitation of Mount Scopus, which because of its association with the Hebrew University had become a symbol of cultural renaissance for Jews. Also because the area had been an outpost of Israeli territory from 1948 to 1967, Mount Scopus held further significance to Israelis, both as a symbol of independence and as the highest, strongest defensive point in the entire Jerusalem region. Israeli planners immediately proposed construction of a new University campus along the higher crest of the heights, so that the buildings served the purpose of both higher education and military fortification. Interconnected structures, built of stone and concrete, more than a mile long, with tunnels, interior corridors, limited outside access, and underground entrances were placed, so that each part of the complex could offer supporting fire for the other units in case of attack. In the middle of the complex, a huge concrete tower provides a potential site for a communications center and observation post, with view eastward across the entire Rift Valley. The University complex on Mount Scopus is a formidable fortification that now represents the eastern bulwark of the city.

The third objective of the Israeli planners was to establish new Jewish neighborhoods to connect Mount Scopus and West Jerusalem. The rationale was that dense settlement might discourage the imposition of any future armistice line through the area because there would be no vacancy or unoccupied space. Homogeneity of settlement would encourage integration of formerly isolated neighborhoods and facilities. Hence the increased connectivity within the region would reduce the likelihood that politicians would use the area as bargaining pawns.

The fourth objective was to provide a defensive barrier by extending the outer limit of new settlement to high ground around the city. The outer blocks of flats were often designed with defense in mind. To minimize openings in buildings, doors and windows were both few and small. The fortress-like appearance of many new structures was shown in the residential buildings erected in 1986 in the southern suburb of Gilo, which looks southward toward the Arab-dominated West Bank and Bethlehem. The bulk of the planning funds expended in Jerusalem between 1967 and 1985 was spent on these circumferential communities.

The final initial objective for Israeli planning was to make Jerusalem accessible, especially from the west. This objective was an outgrowth of the military problems encountered in 1948 when bitter battles were fought over the narrow, twisting roads leading from the Coastal Plain to Jerusalem. The Israelis had to rely on difficult secondary roads whenever Jordanian forces controlled the main route. After the 1948 war, the Israelis had constructed alternative routes, but the easiest and shortest route could not be planned until the fortress of Latrun was under Israeli control. Planners met the goal of providing better access to the city by building new roads and improving existing ones. A modern roadway southward allowed rapid and easy access to and from Bethlehem. The development of new roads brought in its wake the problem of increased traffic congestion. Some traffic has been drawn off by circumferential roads, especially the one linking via a northern route the Tel Aviv road to Jericho. This highway largely replaces the older southern circumferential route that extended eastward from Bethlehem road trough a region densely settled by Arabs. Traffic congestion continues to be a major problem in Jerusalem, where both population and vehicular ownership are increasing. These five objectives governed the 1968 plan that the Israeli authorities promulgated. This plan was the first attempt since the Kendall proposal late in the British Mandate period to regulate development for the entire area of Jerusalem.

Modern planning in Jerusalem had mixed success. With shifts of political control, planning orientations have undergone abrupt changes. Reunification of the city in 1967 did not bring an end to the divisions between Jews and Arabs. The animosities are deep and have survived the recent geographical shifts. Removal of political barriers in various parts of the city has demonstrated the influence of ephemeral circumstances on urban development between 1948 and 1967. With the removal of artificially imposed barriers, trends can operate throughout the municipal region, and planners have been able to demonstrate that they not only respond to events but also shape them. The concepts of a business center integrated with the existing commercial activities around the Old City and of restricted development to the west have been revived. A road paralleling the Old City walls has returned to its former importance with lively shops and heavy traffic. Whatever the directional impetus that planners may suggest for the development of Jerusalem, expansion is likely to continue along the favorable, open slopes of the north–south mountain range (Fig. 3.7).

After the War of 1948 the Jordanians decided to make plans for East Jerusalem, which was then annexed to the Hashemite Kingdom of Jordan. Under the British, Jerusalem had been the commercial and economic center of Judea, Samaria, and Transjordan. It had provided the main outlet to the Mediterranean via the routes leading through it to Yaffa and Haifa, by which all supplies were conveyed to the city. Jerusalem also served as a major purchasing center for the Arab population. With the annexation of the West Bank to Jordan it ceased to be a central city and major marketplace, and became a border city, an economic backwater with all supply lines directed towards Amman. This economic subordination to the East Bank also affected the city's physical development and gave it an eastward orientation. It began to spread towards the eastern flanks of the Temple Mount, the

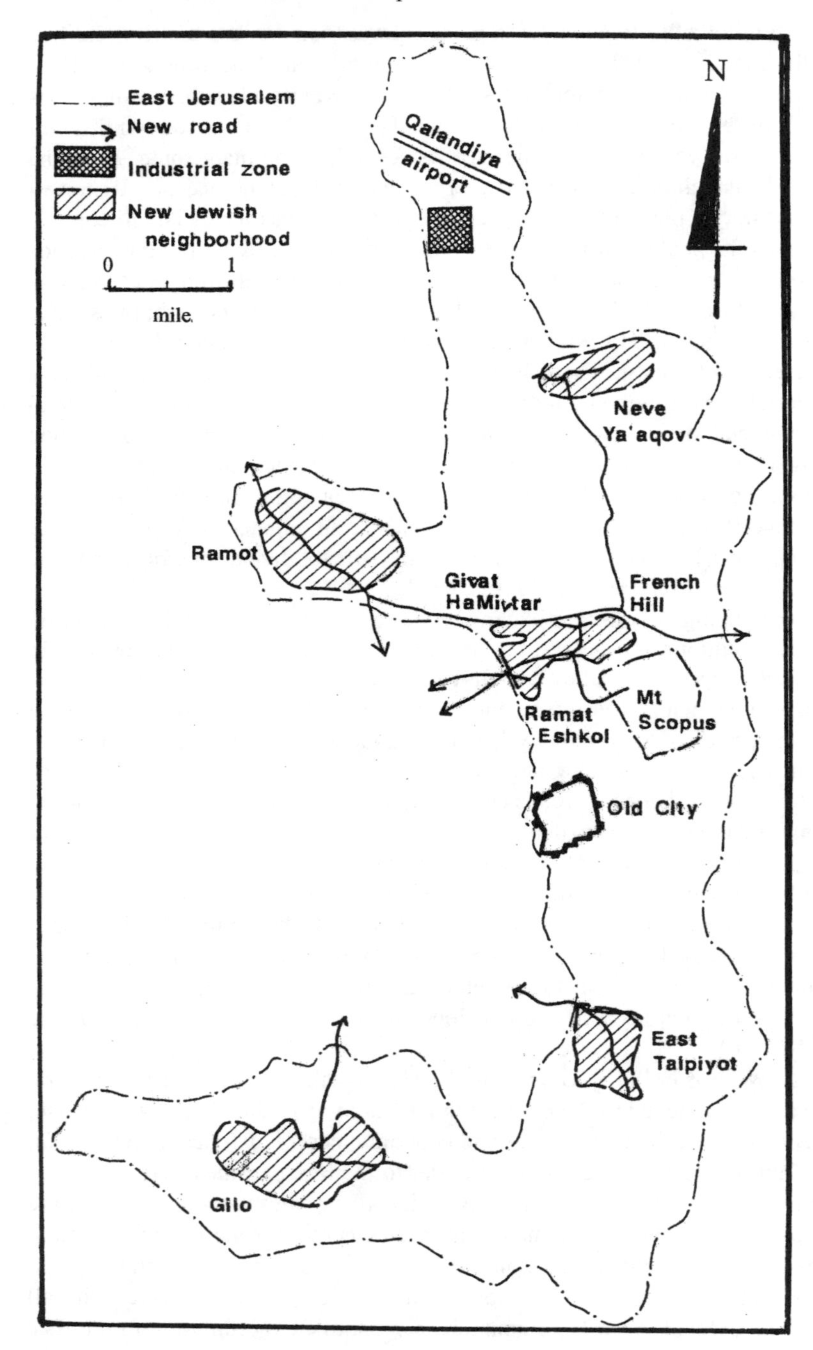

Fig. 3.7 Jewish neighborhoods in East Jerusalem

Valley of Qidron, the Judean Desert, and the busy road to Jericho and Amman, as well as the long traffic arteries to the north and south which were undesirable from the British town planning point of view. In the east and southeast the terrain was highly unsuitable for urban development, so that building took place mainly along the saddle of the Jerusalem Mountains, on both sides of the Jerusalem–Ramallah road. Little development took place toward the south, as the direct connection with Bethlehem was severed.

Most of Jerusalem's Arabs had always lived in the Old City. Great efforts were made to improve their living conditions and raise the standard of public services. Since there was not enough space for commerce and trade, new areas formerly assigned to residential uses in the north of the city were converted to this purpose. The government of Jordan eventually decided to incorporate an area of 34,750 acres (139,000 dunams) for a new outline scheme proposed in 1966 by the British Mandate town planner Henry Kendall, whose main objectives were: residential buildings along the mountain ridge to the north; agriculture in the valleys; heavy industry near Anata; and arterial roads to Ramallah, Bethlehem, and Amman. In adapting the new conditions dictated by the armistice lines, East Jerusalem was forced to abandon its natural economic center in the west and expand to the north, to the south, and to the east (Fig. 3.8).

The new town plan conceived under these circumstances for East Jerusalem was thus based on urban dispersal along the mountain ridge and the development of new settlement nodes on the flat mountain spurs. These nodes were to be linked by means of a main north–south artery, by-passing the Old City. This meant ribbon development along the mountain ridge, and sub-centers with residential and service functions. The entire development was designed as a ring encircling the Israeli part of Jerusalem from the east, while linking the north and the south of the West Bank and connecting the two with Amman. The residential areas were divided into neighborhood units of 1,000 acres (4,000 dunams) each, comprising the vicinity of Qalandiya airport and the villages around it. These units were supposed to include service and industrial centers, parks, residential buildings, and the like. The Mount of Olives was designed as a public open space in the spirit of British former guidelines, and as a site for religious institutions and a nature reserve.

Planning perspectives and problems of the reunited city

On 5 June 1967 another war between Israel and the Arab countries of Egypt, Syria, and Jordan broke out and lasted six days. Shortly after its conclusion, Israeli annexation of East Jerusalem and the Old City brought Jerusalem under a single political control. A new municipal boundary was drawn to include all the uninhabited no-man's land and to incorporate the strategically important areas of Mount Scopus on the northeast and other heights on the south. Military officials and politicians, not planners, made hasty decisions about the exact location of the new boundaries of the reunified city. Two goals guided those decisions: military considerations, especially the inclusion of heights to facilitate defense, and a desire to maximize the amount of territory but to minimize the size of the Arab population.

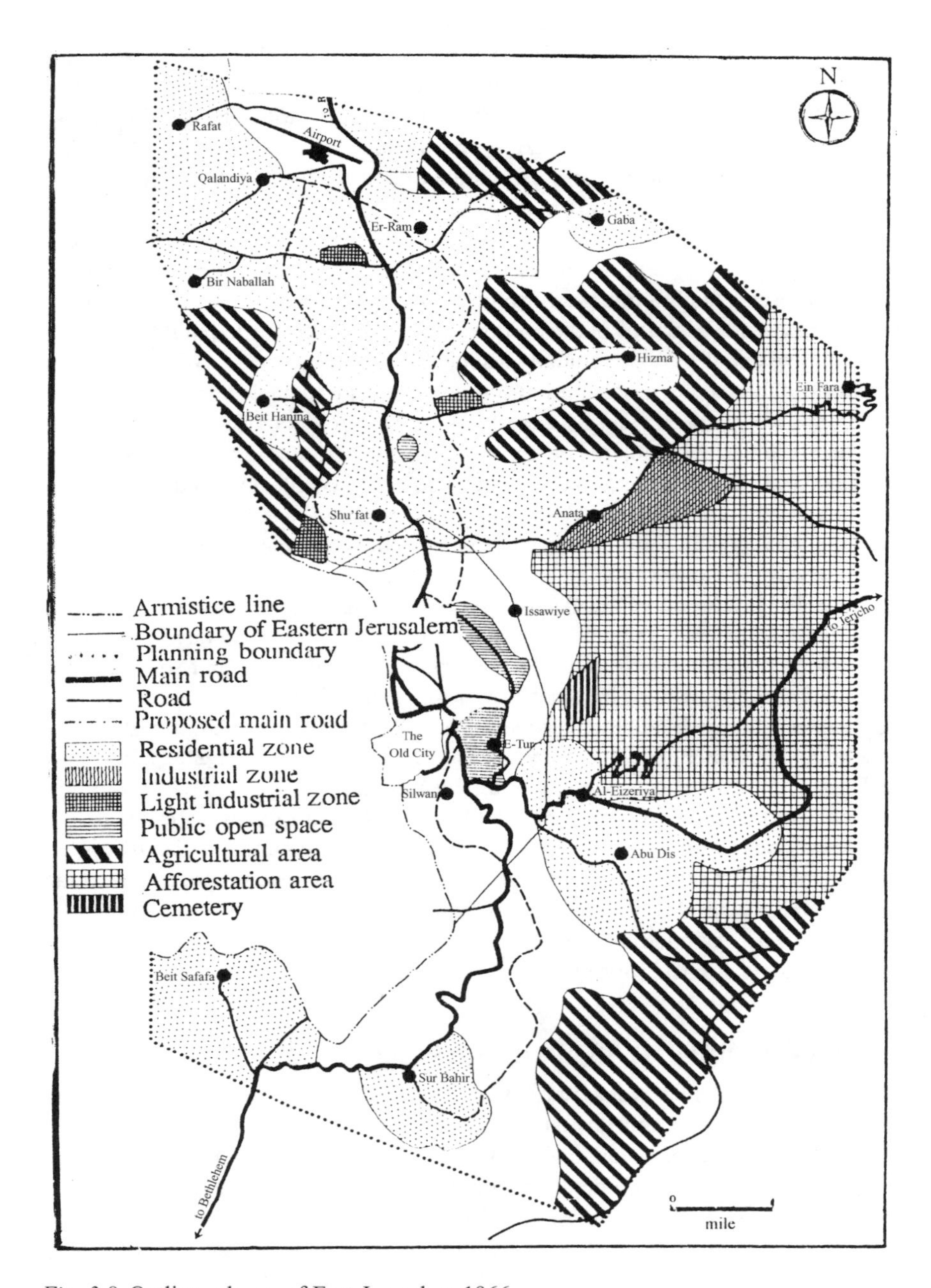

Fig. 3.8 Outline scheme of East Jerusalem 1966

The post-1967 boundaries, especially as compared with those of the divided sections, appeared to be eminently satisfactory. The new eastern boundaries were the same as during the British Mandate, while the western boundaries were those fixed by the 1959 outline scheme. The present boundaries thus comprised the eastern crest – the Mount of Olives and Mount Scopus – the Old City and the village of Silwan, as well as the villages of Sur Bahir, Beit Safafa, and Shu'afat, and the narrow urban strip running north to the Atarot airfield. The city thus had a total area of 26,250 acres (105,000 dunams), about three times its former size, and was planned for 400,000 inhabitants, Jews and Arabs, by the year 1985. The new boundaries were determined mainly by the desire to set up a single geographic entity, to create a geographic security belt, and to secure direct success to the airport – the only one in the Judean–Samaria massif.

The new boundaries of Greater Jerusalem, with their totally different geographic-urban layout, presented the town planners with a fresh challenge. Instead of being a marginal city lying on the eastern end of a narrow corridor, Jerusalem once again straddled the road running along the mountain ridge, with free access from north to south and from east to west. It was no longer confined in its growth to one single direction and now contained considerable land reserves for a large population and for the countrywide functions of a national capital. It was no longer a blind alley, and new traffic arteries could now be developed to connect it with the rural system of Judea and Samaria.

Many proposals have been prepared for the establishment of urban settlements around Jerusalem, as well as urban and semi-urban settlements in different parts of the region. From a social and economic point of view, urban development has the advantage over other kinds of development in being able to absorb many people in a relatively small area. Beginnings at urban settlement were made in East Jerusalem as early as 1967, but it was only in the 1980s that the scale of these developments increased.

After the reunification of Jerusalem it became urgently necessary to make decisions regarding the planning of the city and its environs, but for the first months after the Six Day War there was no clear-cut policy in this respect. No time was lost in pulling down the barriers between the two parts of the city, and the city fathers saw to the immediate physical joining of East and West Jerusalem and to the management of the whole city on the basis of the existing infrastructure. First priority in building and reconstruction was given to those parts of the city where adverse strategic conditions, existing since the War of Independence, needed correction. New quarters were built in the eastern part of the city so as to create a continuous built-up area between the city and Mount Scopus. A decision was also made to rebuild the Jewish quarter of the Old City, independently of any considerations regarding other parts of East Jerusalem.

Shortly afterwards it was decided to build four residential neighborhoods within the new municipal boundaries, two in the north, one in the south, and one in the east. These quarters were built on high ground enclosing the city from these directions. The Jerusalem Municipality also planned the industrial zone of Anatot and began to develop another one near the Atarot airport. These steps were contrary to established planning policy of consolidating the city itself and preventing it spreading over a wide area, but political and historical reasons dictated the steps taken at that time.

After these quarters had been built, Israeli policy-makers turned their attention to ensuring a Jewish majority in Jerusalem. According to the national plan for the dispersion of the population, the population of the Jerusalem district should be not less than 12 per cent of the total population in Israel. The government decided to work toward increasing the population of the city in order to present a numerical balance between Jews and non-Jews, which meant increasing the annual growth rate by 3.7 per cent.

This policy may be termed the "thickening of Jerusalem". Government and other bodies have initiated plans to widen the Jerusalem Corridor northward and southward to provide room around the city and allow future metropolitan development, including new suburbs, rural settlements, and even new towns. The guiding principle in the development of the Jerusalem surroundings was the control of the heights and the traffic crossroads on the mountain backbone. Of particular importance in the view of the planners was control of the main northwest and southwest traffic axes which connect Jerusalem with the lowland and the Coastal Plain.

A comprehensive plan was then drawn preserving the unique archaeological, historical, and architectural character of the Old City while incorporating the holy places in the overall design on the base of the pre-1948 British concept. This plan was the first attempt since the Kendall proposal late in the British Mandate period to regulate development for the entire urbanized area of Jerusalem. The plan was based on the assumption of organic interrelation between three urban entities: the historic nucleus which includes the Old City of Jerusalem, the Mount of Olives, and a surrounding park system; the continuous highly populated urban ring which spreads around the historical center; and a metropolitan area which includes low-density residential areas, agricultural settlements, and small villages. The general aims were to establish an urban structure for a unified city, freely accessible and functionally suitable as the capital of Israel, and to ensure the preservation and enhancement of the historical sites and landscape.

The intention was to plan and build a large city with a considerable growth potential, perched high on the mountains but nevertheless called upon to fulfill major national and country-wide functions. In view of the new demographic structure of Jerusalem, its extended boundaries, and its increased area, profound physical changes were likely to take place which may determine its character for many generations to come. New residential areas were set up and additional public institutions were erected, especially on Mount Scopus and in its vicinity. New industrial zones were established. The environs of the Old City, which continued to be the center of attraction for tourists and visitors, were revamped in a style appropriate to its landscape. The longitudinal axis joining East and West Jerusalem became a center of commerce and tourism and turned into a major traffic artery (Fig. 3.9).

Thus it was obvious that some different planning perspectives had to be applied from those in force between 1948 and 1967. With the removal of the military and

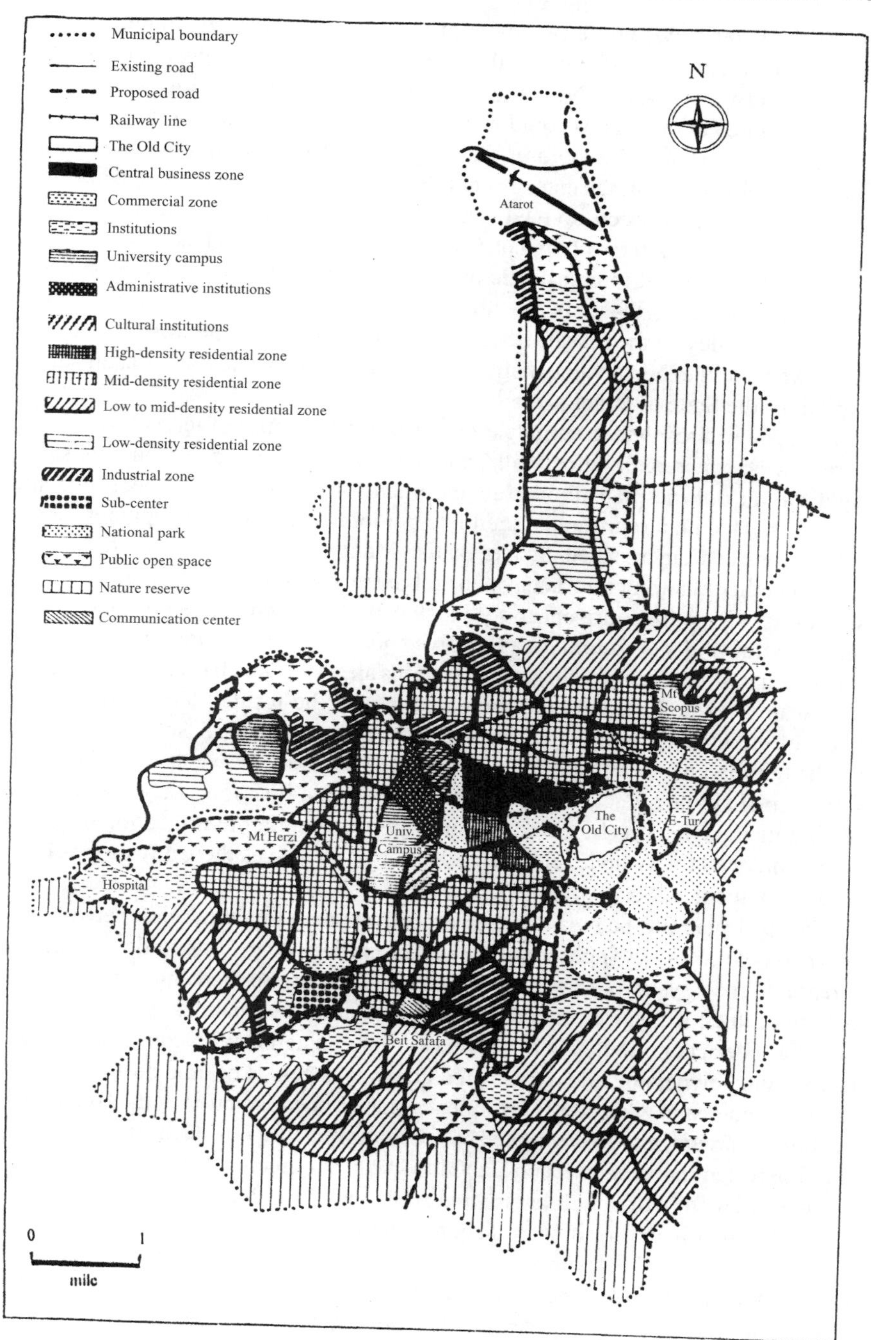

Municipal boundary
Existing road
Proposed road
Railway line
The Old City
Central business zone
Commercial zone
Institutions
University campus
Administrative institutions
Cultural institutions
High-density residential zone
Mid-density residential zone
Low to mid-density residential zone
Low-density residential zone
Industrial zone
Sub-center
National park
Public open space
Nature reserve
Communication center
N
Atarot
Mt Scopus
The Old City
E-Tur
Mt Herzl
Univ. Campus
Hospital
Beit Safafa
0
1
mile

Fig. 3.9 Outline scheme of Jerusalem prepared after 1967

political barrier between the two parts of the city, the extent to which the city's development had been affected by the unnatural conditions imposed upon it had become glaringly evident. Now that the natural physical conditions have been restored, more national roads could operate, especially as the city boundaries were no longer bigger than ever before. The original British idea of a business center integrated with the existing center around the Old City, and with restricted development to the east, has been revived. Thus the city resumed its British traditional course. Already the artery running parallel to the Old City walls has become a main road, where trade and tourist traffic have developed. The city also continued to grow in its natural north–south direction, along the mountain ridge, rather towards the Qidron Valley on the east and the "Jerusalem Corridor" in the west. As a united city it was likely to become the main urban center in Judea and Samaria, and a real capital for the State of Israel.

The 1967 war resulted in complete Jewish political control of Jerusalem. Barbed wire fences, concrete dividing walls, and snipers' nets came down on both sides. By 1968 an outline plan for the development of Jerusalem had been put into operation. This plan represented the first attempt to regulate development for the entire urban settlement since the late British Mandate times. However, the master plan and other planning efforts have not solved many of the problems and divisive situations which have arisen and persisted in Jerusalem. The political act of reunification did not automatically solve the problems of internal division in Jerusalem. Symptomatic of these difficulties is an area which has come to be called the "seam area". The seam represents that part of the former demilitarized zone north of the Damascus Gate of the Old City. The designation "seam" represents the Israeli planners' conception of this area as a binder between East and West Jerusalem. In point of fact, the seam continues today to function as a boundary zone separating the two parts of the city. Thirty-eight years after reunification the seam area remained largely undeveloped, and not until 1981 was there any proposal for its development.

The 1981 plan for the area had four objectives: mending the lesion between the two parts of the city by incorporating it into a unified urban system; developing an integrated road system in the area and ensuring access to the center; designing a pattern of intended land uses; and establishing built form and design principles in the area. The accomplishment of the first of these objectives is complicated by two factors, land ownership and the planned highway access. The land north of the so-called Mandelbaum Gate site is now mostly under the jurisdiction of the Israel Land Authority, having been expropriated by the State after 1967, whereas the land to the south between the Gate site and the Old City has a much more complicated and fragmented pattern of mixed Jewish and Arab, private and institutional ownership, some of which is untraced or in dispute. The United Nations even lays claim to some land and buildings within the zone, although these claims are not considered valid by the Israeli government (Efrat and Noble, 1988).

The other factor is equally vexing. The open space of the seam is an attractive location, because of its low development cost with minimum inconvenience and little impingement upon historical or religious sites, for a highway providing access to both Jerusalem's commercial facilities and to the tourist centers of the Old City. Consequently, Highway 1 is now one of the major features of the seam area. It reinforces rather than diminishes the barrier effect of the seam.

Although politically reunified since 1967, the city of Jerusalem remains economically, culturally, and socially divided. These divisions and disparities present an enormous obstacle to those engaged in the overall planning of the community. Between 1948 and 1967 two cities developed with distinctive systems and philosophies of municipal government, different rates of economic development, contrasting approaches to land uses, independent sets of communications lines, and radically opposed orientations. Although considerable thought and effort have been given to the complete reunification of the city since 1967, the reality is that the divisions still persist. Nowhere is the continued division of the city more clearly revealed than in the pattern of employment. Thousands of Arabs of East Jerusalem work in West Jerusalem, and thousands of Arabs commute daily from the West Bank to Jerusalem for work. Together these two groups of workers make up about 15 per cent of the workforce employed in West Jerusalem. Arab workers are not employed in all fields. One-third work in building and construction, usually as unskilled workers, and another sixth are employed in public services, manufacturing, trade and commerce, and in the hotel industry, again at low levels. In building and construction, Arabs account for about 60 per cent of all workers and in the hotel service about 50 per cent. Many Arab workers have learned Hebrew and have consequently achieved a level of skilled employment, such as ambulance drivers, laboratory technicians, X-ray technicians, or waiters. However, the employment of Arabs in white-collar, management or professional positions is extremely low. Even graduates of institutions of higher education find it very difficult to secure positions in private Jewish organizations and the demand for them in governmental or public institutions is very low.

In practice, two largely separated employment markets exist in Jerusalem – one Arab and one Jewish. The Arab employment market, operating in the Old City and East Jerusalem, is oriented to tourism, trade, commerce, transportation, education, handicraft manufacture, and religious services. White-collar employees are mainly teachers, physicians, pharmacists, engineers, and shopkeepers. In the Jewish market conditions are radically different. Employment is subject to greater governmental regulations and is thus somewhat more secure and usually better paid. On average, salaries in East Jerusalem are about 40 per cent lower than those in West Jerusalem. Jews avoid the lowest paid and least desirable jobs, and, as with the "guest workers" of continental Europe, it is the Arabs who find employment at this level (Romann and Weingrod, 1991).

One consequence of an employment stratification based on religious lines, together with a geographical segregation of residences, is an excessive burden on public transportation facilities. East and West Jerusalem are served by separate bus systems, which necessitate both longer journeys and physical transfers by workers. Furthermore, at present the bus system has very few lines which cross the former no-man's land, which reinforces the earlier division of the city. Other services are similarly affected. Not only are there two bus stations, but there are two central police stations and two police forces. Each part of the city has its own fire brigade, responsible only for its side of the city. The Arab hospitals of East Jerusalem treat only Arab patients; the Jewish hospitals of West Jerusalem treat only Jewish patients, except in very special cases when no medical treatment is possible for patients in East Jerusalem. The supervision which the Israeli government exerts over Arab hospitals is minimal. The educational systems are entirely separate. Instruction is even given in different languages, Hebrew in West Jerusalem and Arabic in East Jerusalem. Perhaps more than any other fact of life, the different education systems perpetuate the division of Jerusalem.

Despite these manifestations of separation, Jews and Arabs do need each other's services and products, but in different ways and in different amounts. Jewish entrepreneurs frequently employ Arab subcontractors to supply workers at below prevailing Jewish rates. Such practices are especially common in footwear manufacture, tailoring and garment-making and the plastic goods industry. Most of these relationships are kept confidential and the public is largely unaware of their widespread existence. Trade and commerce take place more openly. Arabs sell stone products, meat, vegetables, and handicrafts to Jews. Jews sell milk and milk products, bakery goods, cosmetics, petroleum products, and a wide variety of other manufactured items to Arabs.

The Arab population faces a large number of restrictions which have two practical effects: availability of work only as employees of Jewish professionals, and the discouragement of Arab professional training. Arab lawyers are not allowed to represent clients in an Israeli court. Only Jewish architects can submit and receive the approval of building plans. If Jewish engineers are employed, Arabs receive better and more rapid consideration in technical matters before the local municipal authorities. Jewish agents are more successful in getting goods released from customs authorities or in representing Arab clients in tax claim cases. Furthermore, virtually all technical and sophisticated repair services, air conditioning, elevator, and computer services are Jewish. Even in the case of money and finance the separation exists. The Arab banks which persisted in East Jerusalem before 1967 were closed, and only Israeli banks have the right to provide services. The Arab population distrusts not only the Israeli banks but even Israeli currency; they prefer to use Jordanian currency, which circulates freely in East Jerusalem. Money changers, who are allowed to deal in both Israeli shekels and Jordanian dinars, provide the facilities for the conversion of funds by the Arab population.

In view of all these features which divide Jews and Arabs, it is hardly surprising that urban planning efforts in Jerusalem have achieved only partial success, and that most of that success has been in West Jerusalem. Much of the difficulty in reuniting Jerusalem lies in the mutual feelings of suspicion between the two groups and the basic lack of understanding and sympathy for Arab culture by the western-oriented Israeli planners. Fundamental to these considerations are the different ways Arabs and Jews accumulate wealth. Jews build savings in bank accounts, buy stocks and bonds, and favor the investment of savings through financial transactions. Arabs prefer to accumulate wealth by buying land and constructing buildings. Thus they have a fierce attachment to property and resist government attempts to interfere with or regulate private property. In the Arab view, urban planning is the servant of property taxation. Consequently, they resist co-operating with planning officials, even if this prevents them receiving improved municipal services. Because of their strong attachment to small plots of land, their traditional hostility to local authorities, the complicated system of land ownership and tenure common throughout the Muslim world, and the frequent secrecy and informality of land transfers, planning is faced with almost insurmountable barriers. Furthermore, the negotiations to undertake even the most basic and critical projects are substantial and very time-consuming, with the result that Arab planning projects often drag on for several years.

In Jerusalem political unification has not solved social and economical problems and it has not resulted in social unification. In part this is because both sides have been unwilling to compromise. It seems likely that as long as each side receives support from other countries – the Arabs from other Arab nations and the Israelis from the U.S. – the difficulties will persist. The problems in Jerusalem are merely one aspect of the large difficulties as represented by the Arab revolt in the West Bank which began first in December 1987 and for a second time in 2000. The problems are compounded by deep divisions which exist even within Israeli society.

The Jewish–Arab struggle in the city and in its environs

Since the Six Day War unprecedented building activity has been conducted in the Jerusalem area with Arab financing and co-ordination between landowners, former mayors, directors of village councils, and mukhtars. Areas that were neglected were now cultivated, and every month dozens of houses were erected in the vicinity of the city. The demand for workers from among the Arabs of the occupied territories grew in the course of time and the inhabitants of Judea, especially from Mount Hebron, began streaming to the building sites in Jerusalem, and gradually moved into the Old City of Jerusalem with their families, despite its crowded conditions. The original residents then moved into the Old City suburbs. The Arab population of Jerusalem has more than doubled since 1967, and by May 2005 numbered about 230,000.

At the same time the demographic balance in the city has changed. The annual increase in the Jewish population was about half that of the Arab, and the ratio of 73.3 per cent Jews to 28.7 per cent Arabs in 1967 shifted to 67 per cent Jews and 33 per cent Arabs in 2003. This trend has continued since 1969, and figures have accelerated with the government-assisted move of Jerusalem residents to nearby towns beyond the "Green Line" (Table 3.1).

In recent years Arab construction in Jerusalem has also acquired a political tinge. The National Guidance Committee of the Arabs of the occupied territories has urged the inhabitants to plant trees and erect buildings in every place designated for Jewish settlement. The Arab villagers of the West Bank made no distinction between State land and private land. For them both were lands to which the occupation authorities had no right. The areas never operated according to an overall plan, had a long tradition of unauthorized building, and lacked awareness of

Table 3.1 Jewish and Arab population in Jerusalem 1967–2003

	1967	*Percentage*	*2000*	*Percentage*	*2003*	*Percentage*	*Increase (%)*
Jews	196,500	73.3	439,600	66.8	464,500	67	136.3
Arabs	71,300	26.7	217,900	33.2	228,700	33	220.7
Total	267,800	100	657,500	100	693,200	100	158.8

Source: List of Localities, their Population and Code, 31 December 2000, Central Bureau of Statistics and Statistical Abstract of Israel, Jerusalem, 2004.

planning, so that the application of construction regulations there was extremely difficult.

In the northwest villages of Jerusalem a few thousand new buildings have been erected since 1967, and also a few thousand on the mountainside north of Jerusalem. In East Jerusalem the spread of Arab construction and the acquisition of land for building purposes were obvious. South of Jerusalem the pace of growth has been smaller, but there too several hundred units have been added.

This accelerated Arab construction had implications for the future planning and development of Jerusalem. Some routes had to be changed owing to this rapid Arab construction that interrupted the continuity of Israeli spread in many places. Arab construction had spatial and political implications, involving the occupation of considerable territory by a relatively small population, control of important roads connecting Jerusalem with the environs, the placing of obstacles between sites of Jewish development, and the creation of difficulties in providing services (Fig. 3.10).

These developments impelled the Israeli authorities to take preventive measures in the form of confiscating land. Jewish private individuals and public bodies have been acquiring hundreds of acres of land, occupying as much territory as possible in order to ensure orderly construction and development of the region in the future. The settlement and development authorities claimed that, within one or two decades, the settlement policy of the government would prove to be a solution to the establishment of rural and semi-urban settlements, based on a comprehensive regional plan, to the east of the Arab population. It will be effective and be able to compete in size with other Arab concentrations.

Besides the spatial and municipal problems that have arisen between the Jews and the Palestinians in Jerusalem, the most crucial one that exists is the conflict regarding the sovereignty of the Temple Mount, which is a political issue of high importance for the two peoples. The permanent policy of the Chief Rabbinate concerning the Temple Mount is to refrain from allowing Jews access to the Mount for the reason that the Jews in our times are unclean, from the point of view of the Law of Moses, because they are in touch with dead people, and therefore they are not allowed to enter the place where the holy Temple once stood. Over the years the exact location of the Temple has been lost, and anyone entering the Mount could unwittingly enter the area of the Temple and the Holy of Holies. But some rabbis

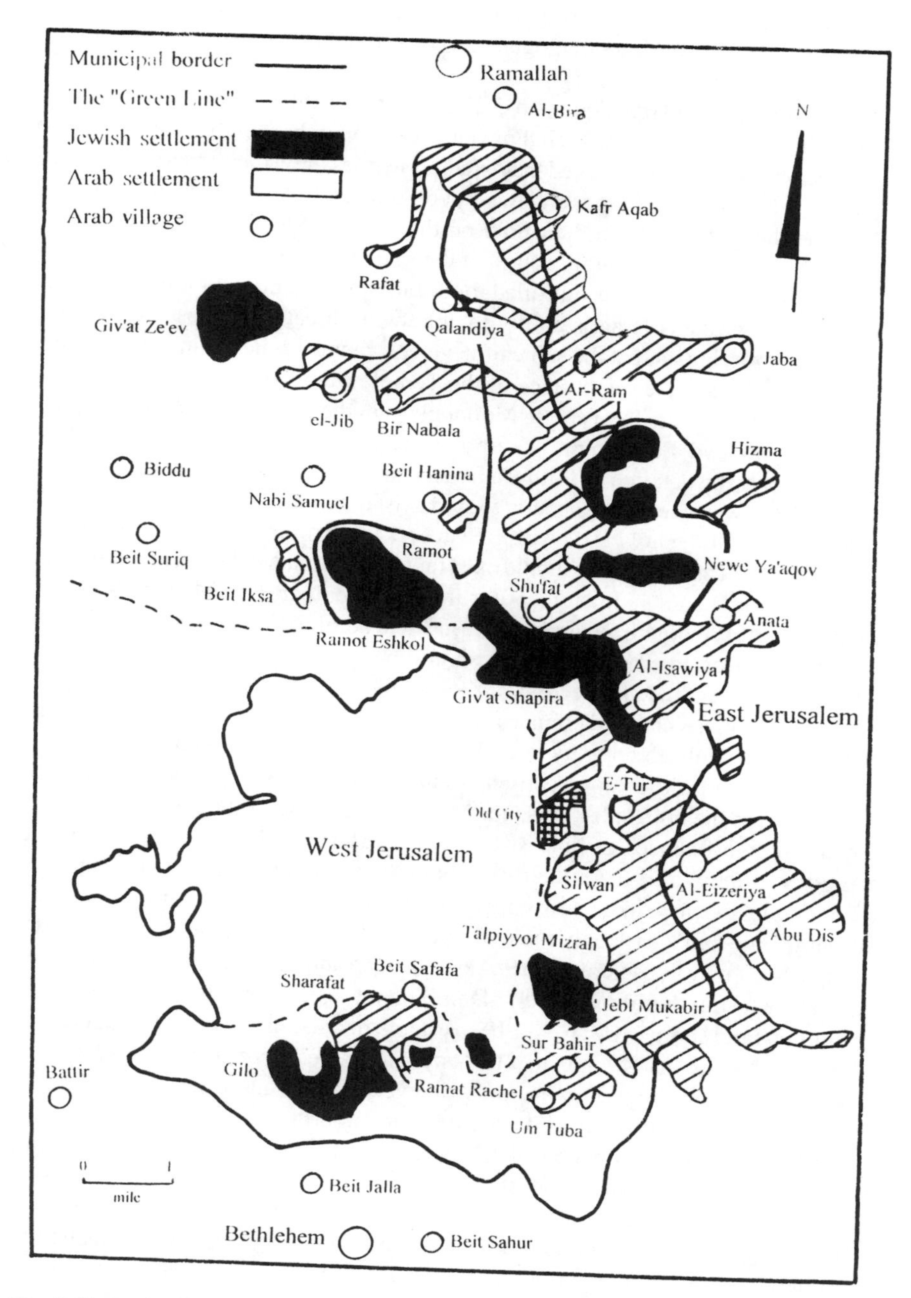

Fig. 3.10 Jewish settlements and Arab villages in East Jerusalem

think that there are some places on the Temple Mount where Jews may stay and pray, and even build there a synagogue, not corresponding to the original site of the holy Temple.

There are rabbis in Jerusalem who declare that the Temple Mount gives strength and ability to whoever possesses it. For years, many members of the Temple Mount movement in Israel have believed that Israel's enemies draw their strength and their ability to threaten and hurt the Jewish people directly from their control over Judaism's holiest site, from their hold on the Temple Mount. According to this theory, the very existence of mosques on the ruins of the Temple and the fact that the Temple Mount has been controlled for decades by Muslim religious authorities permanently weakens Israel's ability to cope with threats and pressure, whether domestic or foreign, and at the same time gives strength to the enemy. Such issues increase very much the importance of the Temple Mount and its surroundings in Jerusalem, and the role the Temple Mount plays in the Israeli–Palestinian dispute.

The Israeli and Palestinian standpoints regarding the holy places in East Jerusalem may be detailed as follows. Israel claims a status quo in all the sites that are holy for Jews; external inspection should exist in these sites; free worship should be allowed in all the holy sites with free access to them; the supreme sovereignty of Israel on the Temple Mount should exist under Palestinian, Islamic, and Jordanian administration; and a similar status for the Holy Sepulcher and for the Christian Quarter should be organized under ecclesiastical administration; responsibility for keeping order on the Temple Mount should be given to the Islamic Waqf with limited Israeli presence for security reasons only.

The Palestinians claim supremacy in the status of the holy Islamic sites in East Jerusalem, and full sovereignty over them. While the standpoints of the two sides are opposite, and while this is a critical issue for the success of any future negotiations between the both sides, it is worth explaining some of the geographical and territorial significances of holy sites for the different religions. Almost all the religions in the world have their own holy sites. There are religions that have sanctified many sites, like Christianity, but there are religions that have sanctified very few: in Islam's case only three: the Ka'aba in Mecca and the two sites on the Temple Mount in Jerusalem, the Al-Aksa Mosque and the Dome of the Rock. The Al-Aksa Mosque building and the Dome of the Rock, and the many religious institutions and shrines which have been established within Al-Aksa throughout its nearly 1,400-year history, are all a testament to the respect that Muslims have for this site. The Jewish religion has only one very important holy site, the Temple Mount and its Western Wall. Holy sites play an important role in religions because they need territory for worship which becomes a holy place where the believers can pray and seek solitude with God.

The attitude of people to religion and territory has some interesting characteristics: most religions need a territorial domain in order to manage worship permanently and effectively; values of religions and beliefs, as a part of culture, have an influence on the way the territory is planned and organized for religious worship; most religions direct their worship and prayers to a certain territory, which is in our case the Land of Israel as the chief designated site for Jews, Muslims, and Christians;

no alternative can be accepted for a holy site, although the believers are dispersed all over the world and migrate from place to place; ethnic religions (passed down in smaller regions and communities) don't have many holy places because their beliefs and traditions are connected with a certain space of historic importance; holy sites are used as the last resort by believers where they are able to express their relations and feelings for God; ethnic religious sites are sometimes to be found close together in cases where historic events have occurred in the same place.

The Middle East is famous as an arena of religious disputes. The striving to dominate the Land of Israel as the cradle of Jewish, Christian, and Muslim religions began long ago in the Roman period. These three religions originated indeed in the same country, but although they were developed later on in different directions, they always expressed in many ways their deep attachment and attitude to this land. For the Jews the ties to the Holy Land of Israel stem from the ethnic-religious fundamentals of Judaism and from the many events in history of the People of Israel which are described in the Bible, and from the origin of customs of the rural Tribes of Israel in ancient times. For the Muslims it is a holy land because according to tradition Muhammad was blessed by the angel Gabriel at the sacred mosque in Mecca and there mounted a white winged beast, Al-Buraq, and sped northwards with Gabriel to Al-Aksa mosque in Jerusalem. For the Christians it is a holy land because history of the life of Jesus Christ is connected with many places in this country. The three religions have a special attitude to the history of the Temple Mount in Jerusalem. The Jews revere it because it was the site where the first Temple was built by King Solomon and was destroyed afterward by the Babylonians in 586 B.C. It is also the site on which, after Cyrus of Persia's declaration, the return to Zion occurred and the Second Temple was built and destroyed by the Romans in 70 A.D. It is therefore a site where two holy Temples were destroyed and only the Western Wall of the Second Temple remained. The Dome of the Rock on the Temple Mount is holy for the Muslims because according to Islamic belief Muhammad went up from this site to heaven, while the Rock on which the Dome was built is also holy to the Jews according to their belief that that was the altar on which Abraham was ready to sacrifice his son Isaac by following God's order. The Al-Aksa Mosque is a holy place for the Muslims because this is the mosque built on the extended southern side of the Mount, oriented towards the central mosque in Mecca, and which is connected with the arrival of Muhammad in Jerusalem. East Jerusalem is holy for the Christians because of the Holy Sepulcher site and the many other places that are connected with the life and death of Jesus Christ.

Despite considerable efforts made by the Israeli government and the municipality to create new and modern city facilities, the artificial reunification of the city has been effected in the same way. The Arabs are not impressed with what has been achieved in the city during the last four decades, and they have expressed their attitude clearly by joining in the uprising. During the conflict the artificiality and basic weakness of the reunification of Jerusalem came as a great surprise to the Jewish leaders in the city. Former mayor Teddy Kollek, often cited elsewhere as a great unifying force in the face of divisions, even had to admit that the delicate state of peaceful coexistence between the Jews and Arabs in Jerusalem has died.

Plate 3.1 The separation fence in Samaria

Because of the uprising of the Arabs, Jerusalem suddenly regressed many years. Along the seam line between East and West Jerusalem, when the armistice line and the no-man's land once divided the city into opposing sections, Arabs attacked Jews with stones, and passing through the streets of East Jerusalem became dangerous for Jews. As a result, fewer Jews visited the Western Wall in the Old City, and none entered the Dome of the Rock, which has become a focus of Arab nationalism. Without a declared war, and after a relatively short time of unrest, the artificial fabric of unity was torn by demographic, geographic, and political realities. Although Jerusalem has been decreed a reunified city, during the uprising it returned to its earlier status as a divided city, divided along the so-called "Green Line". The Israeli illusions of a Greater Jerusalem and a reunified city for the two peoples vanished, probably forever. These facts indicate that the Jerusalem environs are a site of demographic and physical struggle between two populations, aiming at substantive achievements, each with a clear political purpose of holding and controlling the environs of the city.

When countries gain independence, as it happened in Israel in 1948, and may even happen in the future to the Palestinians, the religious fundamentals of a nation become very important in the new political organization of the State. When the State includes in its sovereign territory different minorities which have different religions and traditions, a bone of contention may arise and even lead to national disputes, if religious worship is interfered with. It seems that the Jews and the Palestinians in Jerusalem have many good reasons to hate each other in the conflict regarding the sovereignty of the Temple Mount, and no reasons to like the position of religious neighbors which history has imposed on them.

The Jewish–Arab struggle for the Jerusalem area has a demographic aspect as well. In May 2005 Jerusalem had about 705,000 inhabitants, of whom the Jews numbered 475,000 and the non-Jews about 230,000. Furthermore, the Jewish population of the city is ageing, while the Arab population is becoming younger. The 160,000 Jews who now live in East Jerusalem comprise a third of the total Jewish population in the city. By the extension of the municipal boundaries from 9,500 acres (38,000 dunams) before 1967 to 27,500 acres (1,100,000 dunams) after the Six Day War, about 4,250 acres (17,000 dunams) of land were confiscated by the Israeli authorities for the establishment of seven new Jewish neighborhoods which were built later in the 1970s. Jewish settlement in East Jerusalem was seen as a political act with the aim of establishing the enlarged municipal boundaries. The official guidelines were: not to settle Jews in high-density Arab areas; to keep the permanent demographic ratio between Jews and Arabs around 72 to 28; to occupy maximal land with minimal Arab population; and, above all, to prevent the division of the city in the future. Most of the confiscated land which was added to the city was taken from 28 neighboring Arab villages, and partly from the towns of Bethlehem, Beit Jala, and Al-Bira. As a result of this act, 17 Arab villages were bisected by the new boundary.

In regard to the Jewish areas of settlement in the region, in many places around Jerusalem Jewish settlements were erected. The suburb of Giv'at Ze'ev, for instance, housed about 10,800 inhabitants in 2003. East of Jerusalem the town of Ma'ale Adummim has been rapidly populated, with about 32,000 people by 2005. The Jewish expansion over the region was designed to ensure control of access to Jerusalem, there being no desire to return to the pre-1967 situation, when Jerusalem was a cul-de-sac cut off from its environs.

It should be stressed that thousands of Israelis reside not only in East Jerusalem but also in suburbs and settlements adjacent to the northern, eastern, and southern boundaries. While inside Jerusalem a third of the population is Arab, in the near periphery of the city, between Ramallah in the north and Ma'ale Adummim in the east, or in the so-called "Jerusalem Metropolitan Area", there live about 750,000 people, half of them Jews and half of them Arabs, in separated communities throughout in the whole area.

The Israeli authorities were interested in a rapid construction of housing in Jerusalem and its environs and in a fast Jewish populating of the added areas in the town and its periphery to prevent the isolation of Jerusalem by Arab building in the south, east, and north. In the so-called "influence zone" of Jerusalem, between Ramallah in the north, Hebron in the south, and Bet Shemesh in the west, which is much wider than the above-mentioned Metropolitan Area, there reside about 1,125,000 inhabitants, 55 per cent of them Jews. In Jerusalem itself live 47 per cent of the total "influence zone" population, of whom 72 per cent are Jews and 28 per cent Arabs. It is thought that by the year 2010 the Arab proportion of the population may increase to 31 per cent, as against 69 per cent for Jews, in the "influence zone" of Jerusalem, except for the small part of the western mountainous Corridor, where

90 per cent of the inhabitants are Arabs. The Israeli policy in that case was twofold: to increase the Jewish population in Jerusalem by rapid housing and encouragement of new immigrants to settle there, together with an increase of Jewish population in the periphery, which consists of the metropolitan area and the "zone of influence", by establishing and populating new settlements which belong to the occupied area of Judea. It was intended, actually, to develop an axis of Jewish urban sprawl from Ma'ale Adummim to Jerusalem, and another from the Ezyon bloc to Betar Illit and Jerusalem. The city's head engineer declared in 2005 that it will not be possible to build new residential neighborhoods, or to expand construction of Jewish neighborhoods in East Jerusalem. The implication is that the neighborhood that was designed to create Jewish residential contiguity between Jerusalem and Ma'ale Adummim will not be built. There are at least three reasons why construction of Jewish neighborhoods is no longer possible, according to the engineer's statement, in the eastern part of the city: there is no publicly owned land, other than pockets within already existing neighborhoods; expanding construction would entail large-scale confiscation of private land which in the present geopolitical climate is not feasible; and it would not be right to build Jewish neighborhoods side by side with Arab neighborhoods in Jerusalem.

Partition plans for the holy city

During the first part of the twentieth century, each of the three religions, represented by a Christian, a Jewish, and an Islamic polity, has attempted to determine the orientation of development in the city. The city's particular physical characteristics and the religious aspects of the settlement have produced a unique combination of factors that affect decisions of politicians, regardless of the controlling administration. These conditions are likely to remain influential in the future.

A plan for a political partition of Jerusalem had already existed a decade before the creation of the State of Israel, having been drawn up by none other than the Jewish Agency, the official establishment Zionist body in Palestine presenting the Jewish and Zionist interests to the British authorities. The Jewish Agency's plan for the partition of Jerusalem was a part of its overall reaction to the Royal Commission's plan for the partition of Palestine, which was proposed in 1937.

According to the Royal Commission's proposal, the entire city of Jerusalem, both inside and outside the walls, was to be included within the borders of a British Mandate enclave. The reason for this was that Jerusalem is holy to all religions and it was necessary to guard it as a "sacred trust of civilization". The Jewish Agency Executive clearly realized that there was no chance of British consent to a Zionist demand to include the Old City of Jerusalem, in which all of the places most holy to Judaism are concentrated, within the borders of the Jewish State. The Jewish Agency Executive's position in relation to the New City of Jerusalem, in which the majority of the Jewish population and its institutions were concentrated, was entirely different. It had several reasons to demand the inclusion of the Jewish part of the New City within the prospective Jewish State. Among these was the demographic importance of the New City's population for the future Jewish State. At the same time the population of the New City comprised approximately one-fifth of the Jewish population in Palestine, or 75,000 out of 400,000. In the Old City there were only 4,700 Jews. Other reasons for the inclusion of the New City in the Jewish State were the symbolism of Jerusalem and its centrality in the history of the Jewish people, apart from its being the center of the country's political and cultural life at the time (Efrat, 2000).

On this basis, the Jewish Agency Executive assumed that its demand for inclusion of the Jewish parts of Jerusalem outside the walls within the Jewish State would be amenable to the British government. The Jewish Agency Executive thus drew a boundary line that divided the city into two areas: one characterized by largely Jewish concentrations of population and property, the other where the population and property were mainly non-Jewish. In its proposal the Jewish Agency Executive gave up the Jewish holy places in the eastern part of the city including Temple Mount, Mount Zion, the Wailing Wall and the Mount of Olives. The Jewish Agency Executive also forwent the Jewish Quarter inside the walls of the Old City. On the other hand, Mount Scopus, where the Hebrew University complex had been built, was included in the borders of the Jewish area.

In deciding to accept the plan for partition in principle, the Zionist Organization demonstrated the political pragmatism of its leaders, who were prepared to detach the holiest sites in Judaism, the Wailing Wall, the Temple Mount, and the Mount of Olives, from the Jewish State to be. It is arguable that the Jewish Agency's plan for the partition of Jerusalem, while giving up the Old City, sowed the seeds to its agreement a decade later to the internationalization of Jerusalem in accordance with the U.N. Partition Resolution, and its subsequent acquiescence in the partition of the city following the 1948 war (Katz, 1993).

As said above, from1948 to 1967 Jerusalem was politically and religiously a divided city. The armistice line in 1949 confirmed the city's partition and created a neutral zone to be administered by the United Nations between the Jordanian and the Israeli military positions. That no-man's land comprised seven areas, but, along most of the dividing line, hostile positions were immediately adjacent to each other. The armistice line ran through land that was open, undeveloped, or occupied by former roads. The Jordanian army occupied the Old City and East Jerusalem, and the Israeli army controlled Mount Zion, West Jerusalem, and an important enclave on Mount Scopus.

Following the 1967 Six Day War, demonstrating sensitivity to the holy places in the Jerusalem area, Israel proposed that they be granted the status of diplomatic missions. Christian and Muslim clerics serving at the holy places were to be granted a special status, similar to that of diplomatic representatives; Jordan would be considered the "accrediting state" of the Muslim clerics, and the Vatican the "accrediting state" of Christian clerics; and each holy place would constitute a separate and distinct entity with respect to these communities.

A proposal prepared in July 1968 by the advisor to the mayor of East Jerusalem was made with a view to creating a unified zone for the areas within the sphere of influence of metropolitan Jerusalem, and serving as a proper framework for the city's development, establishing independent municipal units within the framework of the extended municipal area, with due attention to the types of settlements it contained and to the desire of the minorities for self-government in East Jerusalem, and making an attempt to meet the Arabs' request for controlling part of Jerusalem while ensuring Israeli sovereignty over the territory within the city's current boundaries. The means to this end were the delimitations of municipal boundaries which would include territories under Israeli and Jordanian sovereignty; the creation of a joint umbrella council for five boroughs (Jewish Jerusalem, Arab Jerusalem, the villages, Bethlehem, and Beit Jala); the granting of limited autonomy to the Jerusalem Arab borough and the village sector, with some of the villages placed under Jordanian sovereignty. The Jewish borough was to include the entire Jewish city, a well as a strip between Sanhedriyya and Mount Scopus, the Old City's Jewish and Armenian Quarters, the Mount of Olives, the City of David, East Talpiyyot–Ramat Rachel area, Mar Elias monastery, Beit Safafa area and Newe Ya'aqov area. This territory was to ensure development and settlement of about 100,000 people, of whom no more than 9,000 would be Arabs, and to be entirely under Israeli sovereignty. For their part, the Arab boroughs were to include the Old City's Muslim and Christian quarters, Sheikh Jarrah, the American colony, Wadi Joz, Shu'afat, urban Beit Hanina and Silwan – all currently under Israeli sovereignty – and Al-Eizeriya and Abu Dis, which were not under Israeli sovereignty. The villages' borough was to include the semi-agricultural villages around the city, some of which would be under Israeli sovereignty, others under Jordanian sovereignty. The Bethlehem and Beit Jala boroughs were to include their municipal areas.

The Greater Jerusalem Council had to deal with the preparation of the program and daily running of the boroughs, as well as with regional and rural development, economy and tourism, fire-fighting, regional sewerage and water projects, and transportation and housing. The State authorities would have the power to annul any decision relating to their sovereign sphere. In 1969, at the height of the Egyptian–Israeli war of attrition, a plan for the solution of the Arab–Israeli conflict was put forward by William Rogers, then the U.S. Secretary of State, only to be rejected by both Egypt and Israel. One of the reasons for Israel's negative reaction was that the plan did not stipulate that Jerusalem would remain under Israeli rule. Rather it stated that the United States would not accept unilateral actions by any party regarding the city's final status, which could be determined only by agreement of all concerned parties, primarily Jordan and Israel, taking into account the interest of other countries in the area and the international community at large. According to the plan, Jerusalem would remain unified, with open access to the unified city for persons of all faiths and nationalities. The plan did not specifically refer to the holy places but did note the need to ensure free access to the city and to take into account the interest of all its inhabitants and of the Jewish, Muslim, and Christian communities in the city's administration.

In 1991–92 a group of Israelis and Palestinians co-operating within a research project published a proposal suggesting that Jerusalem's territory should be quadrupled by the incorporation of almost equal amounts of territory from Israel and the West Bank. The new metropolis would include Ramallah in the north, Mevasseret Ziyyon in the west, Bethlehem in the south, and Ma'ale Adummim in the east. With these new boundaries Jerusalem would have a population of some 800,000, almost equally divided between Jews and Arabs. This population balance would be maintained in the future by means of an immigration policy based on an annual increase of no more than 3 per cent. Metropolitan Jerusalem would then be divided into 20 municipalities; the government of Israel and the prospective Palestinian State would still handle most matters normally vested in national authorities and would maintain dual jurisdiction to adjudicate in the metropolis. The citizenship of the metropolitan city's residents would be determined by the area in which they happened to live, and there would be one physically open area with no checkpoints or physical barriers. The Old City would form its own municipality and be run by a city council, with decisions regarding physical planning and development approved unanimously by its residents and each faith having full administrative power over its holy sites.

Two years later, in June 1994, the Israel–Palestine Center for Research and Information similarly proposed that Jerusalem should not be physically divided and should preserve its open character. Separate areas would be created, based on the composition of the population, in which Israeli and Palestinian authorities would respectively be vested with limited sovereignty, whereas sovereignty over the Old City would be entirely relinquished by both sides with each community maintaining its legal system in those areas where it enjoyed a demographic majority according to the boundaries between municipalities and boroughs. The holy places, as well as religious buildings and sites, would not be under the national sovereignty of either Israel or Palestine. The two municipalities would establish a joint planning commission to liaise between the various religious authorities.

In 1995 three maps, prepared by the Jerusalem Institute for Israeli Studies and describing alternative plans for the final solution in Jerusalem, were passed by governmental officials to the Palestinian Authority. In one of these maps the recognition of Palestinian sovereignty in East Jerusalem was clearly expressed, but also the annexation to Israel of certain territories such as the Ezyon bloc, Ma'ale Adummim, Giv'at Ze'ev, and Betar. The plan suggested five alternatives for Palestinian sovereignty in East Jerusalem, from the easy to the difficult:

(1) Sovereignty over a limited area, along the fringe line of Jerusalem's municipal boundary. East Jerusalem would be connected by a strip of land to the Palestinian territories, to be partly used as a Palestinian government compound. This fringe line might include some villages at the southeast part of the city; the eastern part of the Mount of Olives and its near surroundings; and in the northern part Shu'afat, Beit Hanina, and Kafr Aqeb. All other Arab neighborhoods were to remain under Israeli sovereignty.

(2) Sovereignty in East Jerusalem, excluding its Jewish neighborhoods and the Jewish Quarter in the Old City. The other parts of East Jerusalem, together with the Old City, the Mount of Olives and the Town of David, which contain the most important sites for the three religions, would receive a special status of suspended sovereignty or condominium.

(3) Sovereignty over East Jerusalem, excluding the Jewish neighborhoods and the Old City which would remain under Israeli sovereignty.

(4) Sovereignty over East Jerusalem, excluding the Jewish neighborhoods, the Jewish cemetery on the Mount of Olives, the Town of David, West Jerusalem, and a strip of land connecting the Ezyon bloc to Israel.

(5) Sovereignty in West Jerusalem, excluding the Jewish neighborhoods.

The advantages of these alternatives, from the Israeli point of view, were as follows: reconciliation with the Palestinian, and the Muslim world, and a greater chance to achieve a long-term stable peace agreement; preservation of Israeli sovereignty in the Jewish neighborhoods of East Jerusalem, including the Jewish Quarter, and a substantial part of East Jerusalem; Palestinian recognition of Israel's sovereignty over most parts of the city, including the new neighborhoods built after 1967 and consisting of some 260,000 inhabitants; a possible territorial exchange in return for the connection of Ma'ale Adummim and Giv'at Ze'ev to Jerusalem, and a connection of the Ezyon bloc to Israel after Israel's surrender of all the Arab areas in East Jerusalem; no need for a physical division of Jerusalem and assurance of free access to all parts of the city without disrupting the economic fabric, and without the need to rule the 230,000 Palestinians living in East Jerusalem; the security in the city and its foreign affairs would be kept under Israel's authority; the possibility of gradual long-term progression towards Palestinian sovereignty, starting with a limited government compound as an interim arrangement to a bigger part in East Jerusalem, excluding neighborhoods, as a final agreement.

The plan's disadvantages for Israel were as follows: with the functioning of two political capitals in Jerusalem, the Jewish nature of the city would be diminished and its political status as a Jewish domain might be undermined; Palestinian sovereignty would be established on the Temple Mount, which is a holy place for the Jews; the running of a mutual administration and policing was bound to be complicated and to generate conflicts between the two communities.

Another plan prepared by the same institute took for granted the existing situation in the city, created since the Six Day War, and was based on the assumption that the municipal area of Jerusalem would remain under Israeli sovereignty. Exchange of areas by mutual agreement between Israel and the Palestinians, because of pragmatic and municipal reasons, would be possible.

The advantages of this latter plan were as follows: protection of Jerusalem as a Jewish entity; reinforcement of the idea among Israelis and Jews that other alternatives might weaken Israeli sovereignty in Jerusalem, aggravate tension and violence between Arabs and Jews, and create breaches that could not be healed; the plan might be used as a provisional step in a situation of disagreement between the two sides, enabling a return to other alternatives once the Palestinian entity had proved its stability as a political and democratic body.

The weaknesses of this plan were formidable indeed: it was totally unacceptable to the Palestinians; it might be an obstacle to the Israeli–Palestinian peace negotiations; it was unacceptable to the Arab States and could endanger the peace negotiations with them; it might strain American–Israeli relations; and it might create agitation and ignite a new uprising in the territories.

Yet another plan was similarly based on the assumption that Israel would have exclusive sovereignty in Jerusalem in its present municipal boundaries. In the framework of a mutual agreement, the exchange of limited areas in the city with territories in Judea might be possible; a symbolic center of sovereignty for the Palestinians in the city might be approved; the Temple Mount would be under the super-sovereignty of Israel and the Palestinian–Islamic–Jordanian administration; a similar status would be given to the Church of the Holy Sepulcher and to the Christian Quarter in the Old City; the Armenian Quarter would get a special status, as would the area between the walls and the near surroundings of the Old City.

The aim of this latter plan was to administer functional autonomy under Israeli sovereignty in all quarters of East Jerusalem. Such autonomy would include among other things collecting domestic taxes, administration of borough councils with permanent staff members, culture, education, sport, social services, gardening, health, and religious services.

The idea of functional autonomy had been already accepted in principle by different institutions and organizations involved in Jerusalem's political future. The idea was to delegate some important powers to borough administrations, to develop in them some domestic security with civil guard and to encourage their independence vis-à-vis the municipal authority. Borough administration would be established in all parts of the city, allowing in turn the creation of a sub-municipality for the Old City with an inter-religious and international council.

In this plan it was also recommended that the existing system of borough administration would be dispersed to all city neighborhoods. The administration in the Old City would be established on the basis of the ethnic and religious composition of the inhabitants. The boundaries of each borough would be delineated in consultation with the residents' representatives.

Functional autonomy for the boroughs may have a good chance of being accepted. The present situation in the city is unacceptable to the Palestinians, while recognition of Palestinian sovereignty in East Jerusalem is not agreed by many Israelis. This plan, however, is flexible. It enables proposals for different kinds of arrangements between the two communities, and can be executed gradually according to future circumstances. Its main deficiency, though, is that, if the rules are not strictly observed, it may lead to a weakening of Israel's sovereignty in the city.

For the negotiations which were held in Camp David in September 2000, the Jerusalem Institute for Israel Studies prepared a series of plans, as a basis for a final agreement to be reached between the Israelis and the Palestinians regarding the future situation in Jerusalem. The plans included three alternatives for a territorial solution in the town from Israel's viewpoint, but taking into account different proposals for sharing Israeli and Arab sovereignty.

The first plan described a situation in which Jerusalem would remain, more or less, in its current municipal boundaries under Israel's sovereignty. The access between the Israeli and the Palestinian sides of the town would remain open and free for all people as in the current status quo. This alternative was mostly a continuation of the existing situation at that time, but was expected to be unacceptable to the Palestinians.

A second plan proposed that Jerusalem would still remain under Israel's sovereignty, but with a possible exchange of small areas along the borderline with Judea and Samaria, a region that is now under Palestinian authority. A symbolic sovereign capital center would be established for the Palestinians in Jerusalem to run their administration. The Dome of the Rock and the holy sites on the Temple Mount would be under Israel's sovereignty, but under Islamic, Jordanian, and Palestinian administration. A special status would be given to the Old City, including free access to the holy sites between the walls for all religions.

A third plan proposed the partition of Jerusalem into two capitals, with Palestinian sovereignty in East Jerusalem and Israeli on the western side. Even according to this plan the town would remain without inner physical barriers. Following this alternative a supreme municipality could be established with two municipal branches, one for each side, which would enable them to deal together with common problems in one place, and with particular problems of each side, in the others.

These three plans were submitted to the Israeli governmental authorities as a basis for their decision-making towards the negotiations, in order to reach agreement with a compromise as a possible solution.

In addition to these three plans, in April 2005 the Israeli government was considering again the approval of a former plan named E-1 to connect the town of Ma'ale Adummim to Jerusalem by building 3,500 dwelling units on an area that extends between them, and in so doing block the territorial connection between the northern and southern parts of the West Bank. There is no doubt that such a building project seems illogical from any municipal town planning point of view. At the establishment of Ma'ale Adummim in 1978 east of Jerusalem there was no intention to connect it to Jerusalem and not even to expand its territory toward the steep slopes that descend from the Jerusalem mountain crest. The town was established as an urban settlement adjacent to the Jerusalem–Jericho highway at a distance of 9.3 miles (15 km) from the capital. It was located on an area of 8,000 acres (36,000 dunams) with the aim of preventing the eastwards expansion of the Arab villages Abu Dis and Al-Eizeriya and to function as an Israeli urban outpost east of Jerusalem and opposite the Judean Desert and Transjordan. An industrial zone of an area of 250 acres (1,000 dunams) was allocated nearby for Jerusalem's industries and for workers who preferred to live in that new region. In March 1980 an outline scheme for the building of 5,000 dwelling units on an area of 400 acres (1,600 dunams) had been approved by the government for that settlement. Because of topographical difficulties the houses were built on the top of the ridges with deep wadis dissecting them from all sides. Ma'ale Adummim functioned as an independent municipality in its desert surroundings without any intention to extend westward. Recently, some politicians in the government have supposed that the new highway built to connect the town to Jerusalem in order to allow easier daily commuting for the citizens could be a good reason to use it as a new housing axis between the two cities.

The eastern side of Jerusalem was never planned to be moved out toward the Judean Desert. The British Mandatory outline scheme of 1944 did not allocate any housing zones east of Mount Scopus and the Mount of Olives. The British planning

Plate 3.2 An Israeli checkpoint in Judea

conception regarding the city was limited building expansion on the mountain crest only and eventual development of neighborhoods on flat ridges that should be connected by a main north–south road and by one connection axis eastward to Jericho for communications only. The conception of the British, and later on of the Jordanians, was building along the crest without any expansion sideways. The Israeli E-1 plan should be seen, therefore, as a political plan that stands against accepted building rules that had existed regarding the surroundings of Jerusalem for many years. The extension of Ma'ale Adummim westward on topographical differences of 450–600 ft (150–200 m), at a distance of a few thousand feet, is one of the expansion plans that should be rejected.

The Jerusalem municipality approved in 2004 a western construction plan for the city with the aim of enlarging the built-up area of Jerusalem and to make possible extensive building on Lavan Ridge and Mount Heret, west of the city, a part of the Jerusalem Mountains facing the Jerusalem Corridor. The plan also proposes building near the Arazim Valley at the entrance to the city, and adjacent to Hadassah University Hospital in the En Kerem neighborhood. If the plan is executed, some twenty thousand residential dwelling units will be built, and half a million square feet of industrial and commercial space, infrastructure, and bridges over 10.1 sq. miles (26 sq. km) of natural woodland and forests in the western part of the city. The different projects which are a part of this large plan address the impact on the western borderline of the city. The approval of the western Jerusalem plan means that the Jerusalem municipality, the District Planning Commission and the Israel Lands Administration have abandoned the possibility of strengthening the existing old parts of the city. They suppose that the convenient solution to the many difficulties involved in evacuating areas for building inside the city is to build on open spaces. The Jerusalem municipality maintains that it is continuing to strengthen the city core and that the westward expansion is needed in any case.

The "green" organizations in Israel, which consistently object to building plans, and a broad front of residents of the city and surrounding communities, along with a number of groups concerned with social issues, demonstrated on many occasions against this plan. Hundreds of objections were submitted and thousands of people signed petitions warning of the environmental damage that will ensue if the program is implemented. Objections ranged from the part the project will play in the continued weakening of the inner city to the waste of infrastructure and the damage to the city's strength. In order to save some of the open spaces, the "green" organizations handed the advocates of building a concession by agreeing to a move in which they affectively accept the majority of the building plans initiated by the municipality, in return for the authorities' agreement to preserve part of the territory intact and fence it off as a national park. This will be in addition to the areas in the region that already have a protected status. The hope was that the creation of a line of national parks, forests, and nature reserves would set a final limit on the expansion of Jerusalem and prevent additional destruction of open spaces in the future. Unfortunately, the agreement was annulled after the green organizations discovered that the building plans had been changed in a way that eliminated their achievements.

There is now a danger that Jerusalem is probably going to lose extensive open spaces which will be destroyed, and along with them the distinctive landscape, which is created by its very separation from the surrounding hills and valleys. The importance of these areas has grown in the wake of the plans to build the separation fence, which further reduces the continuity of open spaces in the region and enhances the importance of the area inside the "Green Line". The expansion to the west will not solve any acute municipal and social problems within the existing city, but will only draw more resources to the new areas. It will encourage an additional large population to look for homes in new neighborhoods, where the living standard will be higher. There is no proof that the new neighborhoods will have an effect on the old parts of Jerusalem that have been left behind; it is more than likely that the opposite process will occur, because strong populations have a tendency to segregate themselves in order to preserve their quality of life, and they will turn the new neighborhoods into a different kind of city.

The government and the municipal authorities leaders suggest that the basis for this plan should be primarily demographic; the goal of expanding the capital is to keep the 70 per cent Jewish majority, and in light of the great sensitivity of the balance between various groups that make up the human mosaic of Jerusalem, secular and ultra-Orthodox Jews and Arabs, it is hard to imagine a situation whereby it would be decided to freeze development in the city. Jerusalem is experiencing negative population growth and the Jewish population is being reduced by 8,000 people every year; under these circumstances Jerusalem will lose about 120,000 Jews by 2020. But the reality is a challenge to this belief. Since 1967 the so-called need for expansion has turned Jerusalem from a small and compact city to a political-demographic monster that swallows up land and satellite towns, and has provided no balance to its weakening.

The expected investment in the plan should be directed to strengthening the existing city, especially the weaker ultra-Orthodox and Arab sectors. They should be transformed from a threat that banishes secular families to the westward hills into a legitimate part of the population. Such a population seems to be the real hope for the future of Jerusalem. There is no doubt that investment in infrastructure and education, in cleaning up the city, in creating jobs and building parks, combined with an effort to overcome difficulties on the road to getting building plans within the city approved, is the correct method of strengthening the existing city.

These facts indicate that Jerusalem is a site of demographic and physical competition between two populations, with the clear political purpose of holding and controlling the city and its adjacent environs. It may be assumed that, without a mutually agreed comprehensive political plan and rapid systematic implementation of important aspects of it, Israel will not be able to safeguard the city as a capital. It is also clear that the city's reunification in 1967 did not bring an end to the division between Jews and Arabs. The animosities are deep and have survived the recent geographical shifts. None of the different partition plans of Jerusalem will ensure the city's normal functioning. It is also doubtful whether these plans will allow Jerusalem to remain a universal capital as opposed to a mere spatial political arena where two peoples find themselves embraced in hatred without any logical solution.

While in a normal city, especially a capital, the boundaries usually conform to topography, building zones, homogeneous neighborhoods, efficient arteries that connect vital sites to their surroundings and economic sites with optimal places, in Jerusalem the opposite situation exists. The possibility of partial sovereignty, suspended sovereignty, or a common functional sovereignty will never be an optimal solution for the city. The proposed plans demonstrate, after all, that Jerusalem has become an urban mosaic of distorted decisions unparalleled elsewhere in the world. It seems that Jerusalem has actually become a part of the territory of Judea and Samaria and may be eventually included in some of the categories of the Oslo Accords for the purpose of partition.

Jerusalem had not yet by 2004 prepared an official and approved outline scheme for the city. Meanwhile, many partial and local town plans are prepared and approved from time to time by the municipality council, which very often need changes because of political and demographic events in the area.

In the framework of the preparation of a new master plan, the municipality is keen to enlarge its jurisdictional area to the west, and to move some parts of the Jerusalem district westward in order to get more space for another 75,000 dwelling units, industrial zones, and employment centers for its growing population. The intention is, for instance, to change the small village of Zur Hadassah into a town, to establish the Bat Harim new town with 30,000 dwelling units, to extend the suburbs of Mevasseret Ziyyon, to add housing plots in some villages of the Judean Mountains, which lie west of the city, and to convert agricultural land into building areas. Other projects include the construction of a new main ring road in East and West Jerusalem, the establishment of new neighborhood centers in many parts of the town, more institutions, commercial centers, and other needed facilities. The municipality is also keen to integrate all the partial plans and projects into an urban fabric, so that by the year 2020 about 60 per cent of Jerusalem's population will be Jewish and 40 per cent will be Arab.

In 2004 Jerusalem officials who unveiled the new master plan for the city, the first since 1959, also called for massive intervention in the Old City. The plan envisioned using government funds to offer alternative housing outside the Old City walls to interested Old City residents. The plan involved thinning out the population in all quarters of the Old City, except the only part restored so far, the Jewish Quarter, as a means of slowing down the rapid population growth. The plan noted that a great deal of the illegal construction in the Old City takes place in interior courtyards and on the roofs of existing structures, especially in the Muslim Quarter but also in the Christian and Armenian Quarters. It called for the reconstruction of the Anata refugee camp in northern Jerusalem, although, according to ideas put forward by Israeli politicians in recent years, Anata will not be within the Jerusalem city limits and will be transferred to the Palestinian Authority. The plan also proposed tripling the size of neighborhood parks, which cover an area of 660 acres (2,640 dunams). The plan recommended keeping the present skyline, with its view of the city's landmarks. It limited the height of buildings in some areas, while allowing high-rise construction in others.

The four-decade-long territorial conflict in Jerusalem has disestablished the special urban properties of the city to the point of making it a "no city". Further expansion of the city to its periphery will only exacerbate the problems. Any decision on the city's future should be based on the ethnic composition of neighborhoods with minimal friction between Arabs and Jews, so as to maintain Jewish and Arab neighborhoods as independent entities and to protect the Jewish nature of the city in those parts where the majority of Jews live. Should this not be achieved, one might be forced to return to the idea expressed by the late King Hussein of Jordan whereby "Jerusalem belongs to God and not to people".

4 The Gaza Strip – from Jewish bloc-settlement to disengagement

Background

The term "Gaza Strip" dates from the last stages of the 1948 war between Israel and the Arabs. It received political validity in the 1949 Armistice Agreement between Israel and Egypt, when it was recognized as a separate entity under Egyptian supervision. The political existence of the Strip was terminated by the Six Day War in 1967, which brought it under Israeli military administration. The final decision about its future was made in 2004 by the Israeli government, which decided that an entire Jewish disengagement from the Gaza Strip will be carried out by the end of the year 2005.

Three geographical sub-regions can be distinguished, running parallel to the coastline in the Gaza Strip. They are, from west to east, sand dunes, agricultural land, and sandstone ridges. These sub-regions greatly influence the human-geographical formation of the Gaza Strip, and the development of the settlement, the economy, and the communications in this area. The dune belt in this region is similar to that west of the Judean Plain. It reaches an average of 3.1–4.3 miles (5–7 km), and is continuous, save for one gap near Dahir el-Balah. The dunes are 30–60 ft (10–20 m) high, rising in some places to as much as 150 to 180 ft (50 to 60 m). Patches of cultivated land are to be found within the confines of the dune belt, particularly in the flat portion of the Strip. Parallel to the coastline is the "Coastal Depression", which contains few cultivated patches. The agricultural belt in the central part of the Gaza Strip is the southern continuation of the Coastal Depression, which extends in a north–south direction parallel to the Coastal Plain of Israel. The agricultural soil found in this area has been deposited throughout the ages by streams and wadis, whose drainage area lies in the western Negev.

The sandstone ridges bounding the Gaza Strip in the east reach a height of 210–240 ft (70–80 m). In the past they probably formed a continuous barrier, which was later breached by streams, thus creating a number of separate ridges. This geographical formation has a bearing on the water resources and the soil quality of this region. As we progress southwards the proportion of sand to loess in the soil increases, until south of Rafah we find only sand. This soil composition accounts for the formation of shallow ground water, which can be tapped near the surface, especially in the region of the Coastal Depression, or where it borders on the sands.

The groundwater potential of the Gaza Strip was once fairly high, and it is not surprising that over one thousand wells supplied water for irrigation. Between 1948 and 1967 the sinking and operating of wells in the Strip was not subject to government control, and excessive pumping caused intrusion of sea water and the salinating of wells. The Gaza Strip's length is about 29 miles (46 km), and its width is 3–4 miles (5–6.5 km) in the northern section, with a maximum of 8 miles (13 km) at the southern end. The area of the Gaza Strip totals 145 sq. miles (363 sq. km).

With the emergence of the Gaza Strip as a political entity its population underwent profound changes. To the existing sixty to seventy thousand inhabitants at the end of 1947 were added large numbers of Arabs who had, as result of the war, abandoned their villages, towns, and Bedouin encampments in the southern Coastal Plain and the Negev. The refugees swelled the population figure to an estimated 200,000, practically all of them Arabs and the overwhelming majority of Muslim faith. According to the Egyptian 1966 estimate there were 454,960 inhabitants in the Gaza Strip, while 354,000 were actually registered by the Israeli census in 1967. Together with northern Sinai, the figure was then 390,000. By the end of 1968, the population of the Gaza Strip and northern Sinai had decreased to 356,000, this development being attributed to emigration, principally to Jordan. Even after the true figures have been established, the fact remains that the Gaza Strip is today one of the most densely populated areas in the world, averaging 6,200 inhabitants per sq. mile (2,422 per sq. km). The Gaza Strip population differs from that of any other world region in that refugees make up an absolute majority. The 1967 census revealed that families whose heads were born in areas held by Israel since 1949 numbered 207,250 persons, i.e. 58.9 per cent of the total population. Of these, however, only 149,396 lived in refugee camps, while the rest had established their homes in villages and towns.

Another feature distinguishing the Gaza Strip from other Arab regions is the extremely high percentage of urban population. In the census, urban settlements accounted for 282,803 inhabitants or 79.9 per cent of the overall population of the Gaza Strip. Even if the camps are excluded from the calculation, there were 149,890 town dwellers, as against 31,368 villagers. It was found that the birth rate in the Gaza Strip is very high, with the 0–14 years group constituting over half of the population.

Although most of the Gaza Strip population resides in urban areas, farming provides the principal source of income. Not only villagers but also urban dwellers work variously sized parcels of land. Prior to 1967, the Gaza Strip had practically no serious industrial enterprises employing up-to-date working methods. On the other hand, there were numerous small shops, particularly in traditional crafts such as pottery, weaving, food processing, etc. Commerce and mostly small retail shops provided employment for a considerable number of people, especially in urban communities.

As a result of the great population density, the strain on existing soil and water resources is enormous. Every stretch of land fit for cultivation is exploited. This is true even on sand dunes, wherever more fertile soil is hidden at a shallow depth beneath the sand. Out of the 145 sq. miles (363 sq. km) of the Gaza Strip, 107 sq. miles (267 sq. km) were under cultivation in 1967. The composition of the soil in the Gaza Strip determines the geographical distribution of the varieties of agricultural crops. In the north, with a high concentration of dark brown soil, there are mainly citrus plantations; in the central region there are field crops, with few citrus and other plantations; while in the south, where the soil contains loess with sand, we have watermelons, field crops, and dates, as well as other crops tolerant of a certain degree of salinity. As we progress southwards, the grazing area increases. Irrigated crops in 1967 covered 13,700 hectares (137,000 dunams), with citrus groves heading the list with 9,200 hectares (92,000 dunams). This branch of agriculture, which has expanded in the Gaza Strip mainly during the last three decades, produces the principal export item of the area, amounting to two to four million standard cases of fruit annually. Until recently, East European countries were the main customers for Gaza citrus. Of the remaining area, about 1,000 hectares (10,000 dunams) are planted with olives, vines, and deciduous fruit, while 3,500 hectares (35,000 dunams) produce vegetables and field crops. The most important plantations are those of date palms. Wheat is the principal field crop in the Gaza Strip.

Distribution of settlements and population in 1947

The land uses and the settlement pattern of the Gaza Strip are determined by its physiographic structure, which is characterized by sands in the west, alluvial soil in the center and sandstone ridges in the east. The sands are, on the whole, not suitable for farming and have not attracted agricultural settlement; the same can be said of the sandstone ridges with their thin soil layer. There remains the central part of the Strip, where most of the rural settlements and agricultural activities are concentrated. Owing to these geographical conditions, the population in the Gaza Strip has tended to concentrate in the agricultural areas, along the main communications axis and near focal points that enjoy some special local advantage. The population did not spread across the whole width of the Strip, but tended to follow the line of the coastal road, the historical *via Maris*. Such a population distribution in selected focal points along a linear axis is characteristic of desert and semiarid regions, and can be observed in other parts of Israel (Fig. 4.1).

Another distinguishing feature of the settlement pattern in the Gaza Strip is that, while in the west of the coastal region Arab settlements were built on relatively high land and on sandstone ridges leaving the low-lying land for farming use only, settlement in the Strip has concentrated in the plain, in the midst of the agricultural area. One reason for this is the absence in the Gaza Strip of swamps which were common in the northern plain. Another reason may be the ancient main highway passing through the Coastal Depression which stimulated commerce and provided possibilities of employment in times of peace as well as in times of war.

Towards the end of the British Mandate in Palestine, there were only two urban concentrations in the Gaza Strip: Gaza with 34,250 and Khan Yunis with 11,200 inhabitants. The remainder of the population lived in 15 small to medium-sized villages, located on both sides of the coastal roads linking Palestine with Egypt, and at a distance of not more than a mile from the main roads or the railway. Five of

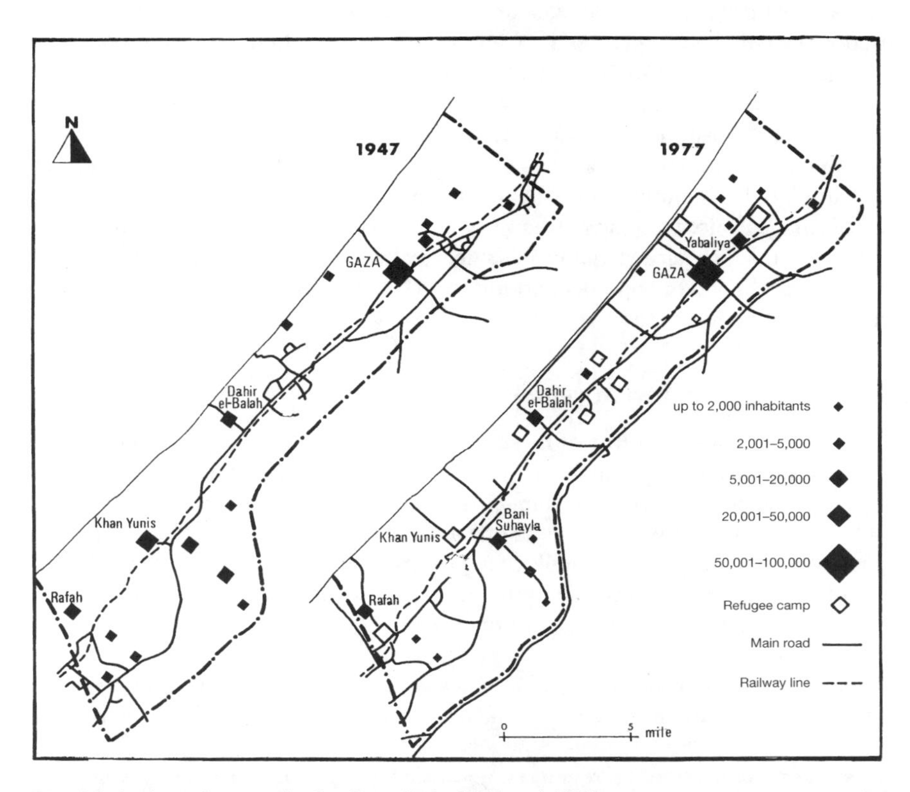

Fig. 4.1 Arab settlements in the Gaza Strip 1947 and 1977

these villages numbered fewer than two thousand inhabitants, and ten between two thousand and five thousand inhabitants. The five largest villages were Yabaliya, Dahir el-Balah, Bani Suhylah, Abasan, and Rafah. The total population of the Gaza Strip numbered 69,700, of whom 65.2 per cent lived in Gaza and Khan Yunis. The population distribution was thus to a marked degree modal and concentrated, as is usually the case in border regions and desert fringes.

The two towns, Gaza and Khan Yunis, occupied a more or less symmetrical position in relation to the groups of villages. Gaza, in the north of the Strip, and Khan Yunis in the south, constituted two focal points in the heart of the farming region. They were based on a plentiful supply of water and on their location at the junction of main roads with the railway line. Gaza was the focal point for connections to Jaffa and Be'ersheva, while Khan Yunis played a similar role in respect of North Sinai and Egypt. Four of the five large villages were strung out at more or less regular intervals of 6 to 10 miles (9.6 to 16 km) along the main communications axis of the Strip. The smaller villages were grouped in four areas: north of Gaza, west of Khan Yunis, south of Gaza, and in the vicinity of Rafah. The inhabitants in the first and second groups earned their livelihood from the cultivation of citrus and field crops. The third group contained mainly concentrations of Negev and North Sinai Bedouins, who had settled on the fringes of the region. In the fourth group lived villagers whose occupation was with the army camps at Rafah.

It can be seen that the population was concentrated around focal points, most of them rural, whose location was determined by the nature of the soil, the main communications arteries, and the sources of livelihood. These settlements formed a clearly graded hierarchy – a large number of small villages, a smaller number of large villages, one small town, Khan Yunis, and the main town of the region, Gaza. The formation of such a hierarchy of settlements was the result of the heterogeneous agricultural and economic background which led to the development of a wide range of settlement types.

Gaza – the main urban center

The town of Gaza, by virtue of its size and its regional and historical importance, is the dominant geographical feature in the Strip. The town is surrounded on all sides by sands and citrus groves. The municipal boundary encloses an area of 2,750 acres (11,000 dunams), of which more than 550 acres (2,200 dunams) are built up. The population numbered in the middle of the 1970s 115,000, not accounting the 35,000 people living in the Esh-Shati refugee camp, which more recently has been incorporated into the municipal area of Gaza. In 2003 Gaza numbered about half a million inhabitants.

The town contains several parts, which reflect its historical development and certain political circumstances. The old historical town was built largely during the

Plate 4.1 The town of Gaza

Ottoman period, over the remains of an ancient settlement. There is a central square, from which springs the main street, Omar el-Mukhtar. This is the main longitudinal axis along which the town developed. On both sides is the principal business center, with rows of shops, some of fairly modern construction. Gaza is situated near the main communications axis of the Strip and in an agricultural region. It has thus the advantages of easy access and economic basis.

During the 1930s and the 1940s the development of Gaza was guided by the interests and the policies of the British Mandatory government. A new and spacious residential quarter, Rimal, was built on the sands west of the town. It contained detached houses built in European style, with plots of a quarter of an acre or larger. This development was not due to any local initiative. Arabs preferred, as a rule, to live in the area of the sandstone ridges, or on agricultural land. The British, on the other hand, gave priority to building on the sands, in the proximity of the sea, so as to enable maximum use to be made of the seashore, including the development of a port, even if only for the export of citrus and other local produce. This also accorded with the general European town planning concept that towns should not be built on land suitable for agriculture. The policy of the Mandatory government was to transfer the center of gravity of the town to an axis leading to the port, whose economic basis would thereby be strengthened, and to achieve a gradual detachment from the old center.

During the same period, the Zeitun and Judeida Quarters were built, expanding the town towards the south, the southwest, and the east. The growth of these quarters was to a large extent due to the activities of foreign institutions, such as hospitals, which were in need of unoccupied land suitable for building. The Jewish Quarter of Gaza, where about fifty Jewish families had lived until the 1929 riots, also expanded in the same direction. Two other quarters, Turkeman and Tuffah, sprang up in the southern part of Gaza, around the nucleus of old and dilapidated houses dating from the nineteenth century. They are now slum areas, with mud houses, and are in the nature of semi-urban settlements for the Bedouin of the area. Today most of Gaza's automobile repair shops and service stations are concentrated there.

An additional urban element of Gaza is represented in the Esh-Shati refugee camp, which was established in the 1950s as one of eight camps in the Strip. It is situated at some distance north of the town. The camp has been incorporated in the Gaza municipal area, in view of its importance in all matters relating to the workforce, employment policy, services, finances, and administration. The camp inmates consider themselves as temporary residents and make no attempt to take part in the life of the town. The Gaza Municipality, for its part, was never interested in accepting the refugees as an integral part of the town. The Esh-Shati inhabitants do not build outside the limits of the camp, but add rooms to their already crowded quarters inside the camp. Even those who find work outside prefer not to settle elsewhere, and return to live in the camp.

In the development of Gaza we can recognize the same elements which characterize most Middle Eastern towns: situation near a communications crossroads, environmental advantages, and a compact town plan. Had it not been for the intervention of the British, which imposed a linear development, Gaza's original pattern would have remained unchanged until this day. After 1948 the town turned away from the "Green Line" and directed its development in a western direction, while at the same time spreading along a north–south axis. In Gaza, as well as other towns of the Strip and the West Bank, the refugee population has not been integrated within any municipal framework, and there has been practically no absorption in the local population.

The Gaza Strip between 1948 and 1967

The consolidation of the Gaza Strip as a political and administrative unit brought about changes in the settlement pattern and in the distribution of population. The rapid influx of population brought about a marked increase in the proportion of urban and rural dwellers. Only about one-sixth of the inhabitants of the Strip are farmers. Although conditions in this region are in favor of agriculture, there was little development in farming between 1948 and 1967. The existence of a relatively large population, in excess of the absorptive capacity of the region, was made possible by the high degree of urbanization and by the fact that, for most of the refugees, the main means of support was the aid administered by the United Nations.

The growth of the towns and villages in the Gaza Strip has been remarkable. First place is taken by the town of Gaza, by virtue of its being the main urban center of the Strip; its population, which numbered 34,250 in 1945, more than trebled, and in 1967 numbered about 115,000. During the same period Khan Yunis grew by 160 per cent from 11,200 to 29,700, Yabaliya by 200 per cent, Dahir el-Balah by 320 per cent, and Rafah by 350 per cent. In the course of a few decades the population distribution of the Gaza Strip underwent substantial changes. The number of settlements increased to 27. Gaza kept its place as the largest town in the Strip, followed by Khan Yunis. The large villages grew about threefold, with exception of Abasan, whose growth was slower on account of its distance from the main routes of communications. The small villages also increased in size and, on average, their population doubled during the same period. On the whole, it can be said that the hierarchy of the Gaza Strip settlements did not change basically, although their number and size increased.

The refugee camps which were established in 1948 added a new element to the population and settlement pattern of the Gaza Strip. Each camp covers a large area and houses twenty thousand or more refugees. The camps were originally eight in number: four large camps, Yabaliya, Esh-Shati, Khan Yunis, and Rafah, and four smaller camps, Nusayrat, Al-Burayj, Al-Mughazi, and Dahir el-Balah. Two large camps were built in the north of the Strip and looked to Gaza and the surrounding agricultural land as a source of livelihood. Another two camps were located in the south, one near Khan Yunis and the second near Rafah, and were intended to supply labor to the nearby army camps. Smaller refugee camps were established in the central part of the Strip, where there had been no large urban settlements. The refugee camps were a notable addition to the population of the Gaza Strip. They were built at the time as a temporary measure, in a haphazard pattern of narrow intersecting streets, and closely packed one-storey houses. The camps were generally located near existing Arab settlements or in abandoned army camps and they constituted a workforce reservoir for agriculture and services in the Strip. Up to now the camps have remained unintegrated into the municipal structure of the towns. The uncertainty regarding the political future of the Strip tends to perpetuate this state of affairs; the camps are not abolished nor are they given the status of permanent settlements (Fig. 4.2).

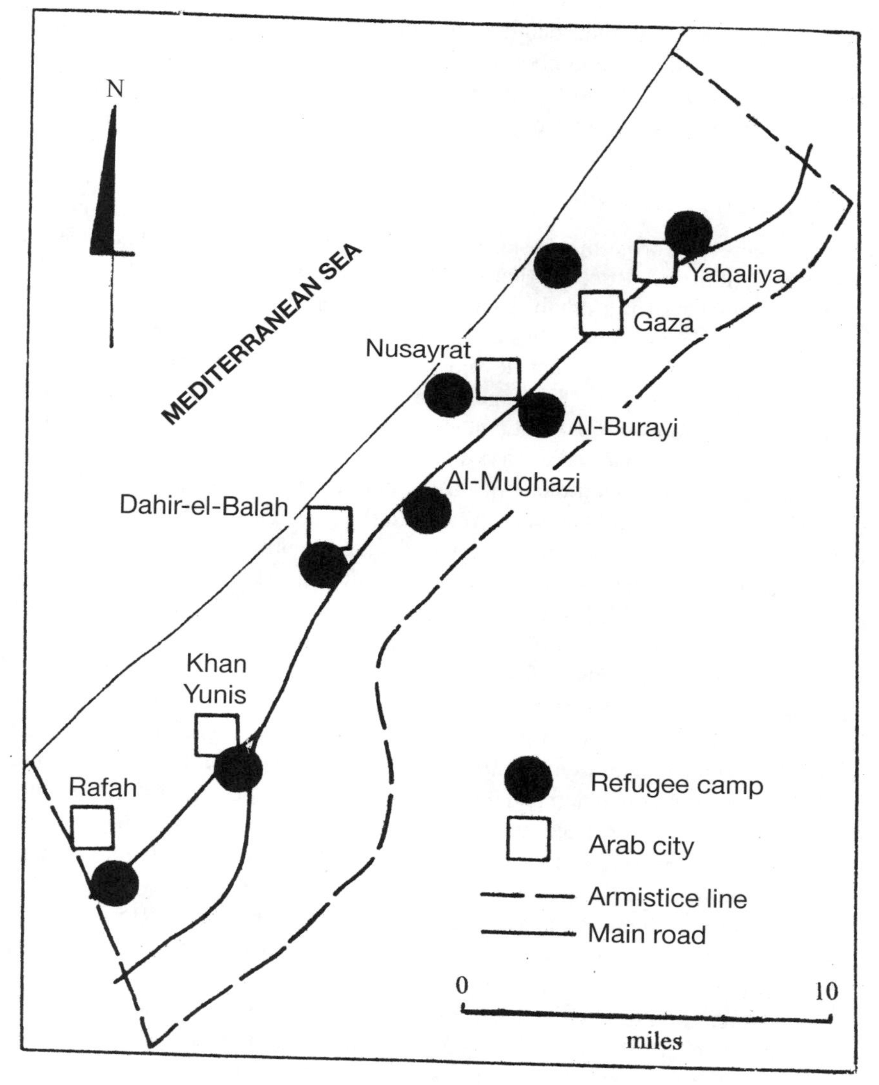

Fig. 4.2 Refugee camps in the Gaza Strip

It can be seen that the Gaza Strip, an artificial geographical entity, which for 19 years was bounded by the armistice "Green Line" and between 1967 and 1995 was subject to Israeli military rule, has changed but little in its internal structure. The region has few soil and water resources, no minerals, and is generally poor. Its economy was formerly dependent on the limited agricultural potential, and any addition to the population could only be based on urban employment in industry or services, and on outside aid. Growth is concentrated mainly in the large urban centers and in the refugee camps, which, as we noted above, are artificial settlements receiving assistance from outside. The lack of substantial investment, the maintaining of the refugee camps in their stagnating state, and the high national population growth, which is in the neighborhood of 45 per thousand per year, have all contributed to intensify the social pressure of the inhabitants on their surroundings, which in turn has nurtured extremist nationalistic sentiments.

The Gaza Strip after 1967

The Six Day War brought substantial economic changes in the Gaza Strip. The opening of the armistice line between the Strip and the State of Israel, and the possibility for the strip's inhabitants to visit Judea and Samaria and even the Hashemite Kingdom of Jordan, besides the investments of the new Israeli administration in construction and other development projects, improved the economic condition of the inhabitants. The population of the Gaza Strip in the middle of the 1970s numbered about 444,000 inhabitants, among them 260,000 refugees (58 per cent). The annual population increase there was 5 per cent.

The Israeli military government took a number of steps with a view to modifying the artificial structure that had been created in the past. The chief of these was to build new and planned residential quarters for the inmates of the refugee camps. Other steps included the improvement of the road network, the setting up of new administrative and health institutions, and the raising of the level of agricultural employment. Agricultural production in the Strip has increased since 1967 by 10 per cent annually and the farmers' profits by about 15 per cent annually. As a result of this, there has been an increase in national and local production and in the rate of employment. About 35 per cent of the Gaza Strip's workforce was then occupied in Israel. Unemployment decreased from 13 per cent in 1968 to 1 per cent in 1975. There was a great demand for laborers in Israel, especially in building and industry. There was even a demand for agricultural laborers in the Strip itself, and those who were dismissed from agricultural work in Israel could easily find another occupation in the Strip.

The continuous increase in the standard of living affected different kinds of people: hired laborers, self-employed persons, refugees, and non-refugees. It may be assumed that the take-off of the Gaza Strip economy from a very low level to a much higher one has now come to an end. The tremendous economic improvement began after the sudden interrelationship between the two economies just after the Six Day War. In the Gaza Strip there was a high concentration of an unemployed workforce supported by UNRWA institutions. Israel's exploitation of

Plate 4.2 The Palestinian refugee camp Esh-Shatti

this unemployment pushed the whole system of social and economic activity onto a new level. After the first ten years of change, it seemed that the region's economy was progressing moderately.

A slow decrease in Israel's economic activity in later years has influenced the Gaza Strip very much, because of its dependence upon Israel. Fewer agricultural laborers from the Gaza Strip work in Israel today. There is a trend to employ more laborers in house construction in Israel. In the past, several factors prevented rapid industrialization in the Gaza Strip: the lack of local entrepreneurs, lack of a skilled workforce, and lack of knowledge, equipment, and machines. To this may be added the lack of a monetary system and capital market which could provide the investment of savings in real property. Political uncertainty and the competition of Israel's industry added to it. It should also be remembered that an economic transition from a handicraft economy under primitive conditions to modern industry is a process which works slowly and takes time.

The Jewish population in the Gaza Strip numbered in 2004 about 7,000 inhabitants and was concentrated in three settlement blocs – the northern area, Nezarim, and Qatif. The northern area, north of Gaza, has a sandy soil with a potential for the establishment of agricultural settlements, and included Ele Sinay, Dugit, and Nisanit. Adjacent to them, on the borderline between the Strip and Israel, was the industrial zone of Erez, the main source of employment for the Palestinians of the Gaza Strip. The Nezarim bloc occupied 875 acres (3,500 dunams) of State land which stretched from south of Gaza to north of Nusayrat and included the only settlement, Nezarim. The Qatif bloc was the largest of the three and included 13 settlements. It extended from north of the town of Rafah to south of Dahir el-Balah. One more Jewish settlement 1.8 miles (3 km) northeast of the Qatif bloc was located in an enclave – Kefar Darom. Jewish settlements in the Gaza Strip were located on State land where no Arabs lived, on land which was vacant or only temporarily cultivated. The total area designated for Jewish settlement in the region amounted to 14,000 acres (56,000 dunams). The three blocs were established on the western sand stone ridge, mostly covered with sand, in places lacking any local advantage.

The Qatif bloc

The largest of the blocs, Qatif, with its 13 settlements, was divided into two groups. The northern part was the oldest, and contained Nezer Hazani, Qatif, and Gane Tal, while the settled southern part included Newe Deqalim, Gedid, Gan Or, Bedolah, Azmona, Pe'at Sade, Shalev, and Rafiyah Yam. Another old settlement, east of Qatif, was Morag, located in an enclave. Settlement in the bloc began in 1970 when a Nahal unit resettled Kefar Darom, which had been in existence before the War of Independence in 1948. In 1972 Nahal units settled Nezarim and Morag. In 1975 interest was reawakened in the settlement of the Strip, as land in the Qatif bloc was handed over to the Hapo'el Hamizrahi Moshav Federation. In 1977 Nezer Hazani was established, and later on Qatif and Gane Tal.

The Qatif bloc occupied 5,000 acres (20,000 dunams) in the southwestern part of the Gaza Strip. On the west it was bounded by the sea, and on the east, north, and south by Arab settlements. It was located on State land which before 1967 was controlled by the Egyptian army. The Qatif bloc had no particular location advantages. It was located where there was land that could be settled after basic preparations. The only advantages it had were the fine seashore suitable for the development of tourism, a pleasant climate, and local water resources. From the Israeli security point of view its virtue was that it created separation between the Arab settlements, restricting their urban and agricultural expansion, and established a continuity line from the coast through the Eshkol and Shalom regions in Israel's territory. The usual settlement form in the Qatif bloc was the moshav, since the land was allocated to the Hapo'el Hamizrahi Moshavim, which were faced with the problem of housing for the younger generation in their older moshavim.

As to the Qatif population, several features were discernible. It was a young population, with many children. The people came from all parts of the country, most from moshavim of Hapo'el Hamizrahi, some from Nahal units of their Moshav Federation, and the rest from the cities or development towns. The ideology of the settlers was based on "Torah and Work" which involved compliance with the religious precepts together with agricultural work, the settlement of the "Greater Land of Israel", of which the Gaza Strip is a separate part, and settlement in the religious blocs in order to facilitate the provision of religious and cultural services.

The Qatif bloc was developed on a local scale only. It was settled by the Settlement Department of the Zionist Organization together with the Hapo'el Hamizrahi Moshav Federation. Most of the planning was directed to the infrastructure of the settlements. As the final plan for the establishment of 13 settlements and populating

Plate 4.3 The Jewish settlement Newe Deqalim in the Qatif bloc

them took shape, simultaneously with the Israeli withdrawal from Sinai, planning was begun with regard to traditional areas in the Gaza Strip held by the State; there were the northern area, the Nezarim bloc, and areas in the Morag vicinity. There was no regional plan for all the settlements in the Gaza Strip, only ideas. The impression left by the various development plans was that there was no consensus on the development patterns; what seemed to be the primary concern of the authorities involved was safeguarding State-owned land and its speedy settlement by Jews.

The Qatif bloc was an example of the establishment of an independent religious settlement region beyond the "Green Line", with mostly agricultural settlements. The bloc faced a large number of problems, such as insufficiency of the chief means of production, land and water. Even if the water problem could have been solved from the national water reserve, there was no solution to the land problem because there was a dense Arab population in the region that was multiplying rapidly and needed land for itself. The dependence of the bloc on means of production from the area outside naturally reduced its ability to exist independently. The Qatif bloc found itself isolated from its surroundings in a changing political situation as it appeared after 2004. The economic basis of the bloc was not very stable either. Agriculture was the main economic sector. The typical farm in the bloc grows vegetables and flowers in greenhouses beside orchards. The bloc was not favorably placed for industrial plants either. It appeared that the establishment of a settlement bloc for geopolitical and security reasons does not always bring economic success.

Moreover, all the planning and development notwithstanding, the total Jewish population in the Gaza Strip did not surpass 7,000. Consequently, the effectiveness of a project of this sort had to be considered doubtful, and, although excellently organized, it got into a traumatic situation.

After Israel's retreat from the Arab cities and villages in the Gaza Strip in 1995, the Qatif bloc remained as an enclave of Israeli settlements in the southwestern corner of the Strip, together with four other settlements which were located in the central and northern parts of the Gaza Strip. After the government approved autonomy for the Arab part of the Gaza Strip, the functions and destinations of the Qatif bloc remained unclear: no reasonable argument was put forward by any official body for the importance of the bloc to Israel's security. Once its importance was, as we have said, as a buffer zone between the Egyptian border line and the dense Arab population which lived in the central part of the Strip, and as a region of concentrated Jewish settlements in an occupied area; but after the decision was taken by the Israelis to withdraw from the Strip, what benefit could Israel derive from the Qatif bloc in its existing form, unless it was to function as a bargain card in the negotiations with the Palestinians on the future of the occupied territories?

Despite the high importance which right-wing politicians attached to the Qatif bloc, that region was characterized by features which it really did not have: it had no Jewish history behind it, and was not a patrimony; even most Israelis had no special emotional relationship with this corner in the southern part of the Coastal Plain; with its 7,000 inhabitants it had no demographic significance as against the 1.2 million Arabs who lived in the Gaza Strip; the bloc was not important in its agricultural production, not even compared to the relatively high production of the Arab rural population; it had no economic and social relations with the adjacent Besor region and with other surrounding communities in Israel's territory; and its spatial and security importance on the Egyptian borderline in Sinai was not great, as a result of the existing peace between the two countries

The area of 14,000 acres (56,000 dunams) which belonged to the bloc, encompassing 15 per cent of the total area of the Gaza Strip, and with its 13 settlements, endangered the Israeli soldiers who were obliged to secure it, and created a difficult logistic problem to the military forces which had to protect the settlers, spreading their troops behind long barbed wire lines and concrete slabs, and safeguarding the transportation of the settlers along twisted and dangerous arteries, with an inevitable cost of wasted money, energy, and power. The reaction of the Israeli public to the deployment from the Gaza Strip, which was quite positive, indicated to a certain extent the need for and justification of the deployment from the bloc too. Except for the right-wing and religious groups' attitude in Israel to this region as part of a messianic conception of the "Greater Land of Israel", the public has taken no special interest in these settlements, especially given the problem of evacuation which existed among the settlers. They envisaged a high probability of withdrawal, sooner or later, promising them large amounts of money as compensation for evacuation (Fig. 4.3).

It seems that a fundamental step had to be taken by the government in order to separate Jews and Arabs in this problematic region, which meant, in effect,

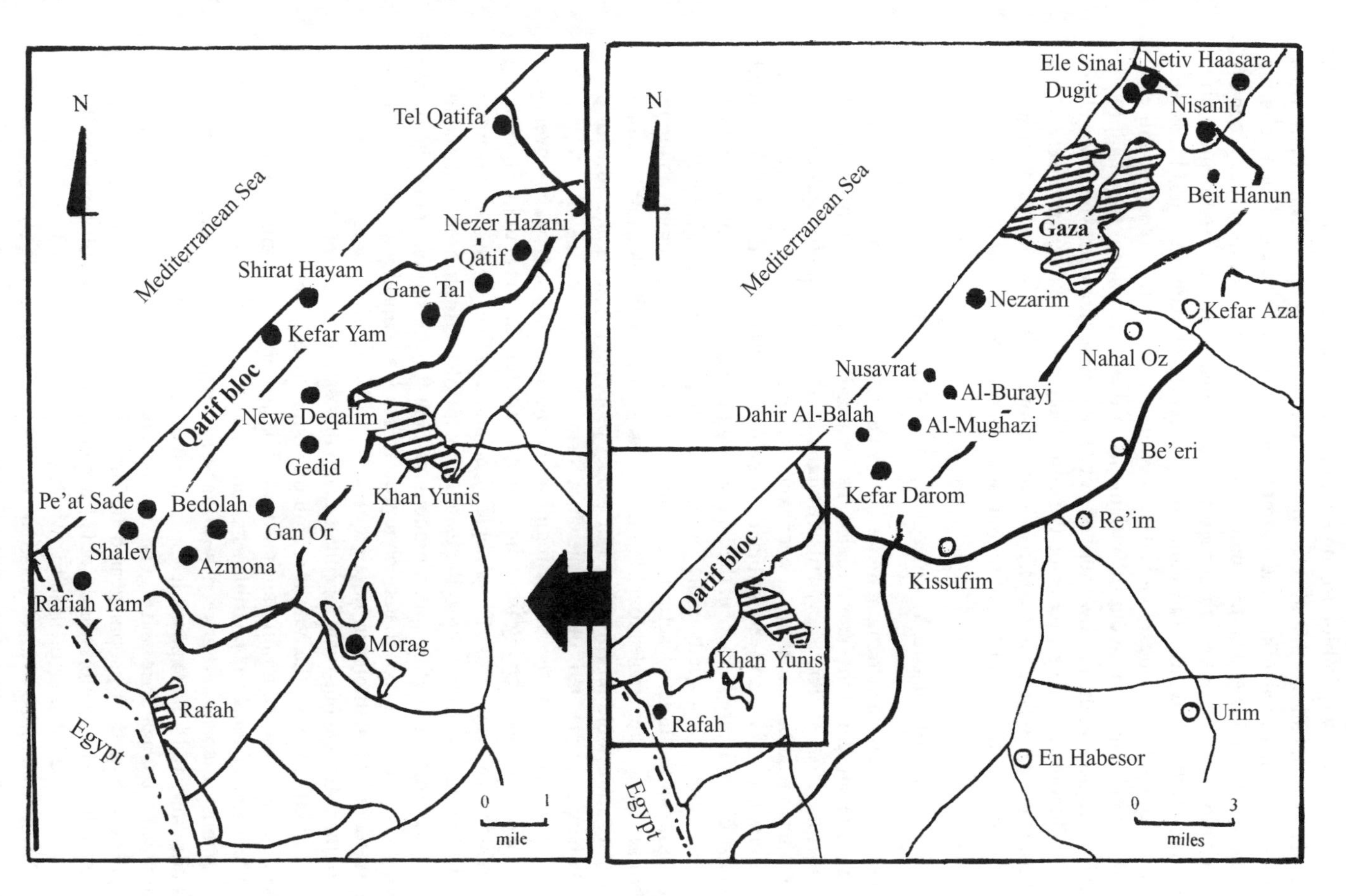

Fig. 4.3 The Gaza Strip and the Qatif bloc

transferring the whole bloc to somewhere else. The recent political settlement history in Israel shows that alternative settlement regions have been found when necessary. The evacuation of the Yamit region in northern Sinai, at the beginning of the 1980s, included a similar number of settlers to those of the bloc. When the evacuation was decided on, the agricultural settlements were offered an alternative in a region very similar to the Yamit area as regards climate, soil, arid landscape, access to main roads, development of economic and service branches, and even with a newly planned layout of settlements in the same system they had, in the Shalom region, in the northwestern Negev. The new settlements which were built in the Shalom region were based on the same sources of livelihood and were a kind of copy of what existed on the other side of the border. The Shalom region absorbed half of the families from Yamit region, and this was viewed as a success.

The evacuation of the Yamit region as a precedent

The civilian Jewish settlement in northern Sinai after the Six Day War in 1967 and the establishment of the Yamit region, its enforced abandonment in 1982, and the scattering of its settlers afterwards throughout the entire country was one of the most serious settlement traumas ever experienced in Israel. An entire development region was utterly destroyed, so that the inhabitants were obliged to decide on their future, either in resettlement in the Shalom region or in rural settlements within the "Green Line". The tragedy of the forced evacuation of the Yamit region was a very big issue at the time. Descriptions of incidents in the Yamit region abounded in terms such as "irreparable blow", "ruin", "trauma" and even "holocaust". The events of that time should be considered in proper proportion and compared with what may happen in the Qatif bloc of the Gaza Strip.

The settlement of the Yamit region after the Six Day War was viewed as a political necessity deriving from the principle that territory is acquired by settling it, which ensures control of a strategic place and at a later stage also sovereignty. This approach led in 1969 to the establishment of the first three settlements in northern Sinai, all before a comprehensive plan for the settlement of the whole region had been evolved. Later, in view of the growing capacity to apply advanced agro-technical methods in desert territory, an ideological program called the "Southern Endeavour" was formulated, and the Yamit region was part of it.

The settlement of the Yamit region embodied two factors, the geographical-political and the economic-agricultural. The geographical aim was to spread settlement as densely as possible as a continuation of the western Negev, in order to establish a separation between the Gaza Strip and the desert, which under peaceful conditions would make possible supervision of the movement of Arab inhabitants between the Gaza Strip and Egypt. The economic-agricultural goal was to raise higher quality crops by sophisticated methods, and to exploit the climate advantages of the region. The region was designed around the central town of Yamit, while the purpose of the establishment of the whole region was geopolitical.

By the time of the 1982 evacuation, the town of Yamit had 3,000 residents and the rural sector of the region a further 2,000. The decision to evacuate the Yamit region after the achievement of a peace agreement between Israel and Egypt led to a hitherto unknown factor, the geography of withdrawal, characterized by the need for people and settlements to relocate, either in neighborhoods or in other parts of the country. The dispersion of the Yamit region population was found to be in concentric circles, whose absorption of the evacuated residents diminished with their distance from the Yamit region. A large proportion of the evacuees settled in the southern district especially in the first three dispersion circles stretching from southwest to north. Most relocated in new villages or in the existing development towns. The surprising thing was that the fourth circle of Greater Tel Aviv and the metropolitan area reabsorbed most of the residents, as evidently most came from there and returned to their places of origin. The urban population of the town of Yamit dispersed more widely than the agricultural population. The patterns of withdrawal from the Yamit region were characterized by settlement shrinkage, considerable movement over short distances, a tendency to settle areas close to the evacuated one or in repeated settlement in a similar geographical area, and by the tendency of the urban population to return to its city of origin. On the other hand, the settlement staying power of the rural population was greater than that of the city-dwellers.

The phenomenon of population evacuation by force may be seen as an event in which people lose their physical and social fabric of life, and an event that has special demographic, behavioral, and spatial characteristics. Research that has been carried out on the mass evacuation and mass relocation of the Yamit region settlers has shown some interesting findings: families tended to be evacuated as whole units, unless separation was needed for a limited time between women and children or between women and husbands; families with children tended to leave sooner than singles; elderly people tended not to leave as soon as young people – because of their stronger relationship to their home and place of dwelling, they are more conservative and hesitate much more to begin a new life somewhere else. There exists a direct relationship between the socio-economic level of the evacuees and their readiness to be evacuated. The richer leave sooner because they can afford to buy or to rent a provisional apartment before they decide about their next permanent home. A necessary political change in a region accelerates the tendency of settlers for evacuation and especially among those who planned their new homes in advance; previous experience of evacuation makes it more difficult for people to be evacuated and it is almost impossible to force them to go through such an experience again. The distance of relocation is larger for people who have lived provisionally in the settlement or in the region as against the permanent dwellers who are deeply rooted in their place; most evacuees are keen to get far away from the place of evacuation where they suffered the traumatic experience. From the point of view of the authorities the efficiency of evacuation is determined by the preparation and planning, by the level of administration and the allocation of budgets for compensation; the more a region is developed, the more efficient the evacuation process may be, unless a panic arises among the settlers because of emotional, political, or national reasons that are hard to restrain. In every evacuation process there will be a hard core of settlers who will resist the evacuation and will use all measures to oppose it and even try to return to the evacuated place after a time.

If the government is to apply the evacuation model of the Yamit region to the Qatif bloc, with the assumption that most of the settlers will continue to be engaged in agriculture, and with the assumption that they will prefer to move to the north-western Negev in the limits of a religious bloc of settlements, it should be possible to establish for them a new rural system of villages in the western Negev, on an open landscape which belongs now to the Regional Council of Eshkol, which is crying out for new settlers, and for more development, infrastructure, factories, and public institutions. Even the filling up of some of the existing settlements in the western Negev along the "Green Line" is still a possible solution, and the Jewish Agency, which is in charge of the establishment of rural settlements in the country, has prepared plans for the evacuees' resettlement. Many of the existing settlements, which are close to the borderlines of the Arab autonomous region along the Gaza Strip, need additional settlers, and so does the inner hinterland in the central Negev. If the settlers of the Qatif bloc are really longing for the redemption of the Land of Israel for the People of Israel, it seems that the western Negev might be the best place for them for carrying out their dreams.

Following the precedent of the Yamit region and the characteristics of people that find themselves in a situation of evacuation, some consequences could be drawn regarding the disengagement from the Qatif bloc. The settlers should be provided with reasonable financial grants to fund their new life and housing after the evacuation; allocation of new sites for settlement according to the demographic composition of the settlers should be planned and prepared; special support should be given to those who intend to settle in Galilee, in the Jerusalem vicinity or in the Eshkol Regional Council region adjacent to the Qaif bloc. New sites should be offered for orthodox families and for seculars, urbanites, and farmers; kibbutzim such as Kefar Aza, Mefalsim, and Or Haner may absorb evacuees in the Sha'ar Hanegev Regional Council; moshavim such as Talme Yafe or Bat Hadar in the Hof Ashqelon Regional Council might be appropriate for secular and orthodox families also; the Regional Council of Har Negev even offered to establish for the evacuees a new settlement region near Nizana, adjacent to the Israeli–Egyptian border. The common features of the options for resettlement lie at a distance of 6–10 miles (10–20 km) of the Qatif bloc and offer different forms of settlement. It may be assumed that farmers of the bloc will prefer to stay as close as possible to the bloc and start again with a new life on agricultural land that will be allocated to them. But most of the others, mainly the outgoing inhabitants of development towns, who came to the Qatif bloc to improve their standard of living, will prefer to return to their urban places in the western and northern Negev with more money in their pockets. The singles among the evacuees might go to the far north of the country to forget their traumatic experience, while the avowed idealists might resettle in the West Bank, despite the danger of being evacuated once again from there when the time comes.

Disengagement from the Gaza Strip

The Gaza Strip was not captured by Israel in the 1948 war. Yigal Allon, a military commander during the War of Independence, used to say that, if he and his men had had another day or two, they would have captured Gaza in 1948. He supposed that, if Israel had captured the Gaza Strip then, there would not have been so many refugees living there, and they would have fled. That was also what David Ben-Gurion thought when he proposed capturing the Gaza Strip in 1955. He essentially suggested deporting the refugees to Jordan, an idea the government rejected. A year and a half later, after the1956 Sinai campaign, Israel was, fortunately, compelled to return it to Egypt. On the eve of the Six Day War, Israel's leaders once again discussed conquering the Strip, and once again considered what they would do with the hundreds of thousands of refugees there. There was then a proposal to deport them to Egypt or to the West Bank or preferably to Jordan or Iraq. The first few months after the Six Day War led to plans aimed at rehabilitating the Gaza refugees, who would be moved outside the Strip. Almost nothing was done, a major mistake that resulted in there being many poverty-stricken refugees to this day. Only one mistake appears to be greater, that the late Prime Minister Menachem Begin did not make the 1979 peace treaty with Egypt conditional upon Egypt's agreement to take Gaza Strip off Israel's hands.

In 2004 the government of Israel, headed by Ariel Sharon, the "father" of the settlements, approved a revolutionary proposal to evacuate all the Gaza Strip settlements within a year and a half. Sharon said that this was a step of critical importance for the future of Israel that should contribute to its security, its political standing, its economy, and the demographics of the Jewish people in the Land of Israel. Prime Minister Ariel Sharon's plan to dismantle the settlements and withdraw the Israel Defense Forces from the Gaza Strip has enjoyed considerable international support, which constricted Sharon's freedom of movement, so that Israel would be obliged not only to plan the evacuation but also to carry it out. When Sharon's legal and political status was clarified, he fixed an accelerated timetable for the withdrawal.

The disengagement plan was entirely the initiative of Ariel Sharon and was a move fraught with all the elements one can conceive: it is simultaneously demographic, historical, religious, mythological, and psychological, and it was the first step toward a return to the 1967 borders according to President Bush's road map. No one is claiming that it was an easy move, but a State is obliged to preserve and protect its democratic character and its authority. It should be mentioned that the settlers are not pioneers but residents who for 38 years have been spoiled with land and money. Water and electricity infrastructures were built for them, and army brigades and divisions saw to their security. Israel's finest sons were wounded and killed to uphold a policy whose time is past and that has turned Israelis into brutal occupiers in the eyes of the entire world.

The background of this plan is that the State of Israel is committed to the peace process and endeavors to reach an agreement based on the vision presented by U.S. President George W. Bush. The State of Israel believes it must take action to improve the current situation. It has reached the conclusion that even after Yasser Arafat's death there is no partner on the Palestinian side with whom progress can be made on a bilateral process. Given this, a four-stage disengagement plan has been drawn up, based on the following considerations.

The stalemate embodied in the current situation is damaging. In order to break the stalemate, the State of Israel must initiate a process that is not dependent on co-operation with the Palestinians. The aim of the plan is to bring about a better security, diplomatic, economic, and demographic reality. In any future permanent agreement, there will be no Israeli presence in the Gaza Strip. On the other hand, it is clear that some parts of Judea and Samaria, including key concentrations of Jewish settlements, civilian communities, security zones, and areas in which Israel has a vested interest, will remain part of the State of Israel. The State of Israel supports the efforts of the United States, which is working along with the international community, to promote the process of reform, the establishment of institutions, and the improvement of the economic and welfare conditions of the Palestinian people, so that a new Palestinian leadership can arise, capable of proving it can fulfill its obligations under the road map. The withdrawal from the Gaza Strip and from the northern part of Samaria will reduce interaction with the Palestinian population. Completion of the disengagement plan will negate any claims on Israel regarding its responsibility for the Palestinian population of the Gaza Strip.

The key points for disengagement from the Gaza strip were as follows. The State of Israel will withdraw from the Gaza Strip, including all Israeli settlements, and will redeploy its nationals outside the area of the Strip. The method of the withdrawal, with the exception of a military presence in the area adjacent to the border between Gaza and Egypt (the Philadelphi route), is detailed below. Once the move has been completed, there will be no permanent Israeli military presence in the evacuated territorial area of the Gaza Strip. As a result of this, there will be no basis to the claim that the Strip is occupied land.

The withdrawal process was intended to end by the end of 2005. The settlements in the Gaza Strip were split into three groups: Group A – Morag, Nezarim, and Kefar Darom; Group B – the Qatif bloc of settlements; Group C – the settlements in the northern Gaza Strip, including Ele Sinay, Dugit, and Nissanit.

Regarding the security reality, after the evacuation the State of Israel will monitor and supervise the surrounding land, will have exclusive control of the Gaza airspace, and will continue its military activity along the Gaza Strip's coastline. The Gaza Strip will be completely demilitarized of arms banned by current agreements between the sides. The State of Israel reserves the basic right to self-defense, which includes taking preventive measures as well as the use of force against threats originating in the Gaza Strip. Military infrastructure and installations in the Gaza Strip will all be dismantled and evacuated, except for those the State of Israel decides to transfer to an authorized body. The State of Israel agrees that, in co-ordination with it, consulting assistance and training will be provided to Palestinian security forces for the purpose of fighting terrorism and maintaining public order. The assistance will be provided by American, British, Egyptian, Jordanian, and other experts, as agreed upon with Israel. The State of Israel stresses that it will not agree to any foreign security presence in Gaza without its consent.

The State of Israel will continue to maintain military presence along the border between the Gaza Strip and Egypt (the Philadelphi route). This presence is an essential security requirement. The physical widening of the route, where military activity may take place, may be necessary in certain areas. The possibility of evacuating the area will be considered later on. This evacuation would be conditional, among other factors, on the security reality and on the level of co-operation by Egypt in creating a credible alternative arrangement. If and when the conditions are met enabling the evacuation of the area, the State of Israel will be willing to consider the possibility of setting up an airport and a seaport in the Gaza Strip, subject to arrangements agreed upon with the State of Israel.

Regarding real estate and infrastructure, houses belonging to the settlers, and other sensitive structures, such as synagogues, will not be left behind. This real estate includes 1,780 apartments, more than 120 public institutions of different size and 30 synagogues. The State of Israel will aspire to transfer other structures, such as industrial and agricultural facilities, to an international third party that will use them for the benefit of the Palestinian population. The Erez industrial zone will be transferred to an agreed-upon Palestinian or international body. The State of Israel along with Egypt will examine the possibility of setting up a joint industrial zone on the border between Israel, Egypt, and the Gaza Strip. The water, electricity, sewerage and communications infrastructure will be left in place. As a rule, Israel will maintain the continued supply of electricity, water, gas, and fuel to the Palestinians, under the existing arrangements and with full compensation. The existing arrangements, including the arrangements with regard to water and the electromagnetic area, will remain valid.

Lately, there has been reconsideration of the decision regarding the future of the buildings, in light of the changes of administration in the Palestinian Authority and the emerging co-operation between Israel and the Palestinians for the disengagement. The defense establishment also thinks that demolishing the buildings in the settlements after evacuating the residents will require a considerable and unjustified effort. But such a plan had two main difficulties. The first was ideological. Resettling refugees could be regarded as giving up the Palestinians' demand for right to return. The second difficulty was that the large clans in Khan Yunis will claim the settlement lands and will not be interested in the Palestinian Authority using what they regard as their property for the benefit of refugees, and those especially from other areas.

In summer 2004 the Israel security cabinet decided on the principle of the disengagement bill and on the payment of advances to settlers from the Gaza Strip and northern West Bank who voluntarily agree to relocate as follows: advances of NIS 9,000–18,000 would be paid against moving expenses depending on family size, with a rent advance of NIS 1,800–2,500 per month, in addition to one-third of the final compensation. Those seeking advances would sign over the rights to their houses to the State via the disengagement administration. Settlers would be able to choose various modes of compensation for homes. A calculation of between NIS

2,700 and NIS 4,500 per 3 ft (1 m) could be made, according to type of home. Settlers who have lived in the territories for more than two years could receive a house in a similar area, with additional compensation of a grant and a loan of NIS 225,000–540,000, with the grant increasing according to years of settlement. Settlers could also choose to have their homes assessed individually. Tenants in public housing would receive compensation according to the type of property rights they have. Those who move to a priority area of Galilee or the Negev could receive an additional grant of NIS 90,000. Settlers who are renters would receive a grant for moving and between 6 and 12 months' rent depending on family size. Salaried employees who lose their jobs as a result of evacuation would receive adjustment allowances of up to twice the average salary in the country for six months. Salaried employees who are more than 57 years of age could receive a pension. Business people who move their business into Israel would be entitled to special grants. Increased compensation would be given to any settler over 18 on the basis of the number of years he or she has lived in the settlement. There would be increased compensation for greenhouse owners, and enlarged fees to hired workers in the settlements on the basis of the number of years in the area.

Regarding economic arrangements, those that are currently in effect between Israel and the Palestinians will remain valid. These arrangements include, among other things, the movement of goods between the Gaza Strip, Judea and Samaria, Israel and foreign countries, the monetary regime, the taxation arrangements and the customs envelope, and the entry of workers into Israel in accordance with the existing criteria. In the long run, and in accordance with Israel's interest in encouraging Palestinian economic independence, the State of Israel aspires to reduce the number of Palestinian workers entering Israel, and eventually to stop their entrance completely. The State of Israel will support the development of employment sources in the Gaza Strip by international bodies.

At the international crossing point between the Gaza Strip and Egypt the existing arrangements will remain in force. Israel is interested in transferring the crossing point to the "border triangle", south of its current location. This will be done in co-ordination with the Egyptian government. The Erez crossing point will be moved into the territory of the State of Israel according to a timetable that will be determined separately.

The implementation of the disengagement plan will bring about an improvement in the situation and a break from current stagnation. If and when the Palestinian side shows a readiness, ability and implementation of actions to fight terrorism, a full cessation of terror and violence and the carrying out of reforms according to the road map, it will be possible to return to the track of discussions and negotiations.

In September 2004 the army was completing plans for redeploying outside the Gaza Strip following the disengagement. The Gaza Divisions headquarters, sited in the Qatif bloc, will continue to operate following the pullout, but will be relocated outside the Strip. The redeployment outside Gaza will be similar to the redeployment on the northern border following the Israeli withdrawal from south Lebanon in 2000. The goal is to reduce sources of friction and to maintain a relatively low physical presence near the fence separating Gaza from Israel, so as not to provide targets for Palestinian attacks. The new army posts will thus be built at some distance and be less exposed to direct attack. The posts will be highly fortified, but relatively few in number. Instead, the Israeli army will use innovative technologies. The army expects that, as in the withdrawal from Lebanon, construction of the new defensive structures will be completed only some time after disengagement.

Israeli public opinion supposes that the goal of the disengagement plan was to perpetuate Israeli control in most of the West Bank and to repel any internal or external pressure for a different political solution. Sharon is consistently trying to realize his vision: Israeli control over the eastern and western slopes of the West Bank and maintaining traffic corridors along its length and breadth. The Palestinians will be left with seven enclaves connected by special highways for their use. This engagement plan will facilitate the realization of this vision at a bargain price from his point of view: he is giving up the Gaza Strip where 37 per cent of the Palestinians live, but whose area is only 1.25 per cent of the Land of Israel.

The country was split between those who were utterly convinced that the occupation is the very venom endangering its existence and those who believed with all their heart that withdrawal from the territories will bring the State's destruction. It is also true that the disengagement from the Gaza Strip divided the nation and split it into two parts. One, tiny and loud, only a few thousand strong, has been convinced until now that it had managed to swallow up the State, and is now terribly offended to discover that it was wrong; the other, huge and quiet, comprising nearly six million people, who are tired of the drug with which they have been injected for nearly four decades on the basis of a prescription for certain salvation; a majority that seeks to be rid of all that. It was thus time for a recovery from the illusion that distorted common sense, the physical borders of the State, and the clear distinction between legal and illegal, between dream and reality. Most of the Israeli public supports the Sharon plan. It naively believes that its realization will bring about the end of the war and a significant economic improvement. The international community also supports the plan. It is tired of the Israeli–Palestinian conflict, and is no longer investing any real input in attempts to solve it. Anyone who supports a unilateral step and regards it as a serious move is accepting Sharon's basic assumption that there is no partner, an assumption that he has made every effort to justify. Anyone who was likely to be a partner received nothing from him, with the exception of harmful compliments. Many people seriously hope that the exit from the Gaza Strip and the evacuation of the settlements will begin a dynamic that cannot be stopped. Such a dynamic would make the continuation of the process in the West Bank unavoidable if the Gaza Strip is handed over to a responsible Palestinian government, through close co-ordination with Israel, and with active and generous support from the international community and the wealthy Arab States. A Gaza Strip which is not a source of terrorism, which is rehabilitated economically, and which is run by a Palestinian government is likely to be a positive model for the future. But a Gaza Strip in chaos, supported by international welfare organizations, and controlled by armed gangs – that is the model that will prevent Israel from even considering a continuation of the process in the West Bank. Continuation of the war after the Israeli exit from Gaza will cause the Israelis to lose any desire to reach an agreement. If it turns out that the conflict has not been solved, that the war with the Palestinians is continuing, that the Israel Defense Forces are busy protecting the settlers, and that the country's political isolation is increasing, Israelis will be left for more years with a government that in effect doesn't want anything else.

In summer 2005 Israel had to do the most ruthless thing it had ever done to its citizens. It had to send its soldiers into the homes of citizens to pull them out and to destroy all they built, all they planned, and all they believed. This brutal act was necessary because the settlements in the Gaza Strip were a historical mistake. If Israel wants to survive and wants to continue a Jewish democratic State, it must correct that error. It must evacuate all of Gaza completely down to the last house. Since the conditions in the area don't allow residents to be left under the protection of the Palestinians, there is no choice but to withdraw them along with the military forces, and, since a substantial proportion of the settlers ideologically oppose this necessary move, there was no choice but to impose it upon them. It is impossible to leave the freedom of choice to individuals. It is necessary to coerce these individuals to accept the will of the majority and the will of Israeli sovereignty. However, that difficult deed must be done properly and correctly. Not with glee, not with indifference, not as matter of fact. That horrifying deed must be done with awe and trembling, with weeping hearts and bowed heads, without treating the uprooted high-handedly, and with the understanding that the Qatif bloc is an all-Israeli tragedy. The question is not a matter of essence. If many of the settlers' leaders understand that, they have lost the campaign. They understand they cannot save Nezer Hazzani and Gane Tal and others. They understand that the process is too strong, and it has passed the point of no return.

According to the government's plan of April 2005, three northern Gaza Strip settlements, Elei Sinay, Dugit, and Nisanit, had to be the first to be evacuated by the army and police in the implementation of the Gaza disengagement plan, according to the withdrawal blueprint. The isolated settlement of Nezarim was also due for evacuation in the first week of the withdrawal. The northern part of the Qatif bloc was slated for withdrawal in the second week, with the southern part of the bloc to be evacuated in the third week. Evacuation of the four settlements around Jenin, in northern Samaria, was expected to begin in the third week, and had to be completed in the fourth week. The northern Gaza settlements were chosen as the first to be evacuated because they were relatively isolated and because their residents were considered less ideologically minded. The residents in these settlements felt that they have played their part in the campaign against disengagement. The evacuation of Nezarim where the resistance was expected to be tougher was also planned to be in the first week. The settlement considered the most difficult for the entire process was Newe Deqalim, the largest in the Qatif bloc, where the ideological motivation was perceived to be very strong. Special sensitivity was being accorded to the evacuation of the Qatif bloc cemetery, together with the evacuation of the synagogues of the settlement bloc. The cemetery evacuation had to take place after the settlements have been emptied, in the fifth week of the operation. Between the fifth and eighth week the army was planning to complete the evacuation of the settlements' infrastructure. Toward the end of 2005, the army forces planned to withdraw from the Strip.

In May 2005 the Israeli government ordered the planning authorities to prepare a regional plan to settle the Jewish evacuees from the Gaza Strip in the Nizan region, between the town of Ashqelon and the Strip, at the southern part of the Coastal Plain, and also to plan the enlargement of the community settlement of Nizan. This planned region has been proposed for the establishment of new settlements for the evacuees who might stay together after the disengagement in a settlement bloc similar to Qatif. In the framework of this new region the government has promised to protect the sandy open space in the vicinity of Nizan and also the existing interrelationship between the environmental values and the urban development of Ashqelon. The execution of this plan depends upon the number of evacuees who sign an agreement with the government authorities to be resettled there. The local and detailed planning of this region will advance gradually according to the pace of the settlers' joining. The government would have preferred to settle the evacuees in the existing kibbuzim and moshavin of the northwestern Negev or in the existing neighborhoods of the development towns rather than to create a new unneeded region adjacent to one of the last nature reserves and open spaces at the southern Coastal Plain. But it seems that sometimes nature has to give up for politics.

Following these facts it may appear that the civilian part of the disengagement plan, excluding its military part, was not prepared properly by the Israeli government. The unclearness that existed concerning the solutions that had to be found for places to where the evacuees should be transferred, the potential of available dwellings in the western Negev and southern Coastal Plain, the contention over the necessity to settle the Nizan area, the search for potential agricultural land for the greenhouse owners of the Qatif bloc, the proposal to settle some of the evacuees in the Nizan region opposite the Egyptian border at Sinai, and the hurried search for free dwelling units in Ashqelon and in other adjacent development towns – all these were reminiscent of the beginning of the 1950s when hurried improvisations in planning and building in Israel were executed, leaving behind them many wounds in the landscape that could not be healed. But while that was done reluctantly after a War of Independence, the declaration of the State of Israel and during the absorption of a mass immigration of hundreds of thousands of Jews, it is hard to accept the fact that such similar improvisation took place in the Gaza Strip after 57 years of statehood. Israel has gained a lot of experience in planning and in the last four decades has prepared many of the master plans and outline schemes for the physical issues that concern a country. Therefore, a comprehensive master plan should now be prepared for the further stages of disengagement from the West Bank that may occur after the disengagement from the Gaza Strip.

After many years the Yamit region faded and disappeared from Israeli consciousness: the evacuation was not seared into Israeli consciousness as a trauma, and that is one of things that should make it possible to launch yet another evacuation process. The settlers want the evacuation to be engraved in the public memory as a great and impossible struggle to prevent any further withdrawal. In Yamit there was a huge gap between those who did the actual resisting, the members of

Gush Emunim, and the people who actually lived in Yamit. The actual residents fought mainly to increase their compensation payments while the Gush Emunim activists went down to Yamit and fought against the withdrawal itself. Yamit was a secular vacation town and towards the end it became a religious city. In the case of the Qatif bloc there is a complete identification between those running the struggle and the residents, so that the struggle against the evacuation will be much more intense.

But the Palestinians don't agree to the disengagement plan. The lessons for them are clear: Sharon's government, with or without the disengagement plan, has no intention of conducting negotiations with them on substantive issues; Sharon's support for the road map peace plan is nothing more than lip service; Israel will continue to establish *faits accomplis*; there is no chance of achieving political change except by the use of power and violence, as happened in the Gaza Strip. There is a risk of an increase in Hezbollah influence in the territories, but there is no alternative. The lesson for the Israeli public is that the occupation of the Palestinian territory will continue, along with the terror and violence; the war will definitely continue even during the implementation of the withdrawal from the Gaza Strip; the possibility that Israel will evacuate the illegal outposts is slight. Not only are the settlers opposed to the evacuation, the government is evading it.

But after all, the Palestinians perceive the disengagement plan in Gaza and the West Bank as a great victory. The Israeli explanation that it is disengagement and not a withdrawal, and certainly not a retreat, does not convince the Palestinians. As far as they are concerned, the army is going to quit the entire Gaza Strip and the State of Israel will be uprooting the settlements. Throughout all the years of the peace process, that has never happened. All the complicated negotiations, all the summits, and all the diplomatic talks never achieved for the Palestinians what the armed struggle has achieved: disengagement.

After Yasser Arafat's death Israel will have a Palestinian partner for negotiations as Abu Mazen was nominated Prime Minister of the Palestinian Authority, but it turns out that Sharon's concept of a unilateral withdrawal was designed to prevent any real progress in the political arena; the Prime Minister's support for the road map, which includes negotiations between the two sides, a clear timetable, and even an international conference, is not genuine; Sharon's disengagement plan deserves support, but eventually it is liable to add fuel to the fire of the conflict. It is clear that Israel must be presented with tougher conditions in exchange for co-operation with the Sharon plan. In order for the Gaza Strip not to turn into a time bomb, the disengagement plan has to be taken from Sharon. Blind support for it means support for the intention of freezing all negotiations. The work against the unilateral aspect of the plan means involving the Palestinians in its implementation, pushing the parties into negotiations in various practical areas, and making the aid from the World Bank and the E.U. countries conditional on the Israeli government combining international, Egyptian, and Palestinian activity.

In Jerusalem, politicians are still arguing about the plan espoused by Ariel Sharon to withdraw from the Gaza Strip and the northern West Bank. The international community, though, is already occupied with the next stage, which will take Israel from the disengagement plan to a deeper withdrawal from the West Bank, to a Palestinian State and to a discussion of the permanent settlement, in accordance with the international road map. Now Sharon has to return to his second round vis-à-vis the Palestinian leader Abu Mazen, from a completely different point. The Qatif bloc and the West Bank settlements of Gannim and Kaddim are already in the Palestinians' pocket; the next negotiations will begin with Bet El, Ofra, and the Jordan Valley settlements. Even after Arafat's death Israel will have to proceed with the implementation of the plan. Sharon wants the process to stop after the withdrawal from Gaza, with the issue of the West Bank left to his successors and with Israel continuing to hold onto the settlements until the Palestinians become "Finns", as one of his advisors said. The price Israel is paying for the new regional order is not the dismantling of the settlements in Gaza and the northern West Bank, but the domestic shock caused by the disengagement, with the clash between Sharon and the settlers at the heart of it. This is a transitional period that will not end with the departure of the last settler from Gaza. If the American administration sticks to this line, Israel will be required to leave all the West Bank.

Execution of the disengagement

More than 15,000 police officers and soldiers were deployed in the Gaza settlement bloc of Qatif on 17 August 2005 to begin the forced evacuation of the settlements. At that time more than half of the settlers in the Gaza Strip – 832 families out of the registered 1,550 registered as residents – had left their homes already. About 700 families remained in the Qatif bloc while many were expected to leave in the next day. A day before, dozens of police and army units had entered the Gaza settlement of Newe Deqalim, the biggest in the Strip, and went from house to house trying to convince residents to leave peacefully by midnight. They also offered to help pack the residents' belongings. Many residents asked the soldiers to leave, and argued with them to refuse evacuation orders. Everything that had happened up to 17 August, the scuffles between the illegal residents who infiltrated into the Strip to counter the disengagement and security forces notwithstanding, was no more than a prologue. The battle to disengage Israel from the Gaza Strip started on that day. Pull-out opponents who had infiltrated the Strip some weeks before clashed violently with security forces after the protesters attempted to block trucks carrying empty containers from entering the settlement. The largest settlement in the Qatif bloc did not appear to fit the description as one of the strongholds of the anticipated resistance. The hundreds who gathered in the center of the settlement seemed like a confused mob. They did not appear like a group of hardened and trained extremists hell-bent on stopping the army's entry. Wherever determination was displayed, the demonstrators backed off. The idea was to progress from the easy targets to the difficult ones and evacuate as many settlements as possible before finishing up at the enclaves of the radicals.

During the execution of the disengagement, police and security service officials were hard at work to identify and locate hard-core elements among the infiltrators, including extremists who used violence against the security forces. The most radical elements that resisted the evacuation forces in the Qatif bloc were individuals who infiltrated the Gaza Strip following its closure to non-residents on 13 July. The largest number of infiltrators was in Newe Deqalim, and some of the Qatif bloc youth joined up with the more radical groups that planned to put up a fight when the evacuation forces arrived.

The infiltrators to the Gaza Strip, Yeshiva students and young hooligans in skullcaps from the hilltops of Judea and Samaria, fought against the soldiers with every means at their disposal. They were subdued with hesitation, stopped, cuffed and locked up in the legal process. Some settlers tried to show that they were hanging on to their houses till the last minute, but they left without opposition when evacuation became inevitable.

The first day of the forcible evacuation saw five settlements – Tel Qatifa, Gane Tal, Morag, Bedolah and Kerem Azmona – completely evacuated. In addition some 150 families were evacuated from Newe Deqalim. In total, 533 homes of 1,523 people – about half of them infiltrators from outside Gaza – were evacuated. While most residents eventually agreed to be escorted out by the soldiers, there were dozens of cases in which troops had to enter a house and carry the family members out one by one, four policemen or soldiers to a person. The first day of the forcible evacuation phase went much better than planners had anticipated, with very few problems and almost no violence. Local dramas were solved relatively quickly and within the unofficial rules of the game recognized by both sides. No barricading incident lasted more than a few hours, while the settlers, who frequently cursed soldiers and police officers and sabotaged their vehicles, refrained in an overwhelming majority of cases from attacking security personnel.

On the next day, 18 August, the evacuation forces planned to focus on the main center of resistance in Newe Deqalim – the synagogue compound, where between one and two thousand people were holed up, most of them teenagers from outside the Gaza Strip. The worst confrontation occurred on the roof of Kefar Darom synagogue. After hours of talks, police officers were hoisted by crane onto the roof, where they were attacked by dozens of youths. About a dozen policement had to be hospitalized after acid was thrown at them; others sustained bruises and light injuries from sticks. Police arrested dozens of teenagers.

On 21 August, on the sixth day of the execution and disengagment, six more settlements were evacuated: Qatif, Slav, Azmona, and the three northern Gaza settlements of Ele Sinay, Dugit and Nusanit. There was little opposition there, and most of the settlers left on their own after reaching aggreements with the security forces. Most of the people evacuated were illegal infiltrators who had entered Nisanit and families that had returned to Ele Sinay. Only the isolated central Gaza settlement of Nezarim remained to be evacuated on the next day, 22 August, and that was carried out as planned. After 35 years, Israeli settlement of the Gaza Strip came to an end with the evacuation of residents from the final inhabited settlement, Nezarim, and the pull-out of the settlers from the Strip was completed. Nezarim was the place that stood for hanging on to every settlement, even the smallest and most isolated. This was the spot, in the middle of the Palestinian territory, that expressed Israeli stubbornness in the Intifada era. This was the place that Ariel Sharon once believed vital to maintain in order to keep an eye on the Gaza port. The port was not built, and now Nezarim has ceased to exist.

In all, it took the Israel Defense Forces and police only four and a half days to forcibly evict some 5,000 settlers and an unknown number of infiltrators. During those days, some 3,000 settlers left Gaza Strip of their own volition. The main reason for the swift achievement lay in the balance of power. The defense establishment allocated a huge force of some 50,000 soldiers and policemen to the task, and this tipped the scales. The complex co-ordination between the forces ensured that they would reach the settlements on time. Those who opposed disengagment could not fight this efficiency and the settlers' psychological warfare also failed to break the well-prepared forces.

After the evacuation of the settlers bulldozers razed more than 30 homes in Nisanit and Dugit in the northern Gaza Strip, making the first large-scale demolitions during the disengagement. Shortly afterward, house demolitions began in all other Qatif bloc settlements. All homes were being leveled to the ground. The complete demolitions were planned to be done within three weeks, and the evacuation of all the Gaza Strip settlers was when the last of them evacuated the settlement of Nezarim on that day.

One may ask if the settlers should have been there. Was it necessary to remove them? The answer is positive. The 30 years of pointless settlement on the Gaza Coast has come to an end. The great injustice done to the Palestinians had to be ended. Israel's great historic mistake had to be corrected. The disengagement was a *fait accompli*. But the significance of this act of total uprooting has yet to enter Israel's consciousness. Nobody knows what damage it has done to both the uprooters and the uprooted, or what imprint it will leave on Israel's soul. The Qatif bloc was a world of its own, a world of work and faith, of patriotic innocence and communal warmth, a world that was established in the wrong place at the wrong time. Now this world was buried in the sands of Gaza.

The complex Qatif bloc case may be seen as a baseless settlement project of a mother-state that chose to place a low-income population in occupied territory, a closed local regime that maintained a colonialist farm economy, nourished by cheap land, cheap water, and cheap labor, all originating in the military occupation. All this was interwoven with the singular settlement enterprise and a messianic cast to the feeling of supremacy. It endangered the mother-state, poisoned its democracy, corrupted its enlightenment, and thwarted its ability to function as a rational entity. These anomalous conditions enabled the development of an anomalous society, a strong, cohesive, and principled society of tenacity, decency, and mutual help, a frontier society of members of the lower middle class who found meaning in the sand-swept territory and fashioned there a narrative of meaning.

By the disengagement from the Gaza Strip Prime Minister Ariel Sharon turned the Israeli reality on its head. He did not apologize to the settlers. The reason for the shift in his position was demography. It is demography that forced the evacuation of Gaza on anyone wishing to live in a State with a Jewish majority and who is not prepared to rely on the Messiah. The approximately 1.3 million Arabs now living in the Gaza Strip are what changed Sharon's mind. Indeed, on the eve of the disengagement, Jews became a minority between the Mediterranean and Jordan. Sharon has also very belatedly reached the obvious conclusion that the immense gap between the villas of the Jewish settlers and the shacks of the Palestinians would end with a huge explosion, a bloodbath, and that was what he wanted to prevent.

There are two faces to the disengagment from the Gaza Strip that, in fact, may be mutually contradictory. The positive aspect is reflected in Israel's success in shortening the military lines logically and ceding territory that effectively was of no strategic importance to the country. Israel was extricating itself from the demographic and economic trap of the Gaza Strip and from an onerous occupation in which farmland and water were plundered from 1.3 million Palestinians. Israel has set itself a precedent in evacuating settlements, and did so, perhaps, at the last minute. The negative aspect of the disengagement is reflected, above all, in the uncertainty of who will rule in the Gaza Strip after the evacuation and whether a new round of violence will erupt. This situation is compounded by the fact that the Palestinians feel, and to a large extent justifiably, that the Israeli withdrawal from Gaza is their victory.

Israel's disengagement from the Gaza Strip was the main goal of the battle, but not the only one. No less important is the rehabilitation of the State's authority and the restoration of the validity of the rule of law. Both of these were undermined for decades by a small minority, Gush Emunim and its settlers, who dictated the national agenda and forced the government to bend policy and security, and social and economic considerations, to their interests. The security forces proved for the first time in a long time their ability to deal with determined settlers and with the hooligans whom they had so far treated with indulgence.

Along with the relatively smooth progress of the disengagement operation, a gap has developed between false predictions and reality; between the threats of a rift, a civil war and mass refusal of military orders, and the discipline that the vast majority of skullcap-clad soldiers demonstrated, and the relative restraint displayed by the settlers. The problematic nature of the dual tactics used by settler leaders and their rabbis was thus unveiled in all its "glory". On one hand, inflammatory rhetoric that depicts the evacuation as an apocalyptic event, comparable to the destruction of the Temple, even the Holocaust; on the other, a genuine effort to moderate and restrain the results of this inflammatory rhetoric on the ground. This dual tactic describes not only the history of the orthodox settlement movement, but particularly what happened during the last few weeks before the evacuation. The leaders prevented violent clashes with the police, but at the same time they persuaded as many people as possible to halt the evacuation with their bodies. The rabbis of the extreme right used all the means at their disposal. At first they called on soldiers to refuse orders and threatened them with eternal punishment if they dared evacuate settlements. Then the rabbis exerted massive pressure on all the skullcap-wearers, especially on teachers at all levels. Rabbis in Yeshiva high schools, male and female teachers, religious educators and public figures – all were silenced in the framework of a spiritual terrorism that accused opponents of messianism of treason regarding the Jewish issue. They have transformed the struggle over the Qatif bloc from a legitimate political dispute into an all-out war between the State and religion. They, and the settler-supporters who do their bidding, inflamed the religious youths who accepted their authority, and didn't shirk from enlisting in the struggle the marginal youths of the religious camp who in any case tend toward violence. It seems that the entire population in Israel is now artificially divided into Jews who support the rabbis and Jew-haters who oppose them.

5 The Palestinian State

The main intention of the Palestinians, when they declared the establishment of a Palestinian State in the West Bank and the Gaza Strip, was to bring about a change in the region, although such a State will lack basic geographical and economic components. A few years ago when Israel had in principle agreed upon the establishment of a Palestinian State in the territories, the agreement was determined by a statement that there would be no return of refugees to the 5 June 1967 boundaries; that the settlements near Jerusalem and those adjacent to the eastern side of the "Green Line" would be annexed to Israel; that the settlers who preferred to remain under the Palestinian Authority would gain a special status, as well as the Palestinians included in the annexed blocs; that Jerusalem as the capital of Israel would never be divided again; and that the Palestinian State would be demilitarized and prohibited from signing military agreements with other countries. But despite all that, the Palestinian Authority is making efforts to establish a State that may create a distorted and unreasonable geographical territory that may not be able to function properly. It is, therefore, worth describing and analyzing from a spatial point of view the main geographical conditions of such a State to be created in the West Bank and the Gaza Strip.

The future Palestinian State will undoubtedly be small in size and high in population density. The total population in the West Bank and Gaza Strip numbered in 2004 about three million. As there are 40 countries in the world with populations of up to three million, it seems at first glance that the Palestinian State might not be exceptional in this list. But if we classify these countries according to their size and population we realize that 9 of them are European countries in a modern co-operative economy, 14 are islands and therefore geographically limited in size and population, and 4 others are wealthy oil countries in the Persian Gulf. All the other 13 are underdeveloped with a relatively small population. As regards size and population, the future Palestinian State might be included in the last group.

The population density in the West Bank in the so-called A and B Areas is about 1,858 inhabitants per sq. mile (726 inhabitants per sq. km), and that of the Gaza Strip, known as one of the most densely populated regions in the world, is about 6,200 inhabitants per sq. mile (2,422 inhabitants per sq. km). The average density of both parts, the West Bank together with the Gaza Strip, is therefore about 2,514 inhabitants per sq. mile (982 inhabitants per sq. km), still a high density compared to other countries. Higher densities than these are to be found in Singapore with 2,236 inhabitants per sq. mile (873 per sq. km) or Bahrain with 2,682 inhabitants per sq. mile (1,048 per sq. km), but their economies are much more developed with a high standard of living compared to the West Bank. A similar population density to that of the West Bank, with 2,339 inhabitants per sq. mile (914 per sq. km), may be found in Bangladesh, which is known as one of the poorest countries on the world. The very high birth rates in the Gaza Strip, which reach to 45 per thousand inhabitants annually, are typical of underdeveloped countries, and are also the main reason for the high population densities.

What kind of a territorial shape may the future Palestinian State have? The shape of countries is determined by their area and length of boundaries. Most countries need a reasonable degree of compactness to be able to function efficiently in their entire territory, to defend themselves from all sides, to provide their populations with services effectively and to develop an efficient communications system. In political geography it is usual to categorize countries by "compactness", a way of describing the relationship between area and length of boundaries. A State may be roughly circular, oval, or rectangular in territory, with the distance from the geometric center to any point on the boundary exhibiting little variance. If the value of compactness of a country (area divided by length of boundaries) is high, it means that the length of its boundaries comparative to its area is short. If the value of compactness of a country is low, it means that its borders are long comparative to its area, and that for each mile of boundary there is only a small area. A country with an oval shape, Hungary for instance, has a compactness value of 48, rectangular France has a value of 112, and Spain with its square shape a value of 136. The compactness of the future Palestinian State with its twisted boundaries around the A and B Areas making a total length of 422 miles (675 km) will be 3.9 – one of the lowest compactness values of countries in the world. The State of Israel has a compactness value of 20.

The Palestinian Authority in the West Bank comprises 60 A and B blocs of different size in which hundreds of villages and cites are separated by C Areas that are under Israeli dominance. All of them are completely separated from the Gaza Strip. So many separated rural enclaves are not known in any country of the world and they also increase to an enormous length the future Palestinian State boundaries without enclosing much territorial hinterland. There are not many countries in the world, except island "countries" such as the Philippines or Indonesia, that contain so many separated territorial units within their boundaries. Once Pakistan was separated into two units separated by a distance of about 625 miles (1,000 km), but later on, the eastern unit became the independent State of Bangladesh. Today, almost no country includes so many remote territorial enclaves as may happen in the Palestinian State. There is no country in the world that needs to secure corridors in a neighboring sovereign country in order to establish commerce and economic ties between its separate units as will happen in the Palestinian State. There is almost no country in the world which is surrounded by another sovereign country, and is enclosed from all sides, as Israel envelops the Palestinian territory and dominates its entrance and exit transit routes (Fig. 5.1).

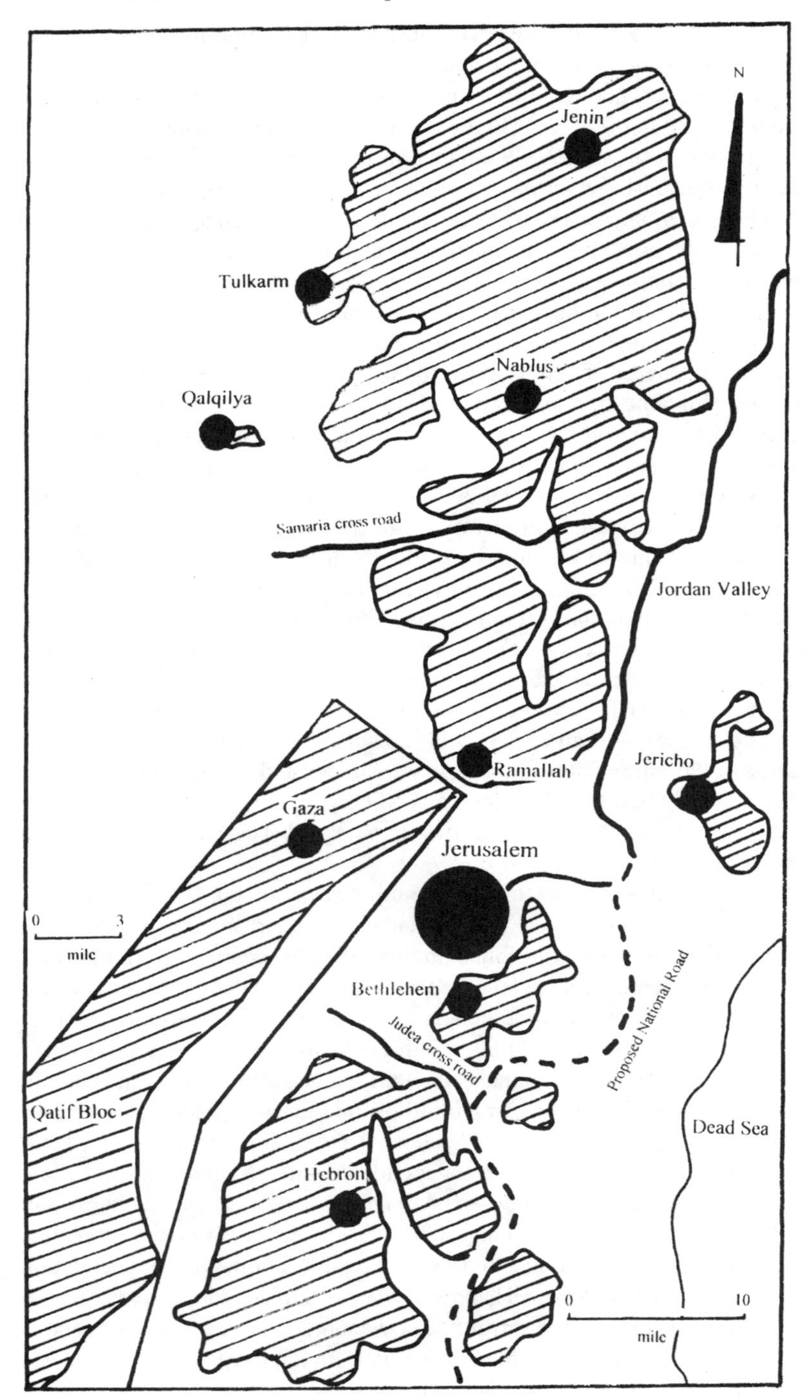

Fig. 5.1 The future Palestinian State

It is quite clear that a Palestinian State with so many territorial enclaves will not be able to manage economic functions and administration. Even if its sovereign territory were greater, and even if some of the enclaves were connected into a continued territorial unit, the main communications arteries that are under Israeli dominance running from north to south and from west to east, and those along the Judean Desert that are under Israeli dominance, might perpetuate their spatial fragmentation. Such a fragmented territory will create a conspicuous disconnection between Judea and Samaria, between Samaria and the surroundings of Qalqilya, and between them and Jericho. The crossing of the region by lateral roads such as the northern and central highways and the northern and southern crossing roads of Judea will, undoubtedly, intensify the fragmentation of the region. The Palestinian State will also be surrounded by Israeli security zones along the "Green Line" in north and west, and also in the Jordan Valley and the Judean Desert, except for a narrow corridor which may be provided to Jericho to the east and to Qalqilya in the west, and with a militarily supervised connection to the Gaza Strip.

The connection between the two main separated parts of the Palestinian Authority is today by the Gaza–Hebron road via the Ashqelon–Qiryat Gat–Tarkumiya axis. The Palestinians commuting on this road are not allowed to leave the road, are allowed to travel only during daylight, and are obliged to pass on their way through several checkpoints. Another road to the north might be provided in the future via the Ashqelon–Qiryat Gat–Ma'ale Nachshon–Latrun–Mevo Horon–Beitunya axis. Even passing from the Palestinian State to the Hashemite Kingdom of Jordan will in future be by a lateral Israeli road under strict security supervision. Roads passing through a neighboring country without diplomatic relations are known only in a few cases in the world, as that between the Congo and the Katanga region in Africa. Other famous such roads of the past were between West Germany and West Berlin in 1945–89, and between West Jerusalem and Mount Scopus in 1948–67. These passing roads were problematic, very broken, and could be used at the mercy of the country that dominated them, which did not always ensure free traffic and communications stability. Territorial connections between parts of a country that are based only on road communications might weaken their functions, dominance, and administration in the area.

The future spatial relationships between the State of Israel and the Palestinian Authority may raise many geographical problems. In the past the discussions dealt mainly with the possible physical connections between the Palestinian fragmented A and B Areas in the West Bank and the C Areas under Israeli dominance. Some initial proposals were raised regarding the arrangements to be made to ensure safe passing roads between the West Bank and the Gaza Strip. It seems that it will be necessary to connect the West Bank and the Gaza Strip by one or two main roads that will have to be decided upon, despite all the physical and environmental consequences of them on Israel's sovereign territory. At Brussels in February 2005 President George W. Bush placed the achievement of an Israeli–Palestinian peace settlement at the top of NATO's list of priorities. He called for the establishment of a democratic Palestinian State with territorial contiguity in the West Bank and said that a State with scattered territories would not work.

Some years ago a plan was drawn up by the former Prime Minister Ehud Barak with a proposal to build an elevated bridge on pillars between the two parts of the Palestinian State, 30 miles (47 km) long, with a four-lane road, a railway line, and all the necessary engineering installations on it, connecting Mount Hebron near Dura and Beit Hanun in the Gaza Strip and allowing free traffic for the Palestinians. This proposed bridge had to be built along the shortest distance between the two parts of the Palestinian State, at an elevation of 15–30 ft (5–10 m) above the ground. Its construction would entail the appropriation of land in a strip 450 ft (150 m) wide, and a total area of about 1,750 acres (7,000 dunams) in Israel's territory. It would undoubtedly impinge on the surroundings, with its hundreds of concrete pillars and engineering installation. It might also do harm to the environment and to the agricultural plots of land along the Sederot–Or Haner–Dorot–Ruhama axis, and might require crossings on existing roads in the region and on the Be'ersheva railway line. The plan was seen as a very unusual solution because long traffic bridges over flat terrains do not exist anywhere. Bridges in the world connect separated areas of land but not separated parts of a territory. Even in cases where a country has separated territory, as Angola and Kabinda in Africa or the two parts of Azerbaijan, or the United States and Alaska, or at one time between West Germany and Berlin, no road bridges were constructed over flat terrain. In order to connect parts of a territory arrangements have been achieved between neighboring countries to enable the passing of traffic, passengers, and goods for the benefit of both sides. It seems that the using of the existing road network in the northern Negev, mainly the Hebron–Be'ersheva–Gaza and the Gaza–Ashqelon–Ramallah roads, or even the Gaza–Arad–En Gedi–Jericho road, with efficient security arrangements agreed upon in terms of peace, might be a cheaper solution to the problem of separated territories and a better and more reasonable connection between the two parts of the Palestinian State.

What kind of a neighboring Palestinian State may Israel find beyond its borders? Should Israel consider that it is possible to administer effectively an independent authority in Judea, Samaria, and the Gaza Strip in these distorted circumstances? The territory which Israel transfers to the Palestinian Authority in the future depends first of all on Israel's own ultimate security needs, disregarding the minimal space that the Palestinians need to run a State. Trends in the Israel establishment incline to accept a gradual change in the fragmented seven urban A Areas and the 176 rural B Areas in the West Bank that were created as a result of the Interim Agreement of September 1995, and to combine them into two bigger disconnected blocs, although they will be bisected from west to east by two Samarian and two Judean cross roads and a Jerusalem–Jericho road, and two connection roads between Nablus, Tulkarm, and Qalqilya that will remain under Israeli dominance. The two mountainous blocs, at an altitude of 1,500–3,000 ft (500–1,000 m), will be surrounded by Israeli territory all sides, by the Jordan Valley in the east, by the Valley of Dotan in the north, and by a longitudinal occupied strip of land in the west, east of the "Green Line". That is, more or less, how Israel intends to demarcate the future Palestinian State in an area of 40–50 per cent of the West Bank.

The objective geographical facts that will influence the future Palestinian State may create adjacent to Israel a neighboring undeveloped Third World State, densely populated, poor, lacking in resources, and blocked physically, with all the social, economic, and political consequences that result. Such a State may endanger its ability to ensure fulfillment of signed agreements, and Israel should be aware of all these facts in any possible peace agreement to be signed in the future with the Palestinian Authority.

After all, the Israeli government prevents the Palestinians from developing a reasonable sovereignty in the region by piling up difficulties for them. Only three urban outline schemes were approved between 1967 and 1993, while for most of the villages boundaries were demarcated through aerial photographs, approving only the existing built-up areas. Lacking approved regional plans is what makes it difficult for the Authority to prevent the hurried illegal building of houses in the villages and towns in spite of the fact that for many years building plans were delayed and private landowners were unable to exercise their right to build dwellings. It is urgently necessary to renew in the West Bank the infrastructure of the towns regarding electricity, water supply, and sewerage. The West Bank needs more industry and employment for the people, especially for those who are prevented from working in Israel. There is a lack of public institutions, especially schools. The population density in the towns is today 2.1 per room, and that will be higher in the future with the estimated total increase of the Palestinian population to an annual rate of 3 per cent in the West Bank and 3.5 per cent annually in the Gaza Strip. In the case of Palestinian independent autonomy and full sovereignty, the return of thousands of refugees from the camps in the neighboring countries is expected. It is estimated that, out of four million refugees who live in the Arab countries, 1.5 million may return within the first decade. If that happens, the population in the territories will be doubled. The housing of the natural population increase will need at least 200,000 more dwelling units; about 150,000 renewed dwelling units will be needed in the refugee camps, and another quarter of a million dwelling units for those who return. The rate of house building will then grow sixfold, and the land allocated for it will be three times bigger than the existing built-up area of today. It may be that even a new town will be needed in the territories to supply dwelling units after all the existing built-up areas are filled up.

Israel's generosity, as expressed in maps drawn by governmental bodies toward a permanent agreement with the Palestinians, is mocking the poor. If Israel holds in the future the long strip of land east of the "Green Line", the Ezyon bloc, the surroundings of Jerusalem, and the Jewish settlement strip along the Jordan Valley, the grant to the Palestinians, even with 90 per cent of the West Bank, will still not be enough for a functioning autonomy. But that is the minimum that Israel has to offer to its neighbor if the aim is to stabilize the situation in the territories and to achieve peace.

6 Occupation and delusions

In the history of the Land of Israel, from the end of the nineteenth century to the present, two main periods of Jewish occupation have occurred in the region. The first one, between 1882 and 1947, which may be named the "Zionist occupation", was characterized by Jewish immigration from Europe to Palestine in five or six waves, by land acquisition and settlement with the assistance of Jewish national and private capital donated by Jews from all over the world. This period was brought to a close at the eve of the War of Independence and by the establishment of the State of Israel in 1948.

The second period of Jewish occupation, between 1967 and today, which may be named the "military occupation" is characterized by the occupation of Judea, Samaria, and the Gaza Strip, and by a gradual penetration and settlement of the territories through seizure of Arab land. What are the similarities and the differences between these two periods of occupation, and what were their results?

The first period of Jewish occupation lasted 65 years and was characterized by a vision and redemption of the Jewish people, with settlement in the Land of Israel and with the hope of enabling Jews to return to their historic homeland after two thousand years of exile. This period was also characterized by intensive activities of land acquisition from Arabs, by the establishment of colonies (moshavot), community settlements (kibbutzim), and smallholders' settlements (moshavim), by the creation of settlement blocs for self-defense against Arab riots, and by the establishing of an economic infrastructure based on agriculture, commerce, and services. In that period the priority of the Zionist leaders was to settle Jews in the Coastal Plain and in the interior valleys of the country, to form an N-shape settlement strip from the Hula Valley in the north though the Valleys of Bet She'an, Harod, and Yesreel, and then along the Coastal Plain as far as the northern Negev, to concentrate Jewish population along the main communications arteries and adjacent to the harbor entrance gates of Jaffa and Haifa, to settle the mountainous areas of Galilee and the Negev Desert, despite all the difficulties of self-defense and political struggle against the Ottoman regime that prevailed till the First World War, against the riots of 1921, 1929, and 1936 and finally against the decrees of the British Mandatory regime and the "White Paper" laws of 1939. But in spite of all that, the final result of the first period of occupation was the establishment in 1948 of a Jewish State in the Land of Israel, which has been recognized by the world community.

The second period of Jewish occupation has existed for 38 years up to the present, and has also been characterized by a vision of settling Jews in the Land of Israel, but with the aspiration to realize Jewish settlement in the occupied regions of Judea, Samaria, and the Gaza Strip. This vision began with a military territorial occupation and was followed by a rapid seizure of the lands that were declared as "State lands", with many settlements established on them in order to consolidate military occupation and security in the region. The settlements were mostly not based economically on agriculture or industry, but mainly on the service sector as community and semi-urban units. They were not established in valleys or plains but mainly in mountainous areas. They also needed self-defense against the Palestinians Intifadas, continuous attacks on Jews and terror, so that blocs of settlement were therefore needed for environmental defense. The occupation met the disapproval of external hostile bodies such as the United Nations, the European Community, and even sections of the Jewish people in Israel and abroad.

A comparison between the two periods of Jewish occupation indicates that behind both of them there was a vision; in both of them means were taken to seize or to acquire Arab lands for establishing settlements; in both of them environmental self-defense settlement blocs were created; and both of them had confrontations with Arabs and external organizations. But while the first occupation was carried out in a slow and gradual way and was based on the readiness and economic ability of the Jewish people in the world to acquire land, the second period of occupation was rapid, drastic, and carried out by military forces, while the settling of the territories was based on the State of Israel's budgets and on governmental decisions. Although the second period of occupation was militarily strongly dominating and almost omnipotent, it was, except in the seizure of land for the establishment of settlements and outposts, generally less successful than the first one, and promised no positive future solution to the dispute between Israel and the Palestinians. But more important is the fact, that, while the first occupation achieved a Jewish sovereign State on a continuous territory of 8,086 sq. miles (about 20,700 sq. km), the second occupation did not achieve any concrete result or acquire more territory, and it is doubtful if it will achieve more territory in a legitimate way in the political situation of today, being threatened by the withdrawal from areas of Samaria.

In spite of Israel's military occupation since 1967, the territories have been occupied twice more since 2000. At the beginning of the second Intifada in 2000 and of the many terrorist attacks on Israelis in the country and in the territories, the government decided to execute a military operation to put an end to terror and to destroy all the places where terror originates, and where suicide bombers are trained and prepared for executing their missions. During this operation the towns of the West Bank were surrounded by military forces and intensive fighting took place in built-up areas, during which many houses were blown up and many Palestinians were killed, although the Israel military forces suffered many casualties too.

After this operation the military establishment considered that it had reached its goal and succeeded in rehabilitating Israel's deterrence after the hurried withdrawal from Lebanon. It considered that the disrupted terrorist infrastructure would ensure at least a few months of rest, an assumption that was too optimistic. After a short time the terrorist organizations started to act again. Their continuous attacks forced the government to attack the Palestinian organizations again because none of the other means taken previously was effective. High-ranking officers made it clear then that the first operation failed and that other steps had to be taken to change the situation in the region. After a new series of suicide bomb attacks in Israel, which caused dozens of casualties, Israel began a new military operation during which the towns of Nablus, Jenin, Qalqilya, Tulkarm, Ramallah, and Bethlehem were reoccupied and encircled, and intensive fighting in the built-up areas in them occurred again.

After this second occupation it was clear that a new policy of permanent occupation in the Palestinian towns, which may last a long time, has been decided. The army then began to administer the economic and social life in the region as a ruling power. This policy fell in line with the military belief that as long as the army is present in all the Palestinian towns it will be possible to prevent the suffering of the population in Israel and to put an end to the suicide bombings. But it turned out that this concept was fundamentally wrong. An occupied population, and especially one such as the Palestinians, that has lost any hope for peace, and that lives without employment and sources of income, may succeed very rapidly in reorganizing and continuing its violent insurgency. But the military establishment considered then that disengagement from the towns of the West Bank might be regarded by the Palestinians as a sign of Israel's weakness: therefore it was out of the question that the dispute should end with a feeling that the Palestinians had won the war.

As a result, after three months Israel found itself again in the occupied towns of the West Bank, making great efforts to destroy the terrorist infrastructure, but being trapped there without any constructive solution. The government considered two options: either to reconcile itself to the terror or to occupy the West Bank. No one in the government proposed a total disengagement from the territories. All the steps that were taken in these two military operations to reoccupy the West Bank were seen as a collective punishment of the Palestinians and a breaching of international agreements. The suffering of the Palestinian population during these military operations cannot be excused and justified by the struggle against terror.

It seems that, after many years of insurgency and terrorism in the territories, the Israeli government is gradually becoming disillusioned with the occupation of the West Bank. Indeed, there is still no common consent in the Israeli government about the next steps, but the efforts, the many plans, and the different possible solutions that are proposed from time to time by officials are perhaps a sign of better results to come.

The first delusion of many Israelis about the occupation is the belief that the Jews in the West Bank are able to settle the occupied territories effectively, although the Palestinian population numbered in 2004 more than three million people, nearly half the size of the Jewish population in Israel.

The second delusion is the assumption that the settlers in the West Bank, who number about 230,000 people, are able to create a demographic critical mass that will dominate the region until the local Palestinian population becomes negligible.

The third delusion is that the dispersion of Jewish settlements all over Judea and Samaria and mainly on their western slopes, will succeed in creating an absolute Israeli dominance on the Palestinian most densely populated urban and rural parts of the region.

The fourth delusion is that the construction of separate by-pass roads in the region for the Jewish settlers will provide them with security and will decrease the conflict between the two peoples.

The fifth delusion is that the legal and illegal outposts that the settlers have constructed to enlarge their settlement boundaries and thereby enlarge the total holding of territory in Judea and Samaria, will ensure their existence there for a long time, that they will be defended by the Israeli military forces forever, that the few settlers who live in the outposts will always be safe there, and that they will be able to retain their position in isolated sites without being evacuated by the government bodies when the time comes.

The sixth delusion is that the more settlers and outposts are dispersed in the peripheral sections of Judea and Samaria, the more land in the occupied territories will be annexed to Israel in the future.

The seventh delusion is that the Palestinians who live in the region will adapt themselves to the sprawling occupation and will be ready for reconciliation, and even be ready to divide the region between them and the Israelis on that basis to reach a final peace agreement.

The eighth delusion is that the Palestinians will agree to the annexation to Israel of the areas in Judea and Samaria where a relatively high concentration of Jewish settlements exists adjacent to the "Green Line", even if remote settlements of the periphery are abandoned and their settlers transferred to them.

The ninth delusion is that reunited Jerusalem will be able to remain united for ever in its present municipal boundaries in the framework of a permanent agreement with the Palestinian Authority, and that there will be no arrangements that may provide the Palestinians with any form of sovereignty in East Jerusalem and in the holy sites.

The tenth delusion is that the seam line in the west, between Israel and the Palestinian Authority, will safeguard the State of Israel from infiltrators, while on both sides of the seam line there live populations at different economic levels and unequal economically as regards employment sources, level of income, and standard of living.

The eleventh delusion is that the separation fence along the West Bank and the envelope fence in Jerusalem will be an efficient measure to prevent terrorist attacks in Israel in the future.

The twelfth delusion is that the intermittent penetration of Israel's military forces into the Palestinian cities to end terrorism is indeed the best solution and a good chance to teach them a lesson so that they may refrain from terrorist attacks.

The thirteenth delusion is that the two occupation campaigns conducted after 2000 have totally destroyed the terrorist infrastructure in the territories, and that after these operations Israel will remain safe.

The fourteenth delusion is that Israel's disengagement from the Gaza Strip is the final step of withdrawal from the territories, and that no further disengagements from the West Bank will be enforced upon Israel by the American administration in the near future.

The fifteenth delusion, but not the least, is that the Palestinian population will give up in despair at the Israeli occupation and the military penetration into cities, and will finally leave the region forever.

There are politicians in Israel who believe that they may delude all the people all the time. Politics needs indeed a high degree of self-delusion in order to be saved from hypocrisy. Herbert Asquith (1852–1928), a Prime Minister of Great Britain, once said that the Ministry of Defence has three different data systems: one to delude the population, the second to delude the cabinet, and the third to delude itself.

Glossary

Aliyah A term used for Jewish immigration to the Land of Israel.

Dunam A land measurement in Israel and in the Middle East. 1 dunam = $1/4$ acre.

Effendi A title of honor given to a high-ranking official in Turkey and in other Arab countries. In the Land of Israel, an Arab land owner who used to employ shareholder farmers to cultivate his fields.

Green Line The armistice line that was agreed between Israel, Egypt, Jordan, Lebanon, and Syria in 1949 after Israel's War of Independence. The line was demarcated on topographical maps in green, whence comes its name. The line coincided with the international borders of Egypt in Sinai and that of Lebanon, but changed the borders with Jordan. It demarcated the Gaza Strip which was under Egyptian rule and the West Bank that remained under Jordanian rule.

Gush Emunim (Hebrew: Bloc of the Faithful or Bloc of the Believers). A Jewish settlement movement of orthodox people in the West Bank that established settlements in this region and strives for Jewish dominance in the "Greater Land of Israel".

Ha'poel Hamizrahi A Zionist orthodox settlement movement that has established moshavim and kibbutzim in Israel and whose members come from religious communities.

Hezbollah An Islamic terrorist organization in southern Lebanon, supported by Syria and Iran. It excecutes frequent, often military attacks on the nothern border of Israel, aiming to be involved in solving Palestinian problems in the occupied territories.

Intifada An Arabic term for the Palestinian uprising and insurgency against the Israeli occupation in the West Bank and Gaza Strip. The first Intifada broke out in 1987 and the second one, the "Intifada Al-Aksa", in 2000.

Kibbutz (pl. kibbutzim) A communal settlement in which the land is national property and the rest of its infrastructure is collectively owned by its members.

Knesset The Israeli Parliament.

Moshav (pl. moshavim) A smallholders' settlement where each settler works his separate plot of land, lives in his own household, and draws income from his farm's production, but with joint marketing of produce and joint purchasing of farming appliances.

Moshava (pl. moshavot) A village with privately owned land, buildings, farming installations, etc.

Mukhtar The representative of an Arab village or town and the person who is responsible for the internal and external relationships of the inhabitants.

Nahal (Hebrew: initials of "Fighting Pioneer Youth"). Pioneering military units that include soldiers as settlers in peripheral areas along Israel's borders, and who are engaged in security and agriculture.

NIS New Israeli Shekel currency. See *shekel* below.

Outpost A temporary Jewish settlement in the West Bank established by settlers whose aim is to ensure the construction of a permanent settlement on its site in the future.

Potemkin Settlement A visionary settlement. The term is used after the Russian politician Gregory Potemkin (1739–91), who erected such villages in the Crimea Peninsula to impress the Tsarina Ekaterina II.

Sheikh A Muslim leader or an Arab leader of a tribe.

Shekel The official Israel currency. $1 US = 4.62 shekels (October 2005).

Stockade and tower A type of Jewish settlement in the years of riots 1936–9 through which settlements were established in remote areas of the country to ensure the possession of purchased land. These settlements were erected in one day by building of a tower and a stockade on a plot of land that included within its limits tents, barracks, and guard posts.

Sultan A ruler or a "king" in an Arab country.

Tel A hill on which a settlement existed in ancient times.

Torah The holy Jewish Scroll of Law.

Triangle An area in the eastern part of the Coastal Plain which includes three large villages that became towns: Tira, Tayibe, and Qalansawe.

Wadi A steep-sided rocky ravine in a desert or semi-desert area, usually waterless, but sometimes containing a torrent for a short time after heavy rains.

Waqf Muslim holy property that cannot be sold or transmitted to anybody else.

White Paper A British law of 1939 that limited free purchase of land by Jews in western Palestine and limited Jewish immigration to a total 75,000 people during the following years.

Select bibliography

Allon, Y. (1976) "The Case for Defensible Borders", *Foreign Affairs*, 55 (1).
Alpher, J. (1994) *Settlements and Borders – Final Status Issues – Israelis-Palestinians*, Study No. 3, Tel Aviv University: Jafee Center for Strategic Research.
Alpher, J. and Feldman, S. (1989) *The West Bank and Gaza, Israel's Options for Peace*, Tel Aviv University: Jafee Center for Strategic Research.
Arkadie, B.V. (1977) *Benefits and Burdens: A Report on the West Bank and Gaza Strip Economics since 1967*, Washington D.C.: Carnegie Endowment for Peace.
Benvenisti, M. (2000) *Sacred Landscape: The Buried History of the Holy Land since 1948*, Berkeley: University of California Press.
Benvenisti, M. (1984) *The West Bank Data Project – A Survey of Israel's Policies*, Washington, D.C. and London: American Enterprise Institute of Public Policy Research.
Benvenisti, M. and Khayat, S. (1988) *The West Bank and Gaza Atlas*, Jerusalem: The West Bank Data Base Project.
Brawer, M. (1968) "The Geographical Background of the Jordan Water Dispute", in C.A. Fisher (ed.), *Essays in Political Geography*, London: Methuen.
B'tselem. (2002) *Land Grab: Israel's Settlement Policy in the West Bank*, Jerusalem.
Buhang, H. and Lujala, P. (2005) "Accounting for Scale: Measuring Geography in Quantitative Studies of Civil War", *Political Geography*, 24: 399–418.
Chechin, A. Hutman, B. and Melamed, A. (1999) *Separated and Unequal – the Inside Story of Israeli Rule in East Jerusalem*, Cambridge, MA and London: Harvard University Press.
Cohen, A. (1983) *West Bank Agriculture 1968–1980*, Giv'at Haviva, Israel: The Institute of Arabic Studies.
Cohen, S.B. (1994) "Gaza Viability: The Need for Enlargement of its Land Base", in C. Schofield and R. Schofield (eds), *World Boundaries, 2: The Middle East and North Africa*, London: Routledge.
Cohen, S.B. (1986) *The Geopolitics of Israel's Border Question*, Boulder: Westview Press.
Cohen, S.B. (1977) *Jerusalem – Bridging the Four Walls: A Geopolitical Perspective*, New York: Herzl Press.
Cutter, S., Richardson, D.B. and Wilbanks, T.J. (2003) *The Geographical Dimensions of Terrorism*, New York and London: Routledge.
Dumper, M. (1997) *The Politics of Jerusalem since 1967*, New York: Columbia University Press.
Efrat, E. (2000) "Jerusalem: Partition Plans for the Holy City", in E. Karsch (ed.), *Israel Affairs*, 6(3–4), London.

Efrat, E. (1994) "Jewish Settlements in the West Bank: Past, Present and Future", *Israel Affairs*, 1(1), London.

Efrat, E. (1993) "British Town Planning Perspectives of Jerusalem in Transition", *Planning Perspectives*, 6, London.

Efrat, E. (1988) *Geography and Politics in Israel since 1967*, London: Frank Cass.

Efrat, E. (1982) "Spatial Patterns of Jewish and Arab Settlements in Judea and Samaria", in D.J. Elazar (ed.), *Judea, Samaria and Gaza: Views on the Present and Future*, Washington, D.C.: American Enterprise Institute for Public Policy Research.

Efrat, E. (1977) "Changes in the Settlement Pattern of Judea and Samaria during Jordanian Rule", *Middle Eastern Studies*, 13(1).

Efrat. E. (1976) "Changes in the Settlement Pattern of the Gaza Strip 1945–1975", *Asian Affairs*, 63, London.

Efrat. E. (1971) *Changes in the Town Planning Concepts of Jerusalem 1919–1969*, Environmental Planning, Jerusalem.

Efrat, E. (1970) *Judea and Samaria: Guidelines for Physical Regional Planning*, Jerusalem: Ministry of the Interior.

Efrat, E. and Noble, A.G. (1988) *Problems of a Reunited Jerusalem*, New York: Cities.

Elazar, D. (1981) *Two Peoples – One Land: Federal Solutions for Israel, the Palestinians and Jordan*, New York: University Press of America.

Elazar, D. (ed.) (1982) *Judea, Samaria and Gaza: Views on the Present and Future*, Washington, D.C. and London: American Enterprise Institute for Public Policy Research.

Elmusa, S. (1994) "The Israeli-Palestinian Water Dispute Can Be Resolved", *Palestine–Israel Journal*, 3.

Enderlin, C. (2003) *Shattered Dreams: The Failure of the Peace Process in the Middle East 1995–2002*, New York: Other Press.

Evans, G. (1998) *Dictionary of International Relations*, London: Penguin Books.

Fawcet, L. (2005) *International Relations in the Middle East*, Oxford: Oxford University Press.

Frum, D. and Perle, R. (2003) *An End to Evil: How to Win the War on Terror*, New York: Random House.

Gharaibeh, F. (1985) *The Economics of the West Bank and Gaza Strip*, Boulder: Westview Press.

Glacaman, G. and Lonning, D.J. (eds) (1998) *After Oslo; New Realities, Old Problems*, London: Pluto Press.

Gvirtzman, H. (1994) "Groundwater Allocation in Judea and Samaria", in R.J. Isaac and H. Shuval (eds), *Water and Peace in the Middle East*, Elsevier B.V.

Harris, W.W. (1983) *A Palestinian State: The Implications for Israel*, Cambridge, MA: Harvard University Press.

Heikal, M. (1996) *Secret Channels: The Inside Story of Arab–Israeli Peace Negotiations*, London: Harper Collins Publishers.

Hirsch, M., Housen-Couriel, D. and Lapidoth, R. (1995) *Whither Jerusalem? Proposals and Positions Concerning the Future of Jerusalem*, Jerusalem: The Jerusalem Institute for Israel Studies.

Horowitz, D. and Lissak, M. (1990) *Trouble in Utopia: The Overburdened Polity of Israel*, Albany, NY: State University of New York Press.

Horowitz, D. (1975) *Israel's Concept of Defensible Boundaries*, Working Paper, The Hebrew University, Jerusalem: Leonard Davis Institute of International Relations.

Isaac, R.J. (1976) *Israel Divided: Ideological Politics in the Jewish State*, Baltimore: Johns Hopkins University.

Kahan, D. (1987) *Agriculture and Water Resources in the West Bank and Gaza, 1967–1987*, Jerusalem: The West Bank Data Base Project.

Karsch, E. (2000) *From War to Peace, Israel: The First Hundred Years*, vol. 2, London: Frank Cass.

Karsch, E. (ed.) (1993) *Peace in the Middle East: The Challenge for Israel*, London: Frank Cass.

Katz, Y. (1998) *Between Jerusalem and Hebron – Jewish Settlement in the Pre-State Period*, Ramat Gan, Israel: Bar-Ilan University Press.

Katz, Y. (1993) "The Political Status of Jerusalem in Historical Context: Zionist Plans for the Partition of Jerusalem in the Years 1937–1938", *Shofar*, 11(3), Jerusalem.

Kellerman, A. (1994) *Society and Settlement: Jewish Land of Israel in the Twentieth Century*, New York: SUNY Press.

Kimhi, I., Reichman, S. and Schweid, J. (1984) *The Metropolin Area of Jerusalem*, Jerusalem: The Jerusalem Institute for Israel Studies.

Kimmerling, B. (1983) *Zionism and Territory*, Berkeley: University of California, Institute of International Studies.

Kimmerling, B. (1979) *A Conceptual Framework for the Analysis of Behavior in a Territorial Conflict: The Generalization of the Israeli Case*, The Hebrew University, Jerusalem: Leonard Davis Institute of International Relations, Papers on Peace Problems, 25.

Kimmerling, B. and Migdal, J.S. (2003) *The Palestinian People: A History*, Cambridge, MA: Harvard University Press.

Klein, M. (2005) "Old and New Walls in Jerusalem", *Political Geography*, 24: 53–76.

Klein, M. (2003) *The Jerusalem Problem: The Struggle for Permanent Status*, Gainesville: The University Press of Florida.

Lapidoth, R. (1994) *The Jerusalem Question and Its Relations: Selected Documents*, Jerusalem: The Jerusalem Institute for Israel Studies.

Lapidoth, R. and Hirsch, M. (1993) *The Arab–Israel Conflict and its Resolutions: Selected Remarks*, Jerusalem: The Jerusalem Institute for Israel Studies.

Makovsky, D. (1996) *Making Peace with the PLO: The Rabin Government's Road to the Oslo Accord*, Boulder, CO: Westview Press and the Washington Institute for Near East Policy.

Michael, K. and Ramon, A. (2004) *A Fence Around Jerusalem*, Jerusalem: Jerusalem Institute for Israel Studies.

Morris, B. (2004) *The Birth of the Palestinian Refugee Problem Revisited*, New York: Cambridge University Press.

Morris, B. (2000) *Righteous Victims: A History of the Zionist–Arab Conflict 1881–1999*, London: John Murray.

Morris, B. (1993) *Israel's Border Wars, 1949–1956*, Oxford: Clarendon Press.

Mutawi, S. (1987) *Jordan in the 1967 War*, Cambridge: Cambridge University Press.

Nakhleh, K. and Zureik, E. (eds), *The Sociology of the Palestinians*, New York: St Martin's Press.

Newman, D. (2002) "The Geopolitics of Peacemaking in Israel–Palestine", *Political Geography*, 21, Oxford.

Newman, D. (1998) "Creating the Fences of Territorial Separation: The Discourses of Israeli–Palestinian Conflict Resolution", *Geopolitics and International Boundaries*, 2.

Newman, D. (1985) *The Impact of Gush Emunim: Policies and Settlement in the West Bank*, London: Croom Helm.

Palestine Liberation Organization (2000) *The Palestinian Refugees 1948–2000*, Factfile, Ramallah and Jerusalem.

Pearlman, W. (2003) *Occupied Voices: Stories of Everyday Life from the Second Intifada*, New York: Thunder's Mouth Press.

Perlmutter, A. (1969) *Military and Politics in Israel*, London: Frank Cass.

Portugali, J. (1993) *Implicate Relations: Society and Space in the Israeli–Palestinian Conflict*, Dordrecht: Kluwer Academic Publishers.

Portugali, J. (1991), "Jewish Settlement in the Occupied Territories: Israel's Settlement Structure and the Palestinians", *Political Geography Quarterly*, 10.

Rabinowich, I. (2004) *Waging Peace: Israel and the Arabs 1948–2003*, Princeton: Princeton University Press.

Romann, M. and Weingrod, A. (1991), *Living Together Separately: Arabs and Jews in Contemporary Jerusalem*, Princeton: Princeton University Press.

Roy, S. (1986) *The Gaza Strip Survey, West Bank Data Base Project*, Jerusalem.

Said, C. (2002) *The End of the Peace Process*, London: Granta Books.

Sayigh, Y. (1999) *Armed Struggle and the Search of State: The Palestinian National Movement 1949–1993*, Oxford: Oxford University Press.

Shehade, R. (2003) *Strangers in the House: Coming of Age in the Occupied Palestine*, South Royalton, VT: Steerforth Press.

Shlaim, A. (2000) *The Iron Wall: Israel and the Arab World*, London: Penguin Books.

Shuval, H. (1996) "Towards Resolving Conflicts over Water: the Case of the Mountain Aquifer", in E. Karsch (ed.), *Between War and Peace: Dilemmas of Israeli Security*, London: Frank Cass.

Sinai, A. and Pollack, A. (1976) *The Hashemite Kingdom of Jordan and the West Bank, a Handbook*, New York: American Academic Association for Peace in the Middle East.

Smith, C. (2001) *Palestine and the Arab–Israeli Conflict: A History with Documents*, Boston and Bedford: St Martin's Press.

Tessler, M. (1994) *A History of the Israeli–Palestinian Conflict*, Bloomington: Indiana University Press.

Wasserstein, B. (2001) *Divided Jerusalem: The Struggle for the Holy Land*, New Haven and London: Yale University Press.

Watson, G. (2000) *The Oslo Accords*, Oxford: Oxford University Press.

Weitz, R. (1975) *Agriculture in the Gaza Strip and West Bank 1974*, Tel Aviv, Israel: Ministry of Agriculture.

Yiftachel, O. (1992) *Planning a Mixed Region in Israel: The Political Geography of Arab–Israel Relations in the Galilee*, Aldershot: Avebury Press.

Index